Starting Over in the U.S.

After Getting Your Green Card

An Indispensible Handbook for Immigrants

Elizabeth (Elzbieta) Baumgartner

New American Guides. Copyright © 2009 by Elzbieta Baumgartner

Cover design: SKOK Communications, LLC, New York, tel. 1-718-224-2948, www.skok.us

Publisher: Polpress Services, 255 Park Lane, Douglaston, NY 11363, tel. 1-718-224-3492

Editing: Heidi Baumgartner

International Standard Book Number: ISBN 978-0-9770453-0-3

International Standard Book Number 10 digit: 0-9770453-0-7

Library of Congress Control Number: 2008939789

1. Aliens -- United States -- Popular Works. 2. Aliens -- United States -- Handbooks, manuals, etc. 3. Visitors, Foreign -- United States -- Life skills guides.

Legal disclaimer: All information provided in this book is of a general nature and does not constitute a legal advice. Although we try to provide accurate and timely information, there can be no guarantee that such information is accurate as of the date it is received or that it will continue to be accurate in the future. No one should act upon such information without appropriate professional advice after a thorough examination of the facts of the particular situation.

Table of Contents

1. INTRODUCTION...1

PART I. What Needs to Be Done Right After You Get Your Green Card

2. YOUR ROADMAP FOR LIFE WITH A GREEN CARD 4

    2.1. If You Worked in the U.S. on a Temporary Visa in the Past.. 4
    2.2. If You Have Worked Without Papers 5
    2.3. If You Have Been Using Someone Else's Identity.................. 6
    2.4. If Your Help to a Fellow Immigrant Got You in Trouble....... 8
    2.5. If Your Identity Got Stolen.. 9
    2.6. If You Were in Trouble in the Past 10
    2.7. If You Never Lived in the United States Before.................... 10

3. MORE PROBLEMS WITH THE IMMIGRATION SERVICE AFTER GETTING YOUR GREEN CARD 12

    3.1. Now that You Are a Permanent Resident 12
    3.2. Potential Problems with Your Green Card............................ 13
    3.3. Remove Conditions on Your Two-Year Conditional Permanent Resident Card 16
    3.4. Don't Lose Your Permanent Resident Status......................... 20
    3.5. Report Change of Address to the USCIS................................ 21
    3.6. Don't Stumble on the Road to Naturalization 23
    3.7. Forms, Appointments, and Office Locations 25

4. FORMALITIES AFTER GETTING YOUR GREEN CARD 26

    4.1. Paperwork at the Social Security Office with New and Old Cards 26
    4.2. Switch from ITIN to SSN 28
    4.3. What Needs to Be Done at Work.. 30
    4.4. How Not to Get Fired for Having Used a Fake SSN in the Past... 32
    4.5. When You Can Leave Your Sponsor...................................... 34
    4.6. What Needs to Be Done at the Bank...................................... 35
    4.7. Register with the Selective Service 36

4.8.   Convert Your Temporary Driver's License into a Permanent One 36

4.9.   Where and How to Report Your Name Change 38

4.10. Address Change 41

5.   ESTABLISHING YOURSELF IN AMERICA 43

5.1.   Your First Place to Live 43

5.2.   Protect Yourself and Your Family 48

5.3.   Education for Your Children 50

5.4.   Evaluation of Your Foreign Diploma and Continued Education 54

5.5.   Pay Taxes that Are Due 57

5.6.   Build Your Good Reputation 61

5.7.   Go Ahead to Achieve Your Dreams 64

6.   FIND GOOD LEGAL EMPLOYMENT 66

6.1.   Your Legal Status Is Just the Beginning 66

6.2.   Employment Background Check 67

6.3.   Get American Job Experience 69

6.4.   How to Increase Your Chances for Employment 72

6.5.   Job Searching in America 76

6.6.   Places to Look for a Job 80

6.7.   Benefits of Legal Employment 82

PART II. How to Clean up Your Past

7.   SETTLE YOUR SCORE WITH THE IRS 88

7.1.   The Tax and Social Security Mess 88

7.2.   How to Get Your Tax Information from the IRS 90

7.3.   Consequences of Failure to Pay Taxes 93

7.4.   Pay Your Back Income Taxes 95

7.5.   Missing W-2 and 1099 Forms 97

7.6.   How to Mitigate the Consequences of Nonpayment of Taxes 102

8.   CLEAN UP YOUR SOCIAL SECURITY ACCOUNT 105

8.1.   How Earnings Are Posted 105

8.2. Check Wages Reported Using Your SSN 109

8.3. How to Pay Back Your FICA Tax 111

8.4. Earnings Errors 115

8.5. How to Correct Your Earnings Record 117

8.6. Problems that Can Be Resolved 121

8.7. Changing Your Social Security Number 124

9.   GET TO KNOW COMPANIES WHICH GATHER INFORMATION ON PEOPLE 126

9.1. What Are Consumer Reporting Agencies? 126

9.2. Credit, Consumer, and Investigative Reports 128

9.3. Your Rights Under the FCRA 129

9.4. Your Rights to Fix Inaccuracies 131

9.5. How You Are Scored 133

10. STRAIGHTEN OUT YOUR CREDIT HISTORY 137

10.1. Credit, Credit History, and Credit Score 137

10.2. Consequences of Unpaid Bills 138

10.3. How to Deal with Collection Agencies 141

10.4. Financial Obligations of an Immigrant Sponsor 144

10.5. Find out what Credit Bureaus Know About You 146

10.6. Clean up Your Credit Report 149

10.7. How to Improve Your Credit 152

11. CHECK THE "OTHER" CONSUMER REPORTS 156

11.1. How Negative Banking History Can Hurt You 156

11.2. Check Writing History: Consequences of Bouncing Checks 162

11.3. Insurance Claims Report: How Insurers Size You Up 166

11.4. Employment Background Check: How Employers Look into Your Past 171

11.5. Improve Your Tenant History Report to Qualify for a Good Apartment 175

11.6. Medical History: What Others Know About Your Health. 183

12. FIGHT AND PREVENT IDENTITY THEFT 187

12.1. How an Identity Thief Can Harm You 187

12.2. How to Protect Yourself 190

12.3. How a Credit Freeze Protects You.............................. 193

12.4. How Laws Protect Your Rights as a Consumer................... 195

12.5. What to Do First if You Are a Victim of Identity Theft 201

12.6. Report Fraud to Credit Bureaus............................. 204

12.7. Report the Incident to Law Enforcement Agencies 206

12.8. Proving That You Have Been Victimized........................ 208

13. **RECOVER FROM UNAUTHORIZED FINANCIAL TRANSACTIONS** **211**

13.1. What to Do About Stolen Checks 211

13.2. Fraudulent Credit Accounts Opened in Your Name.......... 215

13.3. Unauthorized Charges on Your Credit Card.................. 217

13.4. How to Recover Stolen Money from Your Debit Account. 220

13.5. How to Correct Fraudulent Information in Your Credit Report 222

13.6. When Someone Uses Your Social Security Number.......... 226

13.7. When Someone Obtains Phone Service in Your Name 231

14. **FIX YOUR DRIVING RECORD** **233**

14.1. Types of Traffic Violations.................................... 233

14.2. Traffic Tickets 235

14.3. How You Can Lose Your License and How to Prevent It.. 237

14.4. Your Driving Record 242

14.5. How to Obtain and Clean up Your Driving Record 244

14.6. When Someone Steals Your Identity.......................... 246

15. **CLEAN UP YOUR CRIMINAL HISTORY** **248**

15.1. What Is a Rap Sheet? 248

15.2. How to Check Your Rap Sheet............................... 250

15.3. How to Correct Your Rap Sheet.............................. 253

15.4. How to Clean up Your Criminal Record 256

15.5. What You Should Know About the Immigration Background Check... 260

APPENDIX: ABOUT THE NEW AMERICAN GUIDES...................... **262**

1. INTRODUCTION

Each year, over one million immigrants from around the globe gain permission to reside in the United States by receiving a Green Card, while millions more wait for that privilege in the U.S. and abroad. *Starting Over in the U.S. After Getting Your Green Card* and other books from the New American Guides series are indispensible for all immigrants.

This book is for all Green Card holders who want to establish themselves in the U.S. Upon receiving permanent resident status, newcomers must search for a job, find a place to live, buy a car, and learn about potentially new concepts such as medical insurance or credit history, sometimes while only beginning to speak English. Immigrants must abide by new laws, follow unfamiliar regulations, and cope with different customs when they come to a new country. As a permanent resident, you now have some obligations to fulfill and formalities to take care of. There is a lot to learn upon coming to America, including how not to lose your Green Card.

This book is particularly valuable for **those who waited for their Green Cards and worked without papers in the U.S.** They need to fix their records to reflect their now legal status and valid Social Security number. This book explains how an old, invalid SSN or taxpayer number (ITIN) can be replaced. It describes what needs to be done at the Social Security Administration, Internal Revenue Service (IRS), Motor Vehicle Department, and at your bank and workplace. For example, those who started working without authorization need to know how to pay back taxes they owe, how to change their Social Security number at work without getting fired, how to have unauthorized employment period credited by the Social Security Administration, and much more.

Those who stumbled in the past can use the information found here to undo their mistakes and clean up their records, if possible, in order not to be deported or not to lose their chances for naturalization. Many immigrants escaped from hardship in their homelands only to find that at the beginning life in America is not easy either. Whether because of a lack of papers, misinformation, insufficient knowledge, financial difficulty, or falling victim of fraud, newcomers occasionally overlook paying taxes, misuse Social Security numbers, fail to answer traffic tickets, use someone else's identity, miss paying a bill, or even get arrested. They should know that although their actions are recorded in various databases, there are ways to fix past mistakes, and these methods are described in this book.

Obtaining a Green Card does not mark the end of the road to a better life, but merely the beginning of new challenges, as immigrants are enabled to compete with Americans on equal footing. Again and again, newcomers to the U.S. start from nothing, and through hard work and perseverance, achieve their dreams. Americans often wonder how some immigrants, who arrive to the U.S. with nothing, manage to own homes, run businesses, and send their children to the best universities within a short period of time. The reason for this is not only the hard work, entrepreneurial spirit, and frugality typical to immigrants, but also their open-mindedness, determination, and adaptability. **Readers who desire to achieve** can learn from the book about potential pitfalls they may encounter, and how to avoid them.

Starting Over in the U.S. After Getting Your Green Card is the only book on the market that helps newcomers to the United States to start life anew upon receiving a Green Card and fix the problems created by a period of illegal status and other challenges. Immigrants in America are known for their diligence and rapid success. Like many others, you will also succeed in your new homeland!

Please be advised that the author of this book is not an attorney. The book was written for educational purposes only. The reader should consult an attorney about his or her particular situation.

Part I

What Needs to Be Done Right After You Get Your Green Card

2. YOUR ROADMAP FOR LIFE WITH A GREEN CARD

Congratulations! After a long procedure of filling out forms, filing applications, and waiting, you have finally obtained a Green Card, a proof of your legal permanent residency. Having permanent resident status, you are allowed to work and live wherever you want in the U.S. and find a place in American society according to your own aspirations and abilities.

While you are beginning to build your new American life, you must take care of some formalities required by law. What to do depends on whether you lived and worked in the U.S. in the past while waiting for your Green Card, and if so, which immigration status you had while here. Your course of action also depends on what type of identification number you used to pay taxes: a regular Social Security number (SSN), an SSN which was not valid for employment, or an Individual Taxpayer Identification Number (ITIN). If you lived in the U.S. after your status had expired, if you gave someone else your identifying information, or if you used someone else's name for employment, chances are that you must do some work to clean up your records before you can lead a normal life.

2.1. If You Worked in the U.S. on a Temporary Visa in the Past

Before obtaining your permanent resident status, you may have had a temporary visa that allowed you to work legally in the U.S. If so, you have already applied for your Social Security card and received one with the notation "Valid for work only with USCIS authorization." This means that you have been working legally in the U.S. with the permission of the U.S. Citizenship and Immigration Service (USCIS, formerly INS, part of the U.S. Department of Homeland Security). You also legally contributed to the Social Security system and paid your income taxes. Now the following actions are required:

- Report your permanent residency at the Social Security Administration (SSA), so the agency will change the work authorization status of your Social Security card (see section 4.1).
- Do some paperwork at your place of employment (section 4.3). You don't need an additional work permit because your Green Card proves your work eligibility as well as identity.
- Change your tax residency status at the bank (see section 4.6).
- Change your temporary driver's license to a permanent driver's license (see section 4.8).
- Continue paying income taxes (section 5.5) using the same SSN. There is no need to inform the Internal Revenue Service (IRS, the U.S. tax agency) about your Green Card.
- As a person living legally in the U.S. for some time, you may have a credit history. Check your credit record at major credit bureaus; correct mistakes if necessary. Section 10.6 of this book explains how. You don't have to report your change of immigration status to credit bureaus.
- If you are a conditional resident, file timely for removing the conditions on your permanent resident status (section 3.3).
- Don't lose your Green Card! Be sure that an arrest or a long stay abroad does not jeopardize your status (section 3.4).

2.2. If You Have Worked Without Papers

Several million foreigners reside in the U.S. while waiting for the legalization of their immigration status. They are allowed by law to receive their Green Cards here. For a long time, they support themselves and their family by working off the books. They keep a low profile, avoid government agencies, and try not to leave any tracks behind them. Some use their Individual Taxpayer Identification Number (ITIN) for work, banking, and taxes. In most states, they have no way to get a valid driver's license.

If you ever lived in the U.S. and worked without legal status, after obtaining your Green Card you should straighten your affairs with the Internal Revenue Service, Social Security Administration, and other institutions. Taking the following steps to do so will work to your advantage:

- Apply for a new Social Security number (section 4.1).

- If you worked using an ITIN (page 28), a fictitious SSN or an SSN that belonged to another person, have the Social Security Administration transfer your earnings onto your new SSN (section 4.1).
- Pay your back taxes, if you have any due (section 5.5).
- Rescind your ITIN (section 4.2).
- Change your taxpayer number from your old ITIN into your new SSN in all institutions you dealt with.
- Inform your bank about your new Social Security number and your new tax status (section 4.6).
- Obtain a new driver's license (section 4.8) or state identification card.
- Pay your taxes each year (section 5.5). Write your new SSN on the tax forms instead of your old ITIN.
- Conditional residents should file timely for removing the conditions on their permanent status (section 3.3). Don't do anything that could jeopardize your Green Card (section 3.4).

2.3. If You Have Been Using Someone Else's Identity

Struggling to survive in the U.S. without legal status, some immigrants use fictitious Social Security numbers or use their friends' documents. After they get their Green Card, they fear that they may be considered criminals because they shared personal information in the past.

Is It a Crime to Use Someone Else's SSN?

Using another person's identity (name, Social Security number, or other identification documents) is not necessarily a crime. It depends on your intentions.

Noncitizens who work using fraudulent or invalid SSNs are not treated as criminals in the U.S. If caught, they may be deported because of their unlawful status, but they would not be put to jail for unauthorized work. This occurs even though the use of a non-valid fraudulent SSN violates identity theft laws, which make using someone else's identity a federal crime only when a person "knowingly transfers or uses, without lawful authority, a means of identification of another person with the intent to commit, or to aid or abet, any unlawful activity that constitutes a violation of federal law, or that constitutes a felony under any applicable state or local law" (P.L. 105-318, 18 U.S.C. Section 1028(a)(7)).

State laws are equally lenient. For example, in Tennessee, criminal impersonation is defined as assuming a false identity "with intent to injure or defraud another person."

In other words, using someone else's identity requires the intention to commit a crime and cause injury to another person before it becomes a crime itself. Getting a job doesn't fulfill those criteria, not even for an illegal immigrant.

Attention: Saying that you are someone else is one thing, but using someone else's identification document (ID) for employment is a crime. The law (18 U.S.C. § 1546(b)) makes it a felony offense to use a false identification document, or misuse a real one, for the purpose of satisfying the employment verification provisions in 8 U.S.C. § 1324a(b). However, prosecuting illegal aliens for earning their living has never been a priority of the law enforcement.

🏛 You can find U.S. law code online: http://uscode.house.gov.

📖 For more information read *Surviving in the U.S. While Waiting for Your Green Card* (see page 262).

What to Do Now

If you used the name or Social Security number of another person for any purpose, you must now unscramble your personal information and do the following.

- At the Social Security office, file an application for your own Social Security card and also have your previous earnings applied to your new account. Unscrambling the earnings of two people (yours and those of the SSN's rightful owner) may not be easy, so read chapter 8 for more information.
- Make sure you paid all your taxes. If you don't, the owner of the SSN will be responsible for them. The IRS may demand back taxes from him, including a penalty and interest. See chapter 7.
- You may have no credit history, because all your financial transactions were recorded by credit bureaus under the name of the

  SSN owner. Establish your credit history from scratch (see section
    5.6).
- Establish yourself in the U.S. (chapter 5).

2.4. If Your Help to a Fellow Immigrant Got You in Trouble

Immigrants often help their countrymen who follow their steps into America. Those who came first and already established themselves help newcomers by lending them their Social Security number or identification documents. Those returning to their old country give their documents to new arrivals. Some good Samaritans give other immigrants a place to sleep or financial help. Others offer to co-sign a credit card or an apartment lease, or assist with lending a car to newcomers who would otherwise not be able to get off the ground by themselves. If you are one of these people and your beneficiary turned out to be reckless or irresponsible, read this whole book carefully to be able to assess and fix the damage.

Let's assume that a relative impersonated you. He used your identity to work and didn't pay taxes, got into car accidents, and got arrested. Since his actions went into records under your name, you are now in trouble too. Ask him to stop using your identity. If he persists to act against your objections and causes you harm, you can report identity theft to the police. He will be treated as a criminal.

Here are several tips for persons who attempted to help others and were taken advantage of.

- Don't have too many visitors. Your landlord (the owner of the building) may object to long-term visitors staying in your apartment often. He may raise your rent or even refuse to renew your lease. As a home owner, you may get in trouble for overcrowding your house and be required to pay penalties (see section 5.1).
- If you added a relative as an authorized user of a credit card or a co-owner of a joint bank account or a credit card, or if you co-signed a loan for someone, ensure that he behaves responsibly. If he overdraws from an account, you will be responsible (see 10.2).
- If you gave your relative an identification document (ID) of yours to use, check your bank and credit card statements for unauthorized transactions (see chapter 13). Learn your rights. Remember,

however, that transactions are considered authorized if you gave someone access to your credit card or your bank account. Then you are held responsible for the losses, and the bank will not reimburse you.

- Review your Social Security account. If a relative worked under your name, go to the Social Security office together so the agency divides the earnings between the two of you (see section 8.5).
- If a relative worked under your name for an extended period of time, ask to see his federal and state tax returns. To be sure that your taxes are in order, check your tax history too (section 7.2).
- Remember your financial obligations as an immigrant's sponsor (section 10.4).
- A relative still waiting to legalize his immigration status should be advised to read *Surviving in the U.S. While Waiting for Your Green Card* (see the Appendix on page 262). Fewer problems for him mean less trouble for you.

2.5. If Your Identity Got Stolen

According to the U.S. Department of Justice, identity theft (see chapter 12) is now surpassing drug trafficking as the number one crime in the nation. Identity theft is done by computer hackers, professional thieves, and criminals who often sell fake documents to desperate immigrants. You can be one of millions of Americans affected. If that happens to you, do the following:

- Report identity theft immediately to the police according to the instructions in section 12.7. Close affected credit cards and bank accounts. Learn your rights and stop further damage.
- Dispute credit charges and unauthorized transitions done by the thief (chapter 13). Get stolen money back. The law protects consumers from fraud, identity theft, and errors.
- Check and clean up your credit report. Ask credit bureaus to remove fraudulent transactions from your credit report (section 12.6).
- Check your other consumer reports to be sure that they have not been affected by the fraudulent activity (chapter 9).
- Monitor your credit closely for additional fraudulent activities.

2.6. If You Were in Trouble in the Past

The road to success in America is not always a straight one; it has its ups and downs.

Occasionally, people go through difficult times due to financial problems, illness, unemployment, or business failure. Not familiar with the American law, some individuals get arrested and end up convicted. When you are having trouble, bills get unpaid, checks bounce, or you may be evicted from your apartment. It is difficult to pick up the pieces. Here what needs to be done to ensure fresh start in life.

- Pay your bills and eliminate debt. If you are not able to, negotiate with creditors (see section 10.2).
- If a collection agency is after you, stop its actions and ask for debt verification (section 10.3).
- Check your credit report. You cannot remove truthful negative information, but you can add a statement with explanations to your credit record (see section 10.6).
- Remember that many agencies collect information on people, so your missteps may have been recorded in numerous databases. Check what others know about you, as described in chapter 11, and do what you can to alleviate the damage.
- If you ever got arrested, consult with an attorney. Committing crimes can have severe immigration consequences for every non-citizen, because it can end up in deportation or disqualification for naturalization.
- Conduct a background check on yourself (section 11.4) to make sure that you will not be turned down for employment, apartment rental, or insurance.
- Settle down (chapter 5); get focused on your goals in life.

> *Remember that what you do now as a permanent resident can affect your ability to become a U.S. citizen later.*

2.7. If You Never Lived in the United States Before

If you waited for your Green Card abroad, now you came to the U.S. with clean record. You can set off on the road to success not being dragged down by past. However, that perfectly clean record will work to your disadvantage, because you appear to be a person from nowhere. Your record indicates that no one ever trusted you before in the U.S., no one lent you money, rented you an apartment, or gave you a job. In America, reputation – measured by credit or job history – is very important.

Therefore, in addition to struggling with the everyday challenges of moving to a new place, you must make up for the lost time. You must quickly establish a good reputation, learn English, and advance yourself professionally and financially. It is necessary for immigrants to work even harder than Americans to achieve their goals.

Some details must be taken care of first, to establish a solid foundation on which you can build the rest of your life. Here is what you should do immediately.

- Get your Social Security number at an SSA office (see section 4.1). You will need your SSN every step of the way in the U.S.
- Find a place to live (section 5.1). Get proof of address, as it is necessary for opening a bank account, enrolling children in school, and for many other purposes.
- Get a satisfying job (chapter 6). As a permanent resident, you have the right to work without additional authorization. You can even start working before your Social Security card arrives (section 4.3).
- Apply for your driver's license (section 4.8). If you don't need to drive, obtain a state ID which will be your primary identification document.
- Make sure you obtain your Green Card by mail, with your correct personal information (section 3.2). Before your Green Card arrives in the mail, the I-551 stamp in your passport is proof of your legal status.
- Maintain your permanent residency. Remove the conditions on your status if you are a conditional resident (section 3.3). Don't stay abroad too long (section 3.4), and follow the laws.
- Settle down (chapter 5), get focused on your life goals. Good luck!

Many books can help you in making first steps on American soil. The American government has a useful booklet *Welcome to the United States*. Download the publication from the website: www.uscis.gov/files/nativedocuments/M-618.pdf.

3. MORE PROBLEMS WITH THE IMMIGRATION SERVICE AFTER GETTING YOUR GREEN CARD

3.1. Now that You Are a Permanent Resident

Once you become a permanent resident of the United States, it is important that you understand your rights, responsibilities, and obligations in order to not lose your Green Card.

As a permanent resident, you have most of the rights of a United States citizen, with some exceptions. You are protected by all of the laws of the United States, your state of residence and local jurisdictions.

You have the right to:

- live permanently anywhere in the United States; unlike in many other countries, there is no requirement to register your residence with the police
- work for nearly any employer (some jobs are limited to the U.S. citizens for national security reasons)
- travel outside of the U.S. and return under certain conditions (see section 3.4)
- request immigration visas for your spouse and your unmarried children so they can come to the U.S. to live with you
- apply to become a U.S. citizen once you are eligible (see 3.6)
- get Social Security, Supplemental Security Income, and Medicare benefits, if you are eligible
- apply for a driver's license or state ID in your state (see 4.8)
- have yourself or your children attend public elementary school, high school and college (see 5.3).

As a permanent resident, it is your responsibility to:

- obey all federal, state, and local laws
- report your worldwide income and pay federal, state, and local income taxes (see section 5.5)

- if you are a male aged 18 through 25, you are required to register with the Selective Service (section 4.7)
- maintain your legal immigration status (for that, you must not abandon the U.S. and not commit any crimes)
- carry proof of your permanent resident status at all times (see 3.2)
- support the government; however, you are not allowed to vote in most elections
- inform the Immigration Service (USCIS) within 10 days of each time you move (see section 3.5).

3.2. Potential Problems with Your Green Card

Before Your Green Card Arrives

You successfully went through the interview at the U.S. Immigration and Naturalization Service (USCIS) and walked out with an I-551 stamp in your passport. The I-551 stamp bears a handwritten alien number (beginning with a letter "A") and "Valid Until" date. You are likely to get your Green Card in the mail within a few months. A Green Card, a small laminated document (not actually colored green), is officially called I-551, *Permanent Resident Card.*

While you wait for the arrival of your Green Card, the I-551 stamp in your passport has the same legal meaning as the actual Green Card document. The difference is that the stamp must be renewed after a year and the Green Card must be renewed after 10 years or after two years if it is conditional (obtained based on marriage with a U.S. citizen).

Just like your Green Card, the I-551 stamp is an acceptable proof of employment authorization and can be used for applying for a Social Security Card or state driver's license.

Your Green Card Is Delayed

Typically a Green Card arrives in the mail within a few weeks or months after an immigration interview. If you do not get it before your I-551 stamp expires, you need to extend the I-551 stamp by filing form I-90, *Application to Replace Permanent Resident Card,* with your local Immigration office. The Immigration Service will also make inquiries about your Green Card at that time. Check the box next to *"My authorized card was never received."*

Do not use Form I-90 if you are a conditional resident and your status is expiring!

You can also take your approval notice to a local USCIS office and get a new I-551 stamp in your unexpired foreign passport. Make an Info Pass appointment (section 3.7) at your local Immigration office. The USCIS also recommends calling 1-800-375-5283 to check why you have not received your Green Card.

Green Card Never Received

If you never received your card, you may inquire about its status using USCIS Form G-731, *Inquiry about Status of I-551 Alien Registration Card*. Send it to the address indicated on the form. You also may file Form I-90, *Application by Lawful Permanent Resident for New Alien Registration Receipt Card*, to have your Green Card replaced.

You should know that you do not lose your permanent residency if the card or stamp expires, but you will lack legal proof of your status.

International Travel Before Your Green Card Arrives

As a permanent resident, you can travel outside of the U.S. and come back. For readmission, you need a valid passport from the country of your citizenship and your American Green Card (Form I-551, *Permanent Resident Card*). Traveling outside the U.S. for less than 6 months does not cause any problems.

If your Green Card did not arrive yet and you have only the I-551 stamp in your passport, do not worry. That stamp is as good as the real card, as long as its expiration date did not pass. You should have no problem traveling with only the stamp in your passport.

Misspelled Name, Damaged Card

If your card was issued with incorrect information (misspelled name, erroneous birth date, wrong photo, etc.), you should apply for your card replacement using Form I-90, *Application by Lawful Permanent Resident for New Alien Registration Receipt Card*. Make an InfoPass appointment (section 3.7) and visit your local Immigration office, or send the form by mail with required documents.

You can use Form I-90 if your name changed due to marriage or divorce (include a copy of your old card and a certified copy of your marriage or divorce certificate); if your card was damaged, lost, stolen or never received; or your card is expiring. Read instructions to Form I-90 for further information. The USCIS promises to send you the new card in 30 to 45 days, but it is possible for it to take much longer.

> *If the name on your Green Card and your name on your foreign passport don't match, do not risk traveling abroad! Border officers may not let you back to the U.S.*

Carry Your Green Card with You

You need to make sure that you have your Green Card or your I-551 stamp in your possession at all times. The law says that *"every alien, 18 years of age and over, shall at all times carry with him and have in his personal possession any certificate of alien registration or alien registration receipt card issued to him... Any alien who fails to comply with these provisions shall be guilty of a misdemeanor"* (Code of Federal Regulations at 8 CFR § 264.5).

Considering that your wallet can get stolen and renewal of a Green Card takes a long time, you may choose to make a photocopy of your card and carry it instead of the real thing. That way, even if a law enforcement official asks for an ID, you can show the copy and tell him you have the original at home. When it is impractical to have your wallet with you, you should know where your Green Card is, have it near you, and be able to show it to authorities if asked to.

What Should You Do with Your I-94 Card?

All nonimmigrant visitors entering the United States with a visa fill out form CBP Form I-94, *Arrival/Departure Record*, or I-94 W if you travel under Visa Waiver Program. The departure coupon was attached to your passport on the border and should be returned upon exiting the United States.

What are you supposed to do with the I-94 card now that you received your Green Card? The I-94 is not really relevant any more. It is best to have it with you when you go out of the country, and present it to officials who ask you for it.

Summary: The I-551 stamp in your foreign passport is as good as a Green Card. Make sure that your name is spelled correctly. If the card does not come in the mail, contact the Immigration Service.

3.3. Remove Conditions on Your Two-Year Conditional Permanent Resident Card

Are You a Conditional Resident?

You are a conditional resident if you immigrated to the United States as a spouse of a U.S. citizen before the second anniversary of your marriage, which forms the reason for your immigrant status. If you have children, they also may be conditional residents. The EB-5 investor visa also grants conditional residency.

The difference between conditional and unconditional permanent resident status is that your conditional resident status will expire two years after it was given unless you successfully petition to have the condition removed. The expiration date of this conditional resident status is noted on your Green Card.

If you had already been married for two years when your permanent residency was granted, you are a full-fledged permanent resident and do not need to file any papers to remove conditions, because your Green Card is valid for 10 years.

Required Forms and Documents

Within 90 days of your card expiring, you should file a petition to remove conditions, using:

- Form I-751, *Petition to Remove Conditions on Residence*, if your conditional status was based on a marriage
- Form I-829, *Petition by Entrepreneur to Remove Conditions on Permanent Resident Status*, if your conditional status was based on being an investor or entrepreneur.

The forms are available at www.uscis.gov (see section 3.7). Follow the instructions carefully. In this book we only discuss issues pertaining to spouses of U.S. citizens.

With the I-751 form, signed by you and your spouse, you must present evidence of a true marriage. Submit as many of the following documents as possible (make sure they show the names of both you and your spouse):

- birth certificates of children born of the marriage
- an apartment lease showing joint tenancy, a title to a house, condo or co-op apartment; registration of a car, or other personal property
- bank statements showing joint accounts
- insurance policy taken by one spouse showing the other as the beneficiary of any insurance benefits
- joint tax returns
- affidavits from two witnesses stating that they know you very well and that your marriage is valid
- photos from family events or trips during past two years, showing you together.

Mail the completed packet and fees to the USCIS Service Center for your geographical area (see section 3.7).

What Happens Next

After receiving your application, the USCIS will mail you a confirmation receipt, and the next letter which gives you a one-year extension of your Green Card. Keep this receipt with your card. After the card expires, these two documents will be the only evidence of your legal status. During this year, the Immigration Service is supposed to approve or deny your petition.

Tip: If you must travel abroad, keep the receipt with your expired (or almost expired) Green Card and passport with you, to ensure that you will be able to reenter the United States.

After a while, you will get a notice that your fingerprints must be taken. Do as instructed.

If the USCIS has any doubts about your petition, it will request additional evidence or will send you an appointment date for an interview at the local office. If the evidence you provided is sufficient, your petition will be approved and a new 10-year Green Card will be mailed to you. The card will need to be renewed every 10 years unless you become a citizen of the United States.

If You Didn't File to Remove Conditions

If you fail to file the I-751 form on time, your conditional resident status will be automatically terminated and the Immigration Service can start deportation (removal) procedure against you.

You may be allowed to file Form I-751 after the 90-day period if you can prove in writing to the director of the USCIS Service Center that there was good cause for not filing the petition on time. It is up to the discretion of the director to approve your petition and restore your permanent resident status.

If you neglect to file Form I-751 on time, you will receive a notice from the USCIS telling you that you have failed to remove the conditions. Then a Notice to Appear (NTA) will arrive listing charges against you (marriage fraud) and instructing you to come to a hearing. You must rebut the evidence against you at the hearing and prove that you complied with requirements. At this point you should seek help from an immigration attorney.

Getting Divorced

If your marriage fell apart, and your spouse, for whatever reason, does not want to sign the joint petition, do not despair. The USCIS allows you to file without your spouse's signature to have the conditional status removed from your card.

Couples who are separated or have initiated divorce proceedings may still file a joint petition at the end of the conditional residency period. After divorce, you should file I-751 waiver based on a good faith marriage that ended in divorce. Remember that completing a waiver requires the assistance of an experienced immigration attorney. (Keep in mind that the Immigration Service does not know about the divorce unless the applicants reveal this fact).

If Your Spouse Refuses to Sign the Joint Petition

Conditional residents who cannot file a joint petition due to the U.S. citizen's failure to cooperate can file a timely I-751 waiver (see below) based on being a battered spouse, or file a good faith/divorce waiver – presumably late – once the divorce is final.

You may apply Form I-751 as a waiver under one of four options if you can prove that

- you entered the marriage in good faith, and not to evade immigration laws, but the marriage ended by annulment or divorce (waiver filed only after divorce is completed), or
- you entered the marriage in good faith but your spouse subsequently died, or
- you entered the marriage in good faith and have remained married, but you became a victim of battery or extreme cruelty by your U.S. citizen of permanent resident spouse (or parent), or
- the termination of your status and removal would result in extreme hardship.

Applicants requesting a waiver can file Form I-751 at any time, either before or after the two-year conditional residence period has expired. See instructions to USCIS Form I-751, *Petition to Remove the Conditions on Residence*, for more specific information on waivers (www.uscis.gov/files/form/I-751instr.pdf).

If Your Waiver Is Rejected

If the I-751 waiver is denied and a Notice to Appear (NTA) in immigration court is issued, the immigration judge will review the I-751 "de novo" (from the beginning), and you will be able to present evidence and testimony supporting the I-751 in court.

The NTA will list allegations that the Immigration Service believes render you removable, most probably that you committed marriage fraud (Immigration and Naturalization Act section 204(c)). To rebut these allegations, you should keep all documentation relating to your previous marriage, so you will be able to prove that your marriage was in good faith and that you did not commit marriage fraud. If the immigration judge determines you did commit marriage fraud, you will be barred forever from being the beneficiary of any petition. This means that, should you marry, your new spouse will be unable to petition for you based on marriage.

> **Summary:** *Persons married to U.S. citizen are granted permanent residence on a conditional basis for two years. Before that period is over, both spouses must file form I-751 or the Green Card will expire. There are several exceptions to this rule.*

3.4. Don't Lose Your Permanent Resident Status

You may have your Green Card revoked in one of two ways: by becoming deportable or by abandoning the United States. Therefore, it is crucial that you avoid doing either one.

Don't Become Deportable

The most common way to become deportable is to be convicted of a crime. Even seemingly insignificant law infringements can cost you your Green Card. For example, you can be deported for helping someone enter the U.S. illegally or for possessing even a small amount of drugs. There is no set list of crimes that make someone deportable. The relationship between criminal law and deportability is very complex. If you are arrested for any reason, consult an experienced immigration lawyer to find out whether and how you can avoid deportation.

Don't Abandon the United States

By becoming a permanent resident of the U.S., you are telling the government that you intend to live here permanently. Therefore, you need to be careful about losing your Green Card as a result of being outside the U.S. for too long. You may be found to have abandoned your permanent resident status under these circumstances:

- You remain outside of the U.S. for more than one year without obtaining a reentry permit or a returning resident visa. That is because the USCIS feels an absence of longer than one year indicates a possible abandonment of U.S. residence. Remember, that you may be suspected of abandonment even if your absence is less than one year.
- You remain outside of the U.S. for more than two years after issuance of a reentry permit without obtaining a returning resident visa.
- You fail to file income tax returns while living abroad for any period or declare yourself a "nonimmigrant" on your tax returns.
- You move to another country with the intention to live there permanently.

Citizenship: Overcoming Obstacles to Naturalization will tell you more about how not to lose your Green Card and eligibility for naturalization (see the Appendix on page 262).

Summary: *Once you receive a Green Card, you must meet a few conditions in order to keep it for life. You must not violate certain criminal or immigration laws, you must not abandon the U.S. as your place of permanent residence, and you must meet some other requirements.*

3.5. Report Change of Address to the USCIS

Who Must Report Change of Address

The law requires that all non-U.S. citizens who intend to stay in the U.S. for more than 30 days, except for holders of A or G visas, must report a change of address within 10 days of moving by completing a USCIS Form AR-11, *Change of Address*. There is no fee to file this form. You initially reported your address on the immigration Form I-94, *Arrival-Departure Record*, which you completed when you entered the U.S.

It is very important to comply with this requirement since the initial penalty is a fine of up to $200 and/or imprisonment for no more than 30 days. In addition, unless you can prove that your failure to report was "reasonably excusable or was not willful," you can be taken into custody and deported from the United States.

The law does not require U.S. citizens to report a change of address to the Immigration Service. However, they should keep the Service informed of their change of address if they have a petition pending.

You do not need to report your temporary addresses as long as you maintain your present address as your permanent residence and continue to receive mail there.

How to Report

Form AR-11, *Change of Address*, can be filed by mail or online.

By mail: Get Form AR-11 according to the instructions in section 3.7 and mail it to the address provided on the form. Fill it out legibly; otherwise your file in the main USCIS database will not be found.

You don't need to include any supporting documents. Make a copy for your records and send the form by certified mail with return receipt so you have a proof that the USCIS received it.

Online: Go to www.uscis.gov/ar-11 and click on "Online Change of Address." You will need to have certain information available:

- your receipt notice or other notice from the Immigration Service showing your receipt number (if you have a pending case)
- your new and your old address
- if you have filed a petition for a family member, the names and biographical information for that person.

If you are a non-U.S. citizen, please also have:

- the date when you last entered the United States; if you cannot remember, fill in an approximate date
- the location where you last entered the U.S.

Where to File

Make sure to follow the correct procedure.

U.S. Citizens: If you have moved and you have a pending case, you can change your address online. Having no pending case, you don't have to register your change of address.

Non-U.S. Citizens: If you have moved, you need to do two things:

- File Form AR-11 by mail. This changes your address in the USCIS master database.
- If you have a pending case, you must also file a change of address online or call the National Customer Service Center at 1-800-375-5283 or visit www.uscis.gov/addresschange. This changes your address for the specific application you have submitted.

Suggestions

It is better not to move while you have a case pending, for example, if you applied to bring your family to the U.S. A change of address sometimes is not entered properly by the USCIS and important correspondence can get sent to the wrong address. Missing important notifications can result in long delays or even rejection of your petition.

If you have a case pending and you must move, follow the procedure described above, but also leave your new address with the people living in your former apartment or house and check with them regularly.

 Summary: *The law requires almost all non-immigrants and permanent residents to report any change of address in the U.S. to the federal government. The consequences of not doing so can be severe, although they are not often imposed.*

3.6. Don't Stumble on the Road to Naturalization

Advantages of Naturalization

Naturalization, the process of obtaining American citizenship, is a goal of many immigrants as it results in many advantages. A U.S. citizen can travel freely in and out of the United States without restrictions, cannot be deported, can vote in local and national elections, can become a candidate for elected office, receive full Social Security benefits while outside the United States, may receive more generous public benefits (if qualified), and may seek certain government jobs.

Additionally, as an American citizen, you can petition for your parents and siblings to immigrate to the U.S. Your spouse and children (unmarried and under 21 years of age) qualify for immediate relative classification, which means they do not have to wait on line to immigrate (like the spouses and children of Green Card holders). Your children become American citizens even if born abroad.

When You Can Become a U.S. Citizen

You can apply for naturalization if you have been a permanent resident for the past five years. Over 90 percent of applicants fall into this category. You can also apply after you have been a spouse of an American citizen for three years.

Citizenship is a privilege, not an entitlement. You will qualify for it if you meet the requirements set by the law, including:

- a five- or three-year period of continuous residence and physical presence in the United States
- residence in a particular USCIS district prior to filing
- an ability to read, write, and speak English

- a knowledge and understanding of U.S. history and government
- "good moral character" – a standard of behavior set up by the immigration law
- attachment to the principles of the U.S. Constitution and favorable disposition toward the United States.

Obstacles to Naturalization

The most common obstacles to naturalization are extended **trips abroad**. You can find yourself ineligible for naturalization because of lack of "continuous presence" in the United States, as you cannot be outside of the U.S. for more than 6 months at one time. The "physical presence" requirement means that you must be physically present in the U.S. for 30 months (913 days) within the five-year period. Presence requirements for maintaining your Green Card and presence requirements for naturalization vary and are often confusing.

Other frequent complications pertain to the "**good moral character**" of the applicant. Not only individuals with criminal convictions have a problem obtaining citizenship, but even drivers who committed serious driving violations or individuals who have been arrested for other reasons in the past. Additional issues relating to good moral character involve non-payment of taxes or child support, visa or other immigration fraud, failure to register for Selective Service (if required to do so), voting in an election, falsely claiming to be a U.S. citizen, etc.

The Immigration Service may not only deny you naturalization, but in serious cases may also initiate deportation proceedings or request that you give up your Green Card by signing a notice of abandonment of your status.

📖 *Citizenship: Overcoming Obstacles to Naturalization* explains these issues in great detail (see the Appendix on page 262).

Summary: Legal immigrants are eligible for citizenship after five years in the country or after three years if they are married to a citizen. You become a citizen through a procedure called naturalization. Numerous requirements must be met.

3.7. Forms, Appointments, and Office Locations

The U.S. Citizenship and Immigration Service (USCIS), part of the U.S. Department of Homeland Security (DHS), makes all forms, instructions and information available for free.

Immigration forms, instructions, and fees can be found online, at www.uscis.gov. Click on "Immigration Forms." You can also order forms by calling the USCIS Form Line 1-800-870-3676.

Information: USCIS National Customer Service Center (NCSC) provides automated information and live assistance concerning immigration services and status of pending cases. Tel. 1-800-375-5283.

Appointments can be set up or cancelled online at the website http://infopass.uscis.gov. When you type in your zip code, the system will show your closest field offices to choose from.

Office locations can be found online at https://egov.uscis.gov/crisgwi/go?action=offices. Also, you can find this web page by searching for "USCIS office locator."

4.   FORMALITIES AFTER GETTING YOUR GREEN CARD

After you obtain permanent residency, there may be many formalities to take care of, depending on your situation. Some are minor; others are so important that neglecting them can cost you your Green Card.

4.1. Paperwork at the Social Security Office with New and Old Cards

Immigrants who have no Social Security card or only a restricted card have some paperwork to do at the Social Security Administration (SSA). The SSA (www.ssa.gov) is a federal agency that administers the Social Security programs consisting of retirement, disability and survivor's benefits.

About Social Security Cards

Definition: A Social Security number (SSN) is a number assigned to you by the Social Security Administration. It is the main identification number used by the government to keep track of your earnings, benefits, and taxes. It is also used by banks, schools, and many other institutions for identification. You are asked for your SSN when you want to open a bank account, rent an apartment, or buy a home. Your SSN is printed on a Social Security card.

There are three types of Social Security cards:

- cards with the restriction "Not Valid for Employment"
- cards with the restriction "Valid for Work Only with DHS Authorization" printed on them
- unrestricted cards good for employment.

The SSN for Those Who Applied for It Abroad

Social Security cards will arrive by mail to people who applied for them abroad.

Background information: New immigrants who apply for a Green Card abroad at an American consulate can apply for a Social Security number at the same time by checking off the appropriate box on Form DS-230, *Application for Immigrant Visa and Alien Registration*. This process pertains to persons who are age 18 or older and did not get an SSN before. Upon an immigrant's admission to the U.S. as a lawful permanent resident, the data is transmitted to the SSA. The agency automatically issues a Social Security card and sends it to the address provided on the DS-230 form. The SSA issues about 7,000 new SSNs per month for new immigrants entering the United States after getting an immigrant visa abroad.

Applying for the SSN in the U.S.

A Green Card does not give you a Social Security card automatically; it only makes you eligible for an unrestricted Social Security number. You must request a number at an SSA office. You can find an office near you by calling 1-800-772-1213 or online at www.ssa.gov. Lots of information is provided there in other languages, including Spanish.

Get your Social Security number as soon as possible, because it is necessary for taxes and employment purposes. Fill out Form SS-5, *Application for a Social Security Card,* and apply in person. As a new permanent resident, you will be asked to show the following documents:

- a document proving your identity, preferably a passport
- proof of legal status – your Green Card or the I-551 stamp in your passport.

🏵 You can obtain Form SS-5 by mail by calling the SSA at 1-800-772-1213 or downloading it from www.ssa.gov/online/ss-5.pdf.

Changing the Work Authorization Status of an SSN

Important: If you were originally assigned a non-work SSN (with a legend saying "Not Valid for Employment" or "Valid for Work Only with DHS Authorization"), you should contact the Social Security Administration, so the agency removes the non-work notation from your SSN record and reissues you a new card. Unless you inform the SSA directly of your status change, SSA's records will continue to show you as unauthorized to work and will record your name and earnings to the Non-Work Alien File (see page 106).

To apply for a replacement card, you need to come to an SSA office in person, complete Form SS-5, *Application for a Social Security Card* (see above) and bring evidence of your identity and current work authorization from the USCIS (your Green Card or the passport with the I-551 stamp). All documents must be either originals or copies certified by the issuing agency. The SSA cannot accept photocopies of documents. The SSA will verify your status with the Immigration Service.

 Summary: Get your Social Security number, if you did not have a valid number before. If you previously had a non-work SSN, now go to the Social Security and change the work authorization status of the number. If you don't, your number will still have non-work notation in the SSA records.

4.2.   Switch from ITIN to SSN

What Is an ITIN?

Background information: An Individual Taxpayer Identification Number (ITIN) is a 9-digit number, beginning with the number "9," formatted like an SSN (12-345-6789). An ITIN is intended to be used for federal tax purposes only. It can be obtained only by individuals who don't qualify for a Social Security number, by applying using IRS Form W-7, *Application for IRS Individual Taxpayer Identification Number.* The ITIN doesn't authorize work in the U.S. or provide eligibility for Social Security benefits or the Earned Income Tax Credit.

Although ITINs are not valid identification outside the tax system, many undocumented aliens use ITINs for work. If you have used an ITIN instead of an SSN before, now, after legalizing your status, it is time to replace your ITIN with a good Social Security number in databases of various institutions.

First, apply for a Social Security number at your local Social Security office (see above). After you get your Social Security card by mail in several weeks, apply to rescind (cancel) your ITIN.

Rescind Your ITIN

After obtaining your Social Security number, you are not allowed to use the ITIN anymore and you are supposed to rescind (cancel) the number. The IRS provides instructions in the ITIN letter it initially sent to you as well as in a booklet *Understanding Your IRS Individual Taxpayer Identification Number* (see below).

Write a letter to the IRS using the sample on this page. Mail your letter, proof of identity documents, as well as copies of your Social Security card and ITIN document to the address provided in the booklet: Internal Revenue Service, ITIN Operation, P.O. Box 149342, Austin, TX 78714-9342.

Letter Rescinding Your ITIN

Ref: ITIN (987-65-4321) to SSN (123-34-5678) Change

To: IRS ITIN Unit

My name is Joe Smith, date of birth January 3, 1966. I would like to notify you that I was granted a Social Security number (123-34-5678) by the Social Security Administration and will be using it for all future filing purposes. Please void my ITIN (987-65-4321) as well as associate all prior tax information under the ITIN with the new SSN.

Sincerely

Your name

The IRS will void your ITIN and all prior tax information under your ITIN will be associated with your new SSN. The new SSN will become your primary number and must be used for all future filing purposes.

If Your Name or Address Has Changed Since You Received Your ITIN

If you want to cancel your ITIN but your legal name has changed, explain the change in your letter (marriage, divorce, etc.) and include copies of updated important documents – marriage license or divorce certificate. You can write: *"Please be advised that since I received my ITIN, I got married and changed my name to... A copy of my marriage license is enclosed for your review."*

The IRS ITIN Unit is not very concerned with your address change, but just in case you can write: *"Please note that currently I reside at a different address: 23 Pine Street, Milton, NY 12976."*

To be sure that the IRS will have your current information, follow name/address change procedure described in sections 4.9 and 4.10.

Your Credit History and the ITIN Cancellation

If you were using your ITIN for banking in the past, you may have a credit history (see 10.1). Make sure that switching to an SSN does not create havoc in your records by creating a new credit file.

Write to all three credit bureaus – Experian, Equifax and Trans-Union – informing them about your new SSN (addresses can be found in section 10.5). If you continue using the same name, date of birth, and address and you inform the bureaus of your ITIN/SSN combination, then your new credit information will be merged with your old ITIN record. Both ITIN and SSN will be listed and your creditworthiness will not be affected.

A month or two after switching the numbers, check your credit history to assure that it was corrected (see section 10.5).

Where to Learn More

📖 *Understanding Your IRS Individual Taxpayer Identification Number ITIN.* Order this free booklet by calling the IRS Forms Hotline 1-800-829-3676 or download it from www.irs.gov/pub/irs-pdf/p1915.pdf.

Summary: *After obtaining a Social Security number, you no longer need your ITIN and you shouldn't use it anymore. Write a letter to the IRS asking to rescind the number.*

4.3. What Needs to Be Done at Work

Can You Start Working While Waiting for Your SSN?

Let's assume that you received your Green Card, filed an application for a Social Security card and received a job offer before card arrived in the mail. Can you start employment without a Social Security number?

Yes, you can. Neither immigration law nor federal tax law requires you to have a Social Security number to start employment or receive payments. The Internal Revenue Code does not obligate an employee to have an SSN to begin working, but requires only that he files an application for an SSN within 7 days of commencing employment for taxable wages (see 26 USC § 6011; 26 CFR § 31.6011(b)-2). You need the SSN to continue employment because the reporting of your wages (on forms W-2, 1099, etc., see section 7.5) requires your SSN for identification.

Form I-9, *Employment Eligibility Verification,* (see below) needs to be filled out for every new employee. It does not require an employee to present an SSN card but, rather, lists the Social Security card as one of several documents that establishes employment eligibility.

Although it is not mandatory that you have an SSN when you are hired, your employer may insist that you have. The reason is that the company may not be able to generate a paycheck without the number. Some types of payroll software may be able to use a "dummy" SSN to generate a paycheck. You must provide your actual SSN as soon as you get it from the Social Security Administration.

✧ More information can be found at www.ssa.gov/employer.

Update Form I-9

Form I-9, *Employment Eligibility Verification*, is designed to determine worker's employment eligibility. Employers are required to complete this form for each employee, including U.S. citizens, and keep it for their records.

When your status changes from temporary to permanent resident, you should show your employer your new document showing your new work authorization: the Green Card or the I-551 stamp in your passport. Your employer is supposed to verify your document and record its title, number and expiration date.

> *The I-551 stamp in your passport is acceptable proof of employment authorization when you complete Form I-9 for your employer.*

When Your Green Card Expires

The I-551 Permanent Resident Card contains an expiration date, making the card valid for 10 years from the date of issuance. After it expires, you will be required to obtain a new card. However, because employment authorization is unlimited for I-551 holders, there will be no need to update the I-9 form.

When Your Conditional Green Card Expired

A conditional Permanent Resident Card (see section 3.3) also gives unlimited employment authorization (as long as the person maintains his legal status).

When you apply for an extension of your conditional Green Card, you can continue working because your Green Card did not expire. When you get either a Notice of Action or a renewed I-551 stamp, it becomes your new proof of status. For that reason the removal of conditions on your Green Card has does not have to be reported at work.

Summary: *After you get permanent resident status, the I-9 form should be updated at work. There is no need to do that after changing your conditional Green Card to a regular one. You are allowed to start employment before your Social Security card comes in the mail.*

4.4.   How Not to Get Fired for Having Used a Fake SSN in the Past

Changing Your SSN at Work

After legalizing your immigration status, you are eligible for an unrestricted Social Security number. If you once gave your employer an ITIN or a fake Social Security number, now is the time to submit your legitimate SSN. You can be truthful with a boss who knew about your undocumented status. However, some unaware employers may be quite disturbed learning that you lied on your job application and that you weren't honest with them.

The Social Security Administration sometimes, although rarely, issues a replacement SSN in cases of pervasive identity fraud, harassment, or life endangerment (see section 8.7). The SSA has instructions for how employers can correct their records when an employee has a new or updated Social Security card.

How to do it: If your employer has previously filed a W-2 wage report for you (see section 7.5) showing a different name or Social Security number, the SSA says to do the following. The employer should prepare and file Form W-2c, *Corrected Wage and Tax Statement,* showing the previously used name or number (see page 100). One W-2c form is sufficient to correct reports for all prior years.

If you worked for someone else under any previous name and/or number, you should contact the nearest SSA office to correct your earnings. Six months later, ask for an *Earnings and Benefit Estimate*

Statement from the SSA (section 8.2), so you can be sure that your past earnings have been recorded to the proper name and number.

The process of correcting your SSA account, as well as paying back taxes and cleaning up your credit report, is explained in chapter 8.

At this point, your employer should update your Form I-9, *Employment Eligibility Verification*, which contains the employer's certification that to the best of his knowledge you (the employee) are authorized to work in the United States. If your Social Security number has changed, the employer should correct your Form I-9, then initial and date the correction.

Can You Get Fired for Using a Fake SSN?

Some companies have a policy that workers who presented false information on an employment application or on Form I-9, *Employment Eligibility Verification*, are subject to termination. Lawyers advise companies to follow such policies with caution. In the court case of *LULAC v. Pasadena School District* (662 F. Supp. 443, S.D. Tex., Apr. 14, 1987), the court held that termination of workers who had provided false information on job applications was discriminatory. Since a large percentage of undocumented immigrants who used false Social Security numbers for work were Hispanics, terminating those employees was especially disadvantageous for Hispanics.

The court decided that the company's discharge of Hispanic employees violated the Immigration Reform Act's provisions forbidding employer discrimination on the basis of citizenship status. Furthermore, the court found that the employer had not uniformly enforced the termination policy. The case became a warning for large companies against punishing immigrant employees who legalized their status.

Many lawyers will gladly take a discrimination case against a big company, but they are not interested in suing small firms where a lesser number of terminations does not establish a discriminatory pattern. Remember that a company can fire you for any reason. Some individual employers and small companies do just that when they learn that workers cheated them by working without authorization.

Justifying Change of SSN

Very important: Many employers don't know that a valid SSN doesn't change when an immigrant receives a Green Card. If you need to justify to your employer why your SSN has changed, look at *Instructions for Forms W-2c and W-3c* (www.irs.gov/pub/irs-pdf/iw2cw3c.pdf). On page 2 under "Special Situations," you will read: *"If your employee is given a new Social Security card following an adjustment to his or her resident status that shows a different name or SSN, file Form W-2c for the most current year only."* When changing your SSN at work, show the instructions to your employer so he sends Form W-2c to the IRS.

Summary: You should give your new Social Security number to your employer, so he reports your earnings properly to the SSA. Some employers are not happy to learn that their workers used fake papers, so show them Form W-2c.

4.5. When You Can Leave Your Sponsor

Suppose your employer petitioned for your permanent residence. For several years you were a loyal, hardworking employee while waiting for your Green Card. You were not paid much, but you were grateful for the opportunity. Now, that you received your Green Card, you would like to quit this job and move on in life. Some bosses are quite prepared for the worker's departure seeing it as a natural completion of the deal.

How long do you have to work for your employer who sponsored you for a Green Card? The law does not require any specific period of time. The rule rather pertains to your and your employer's intent throughout the application process. By petitioning for you, the employer confirmed his intent to employ you for a permanent (opposed to a temporary) position when the Green Card is approved. In return, you confirmed your intention to accept that permanent position after the approval of your permanent residency status.

There is no time period required to stay with the employer after the Green Card is approved. However, if you leave the job quickly after the approval, your intent could be questioned. Therefore, it is prudent to remain in that job for at least a year or two – a solid time period to indicate true intent.

When you are eligible and apply for citizenship, you will go through a naturalization interview. The immigration examiner may inquire when and why you left your sponsor. Seeing a solid work record, he will not question your intent.

4.6. What Needs to Be Done at the Bank

The Bank Has Your Valid Social Security Number

If you provided the bank with your valid Social Security number while opening an account (even an SSN not valid for employment), and never filled out Form W-8, *Certificate of Foreign Status of Beneficial Owner for United States Tax Withholding*, at the bank, then you don't have to report anything to the bank after legalizing your status. From the tax reporting point of view, nothing has changed.

The Bank Has Your ITIN or Doesn't Have Your Number

When you first opened your bank account, chances are that as a foreigner with an ITIN or no number at all, you filled out Form W-8 and your were treated as an "exempt foreign person," for whom bank interest is not reported to the government.

Now, upon legalizing your immigration status, you are no longer an "exempt foreign person" for tax purposes. You have to notify your bank within 30 days about the change of your status. For that, at the bank, you should fill out Form W-9, *Request for Taxpayer Identification Number and Certification*, in which you provide your new SSN. The reporting will then begin, which means that the bank will inform the IRS about the bank interest you are earning. You are supposed to pay taxes on that interest.

If you don't have your SSN yet, fill out Form W-9, *Request for Taxpayer Identification Number and Certification* at the bank, to testify that you are waiting for the number to be issued. Write "APPLIED FOR" on the form. You will have 60 days to get your number and give it to the financial institution. When you receive your SSN, complete another W-9 form at the bank.

If the bank does not receive your number within 60 days, it may start backup withholdings, which means that it will send 30 percent of your interest earnings to the IRS.

If this procedure seems complicated to you, just tell your bank that you just received a Green Card. They will know what to do.

4.7. Register with the Selective Service

Important: If you are a man 18 to 25 years old, you must register with the Selective Service, commonly known as draft registration. Failure to register constitutes a ground for the government to deny you naturalization as well as for other legal penalties. When you register, you tell the government that you are available to serve in the U.S. Armed Forces. The United States does not have a military draft now. Permanent residents and citizens do not have to serve in the Armed Forces unless they want to.

Failure to register makes you ineligible for naturalization as it reflects poorly on your "good moral character" (see page 24).

☘ You can register for the Selective Service at a U.S. Post Office or over the Internet at <u>www.sss.gov</u>. To speak with a representative of the Selective Service, call 1-847-688-6888.

4.8. Convert Your Temporary Driver's License into a Permanent One

Having a Green Card, you are free to get your driver's license. You cannot convert your foreign license into an American one; you have to apply for a license here and pass a driving test and written exam. In most states, the only foreign driver's license that can be converted is a Canadian license.

Driver's License for Former Temporary Visa Holders

Chances are that you already have a temporary driver's license. After obtaining your Green Card, you can get a permanent one.

Background information: Foreigners on certain temporary visas are issued a temporary driver's license – one with the expiration date limited to the period of time they are authorized to be in the United States. In other words, their license expires when their visa does. This ensures that state identification documents become invalid if persons have overstayed their authorized visit to this country.

Students, participants of exchange programs, and temporary workers may be admitted for "duration of status." Their driver's license (or state-issued identification document) expires on the date the education, exchange, or worker program terminates. If the applicant is unable to provide the exact date when the program ends, the driver license's expiration date is set to one year from the date of the application. The license can be renewed as long as the applicant provides documentation showing he is still enrolled in the program.

Regardless of what kind of temporary visa you had, you should renew your driver's license after getting your Green Card. The new one will be valid for five years.

Check your state's rules for license renewal (www.dmv.org has links for all states). Go to your state Department of Motor Vehicles in person, and bring your Green Card and other required documents. Your new driver's license is going to be sent to you by mail.

Driver's License for Conditional Residents

Immigrants with conditional Green Cards (see section 3.3) can only get driver's licenses which expire with their Green Cards. This can potentially cause problems.

Example: Let's assume that your conditional Green Card expires on April 1. You filed for removal of conditions several weeks before that date, but you haven't received any communication from the Immigration Service yet. On April 1 your driver's license expired. You went to a local DMV to find out if they can give you a temporary extension for your driver's license. The DMV officer said that he cannot do it without the proper paperwork from the USCIS, such as Notice of Approval or a new Green Card. What should you do to have your license renewed?

Solution: To avoid such a situation, you should file Form I-751, *Petition to Remove Conditions on Residence*, as early as you can, starting 90 days before the date of expiration of your conditional Green Card (see section 3.3). Hopefully, you will receive Notice of Approval (NOA) on time. Your NOA extends your conditional Green Card for another year and should be accepted at the DMV as a valid immigration document. If the DMV officer is not familiar with an NOA letter and does not want to accept it, try another office which might be more know-ledgeable.

If you did not receive anything from the Immigration Service, make an InfoPass appointment (section 3.7) at your local USCIS office and ask for a new I-551 stamp in your passport so you can renew your driver's license.

4.9. Where and How to Report Your Name Change

Many immigrants get their Green Cards through marriage and as-sume their married name. Others choose to Americanize their name to make it easier to use in the U.S.

If you changed your legal name, you need to inform all government agencies and companies you are doing business with. It is actually a routine procedure, as millions of Americans change names due to marriages, divorces, adoptions, or court orders.

You should inform the following people and institutions about your name change: your employer, banks, retirement plans, credit card companies, your mortgage company, voter registration (citizens on-ly), your health-care providers (doctor, dentist), insurance companies (health, life, auto, and home insurance policies), utility companies (phone, cable, gas, electric, etc.), and any organizations you may be a member of. Legal documents such as contracts and wills should be updated (change the beneficiary to your spouse at the same time).

The more established you are in the U.S., the more places you have to inform of your name change. A newcomer, on the other hand, faces few formalities.

Documents You Need

To change your last name based on marriage, no formal name-change procedure is required. Because a woman traditionally takes her hus-band's name when she is married, a certified copy of a marriage li-cense is sufficient documentation for a woman's name change. Just take certified copies of your marriage license to the various authori-ties (Social Security, DMV, etc.) and apply for new IDs. Your new So-cial Security card and new driver's license will be useful as identifica-tion for changing your name on other important documents.

To register a name change, you need copies of documents that show your old name and your new name. Your old name can be shown on your driver's license, birth certificate, foreign passport (still valid, even with expired visa), or state ID. For proving your new name, you need a certified copy of a marriage license, a divorce certificate, or an official court related document validating the name change.

If you have to prove your address, use utility bills (cable, electric, but no phone bill) or rental lease.

For an SSN change you need your old and new Social Security card. If you lost your old card, provide official correspondence showing your previous SSN, for example a letter from the IRS or the Social Security Administration.

How to Apply

In person: Some institutions, such as the Department of Motor Vehicles, require in-person appearance. Even if it is not required, a personal visit may be the most time-efficient. When going to the office personally, have original documents with you. However, never send originals by mail; only send copies that are certified, if required. A Notary Public can certify a copy of a document if you show him the original.

By mail: Many institutions have forms for changing personal information. Call and order one by mail or download it online. Fill out all required fields, attach any required documents, and keep a copy for your records. If no form is available, write a letter (see a sample on the next page). Attach it to the last bill, statement, or correspondence for easy identification. As identity theft is frequent, the company may contact you to verify the request.

The Internal Revenue Service (IRS)

You may change your name using Form 8822, *Change of Address*, to submit an address or name change at any time during the year. You can download the form at the IRS website, www.irs.gov or order by calling 1-800-TAX-FORM (1-800-829-3676). Follow the instructions.

If your name was misspelled, you can call the IRS at 1-800-829-1040 and they will correct the spelling of your name over the phone. You can also simply print your name correctly on the next year's tax return.

The Social Security Administration

By law, you are required to get a new Social Security identification card whenever your name changes. Your SSN will remain the same, but the SSA will update its records and issue another card with your new name. If you neglect to change your name, the SSA will send your employer a "no-match letter," informing him about the discrepancy. Then you will have to fix the problem quickly, or you may lose your job.

You can apply in person or by mail. Remember, that the SSA only accepts originals or certified copies of documents, not photocopies. You need to fill out SSA Form SS-5, *Application for a Social Security Card*, which is also used for changing information on your record. Download the form from www.ssa.gov/online/ss-5.pdf or call 1-800-772-1213. Follow the instructions.

If you ever worked using somebody else's name or Social Security number, read chapter 8 for information.

The Immigration Service

To change your name on your Green Card, you must notify the US-

---

Request for Name Change

Ref: Name change at acct. 12345678

To: Credit Card Company

I recently got married and changed my place of residence. For that reason please change your records of my credit card account to reflect my new name and address. Below I have listed the pertinent information you can use to update my card name account records:

Pre-marriage information: full maiden name, date of birth, old mailing address

Married information: new married name, new mailing address

In addition to changing the information, please issue me a new credit card in my new name.

I am enclosing a copy of my marriage license and the latest monthly statement. If you have any questions please feel free to contact me by phone at 1-212-234-5623 or by e-mail: mary.j@gmail.com.

Thank you for your prompt attention to my request.

Sincerely,

Your signature

CIS by filing Form I-90, *Application to Replace Permanent Resident Card.* Make an InfoPass appointment and bring original or certified documents in person. See section 3.7 for directions. The Green Card will be sent to you by mail.

Attention: *If a name on your new Green Card does not correspond to the name on your foreign passport, you will be able to travel outside the U.S., but you may have problems returning to the country.*

After changing your name, you should get a new passport from your country. If that is not possible, travel with a certified copy of your marriage license or court document. Many people don't want to take chances and they postpone their name change until naturalization.

Motor Vehicle Department

Most states require that drivers notify the Department of Motor Vehicles in writing within 10-15 days of any change of name. You must appear in person and present legal proof of name change. A new license will be issued and mailed to you. You will be required to pay a fee.

Check the procedures in your state. You can find your state DMV's website through www.dmv.org.

Summary: After changing your name, you should inform all companies you deal with, especially the Social Security Administration. Follow the instructions provided in this section.

4.10. Address Change

Address change is easy; in most cases no documentation is necessary. In addition to informing all the institutions stated in section 4.9, you should notify the U.S. Post Office. There is no need to inform the Social Security Administration about your move.

Many institutions have forms for address change. Call and order one by mail or download it online. Many bills and statements have address change forms in the back, sometimes on the reverse side of the envelopes they were mailed to you in. Just fill them out.

Post Office

At the U.S. Post Office, fill out an Official Change of Address form. For 12 months the U.S. Postal Service (USPS) will forward all first class mail to you. For 6 months after that, the mail will be returned to sender, but your new address will be listed on it so senders may update their records. For that reason, magazine subscriptions and other mail will be coming to your new place of residence. After 18 months you fall out of the system entirely.

You can also change your address online, at http://www.usps.com, permanently or temporarily. You will need to provide your credit card number as identification. You do not need to change your name at the U.S. Post Office.

Department of Motor Vehicles

You must notify your state DMV when you move to a new address, usually within 10 days, by phone or by mail. State DMVs have Change of Address forms. Download one online or pick one up at your local office.

Check procedures in your state. You can find your state DMV's website through www.dmv.org.

Internal Revenue Service

If your address has changed, you need to notify the IRS to ensure you receive possible IRS refunds or correspondence.

If you change your address before filing your return, you may correct the address legibly on the mailing label from your tax package or write the new address on your tax return when you file. When your return is processed, the IRS will update its records.

If you changed your address after filing your return, you may complete Form 8822, *Address Change Request*, and send it to the address shown on the form. Download the form from www.irs.gov/pub/irs-pdf/f8822.pdf or order by calling 1-800-TAX-FORM (1-800-829-3676).

Summary: *You should report your new address at the Post Office, the DMV, IRS, USCIS, your bank, and other institutions you get important correspondence from.*

5. ESTABLISHING YOURSELF IN AMERICA

Within a few weeks of arriving to America, immigrants are faced with the tasks of finding a place to stay, getting a job, obtaining means of transportation, and arranging other necessities. If with their family, they must send their children to school, and provide for their well-being and safety. Although it takes a lot of determination to start a new life with little money and possibly limited command of English, countless immigrants succeed. With perseverance and hard work, you will succeed as well.

This chapter lists some essential issues for newcomers.

5.1. Your First Place to Live

Finding appropriate housing can be challenging. Cost is the biggest barrier, since housing is expensive and immigrants usually obtain low-paying jobs during their first years in America. Upon arrival, most newcomers spend anywhere from a few days to months sharing cramped quarters with family or friends. This, however, can raise a landlord's objections. Even if the family owns an apartment or a house, overcrowding may cause neighbors to complain.

Homeowners don't like neighbors sharing one-family houses with other families or setting up rooming for immigrants. Neighbors' concerns are not necessarily ethnically motivated, but stem from the fact that overcrowding increases traffic, overloads public schools, and puts strains on social services.

Occupancy Limits

In many places all over the world it is quite acceptable that an extended family shares a tiny apartment or even a single room. This is not so in the United States.

Local housing laws limit the maximum number of people that may live in one dwelling unit (an apartment or a house). Usually, local housing law permits one dwelling to be used by:

- one family (related by blood, marriage, adoption) and not more than one additional person (sometimes two), or

- two adults and their dependents (if any) and not more than one additional person (sometimes two).

Some towns define family very broadly, as including siblings and first cousins. Other places have stricter definitions, for example that family only includes immediate relatives such as spouses, dependent children, and parents.

In addition to these general restrictions, occupancy limits are determined by zoning for the area where the property is located, building classification, the amount of habitable living space, the number of bedrooms, and sometimes even parking requirements. The most restrictive requirement prevails.

For example, in New York City, every occupant should have a livable area of not less than 80 square feet (see Subchapter 3, Article 4 of Housing Maintenance Code, www.housingnyc.com/html/resources/hmc/sub3/art4.html).

A long-time rule of thumb suggested by the U.S. Department of Housing and Urban Development (HUD) was a limit of two persons per bedroom, although configuration of bedrooms and the genders of children are also a factor. This standard is implemented by many cooperatives and multi-family housing complexes. For that reason, some local authorities or your landlord may object to your daughter and son over a certain age sharing the same bedroom.

Sharing an Apartment

Landlords are entitled to set reasonable limits on the number of occupants per rental unit. Therefore, your landlord has the right to object to your sharing your apartment with a person who is not an immediate family member. This restriction may be spelled out in the rental lease. But even if the landlord wants to be flexible, adding a roommate may exceed the local occupancy limit. If it does not, the landlord may allow you to have a roommate but will raise your rent to compensate for usage of more gas, electricity, and hot water as well as for greater wear and tear on the apartment.

Bear in mind that limiting the number of children per unit is likely to be discriminatory. Landlords are not allowed to discourage families with children from moving in; they are also not allowed to refuse to renew the lease only because more children are born into the family or more children arrive from abroad.

Roommates in a New York City Apartment

Generally, one additional occupant is allowed (in addition to the tenant or owner and his family), not to exceed two people per bedroom. Some localities, such as New York City, allow more.

In New York City, apartment sharing is regulated by the Real Property Law (RPL), paragraph §§235-f, also known as the Roommate Law. It essentially states that landlords of New York City apartments may limit the total number of people living in an apartment to comply with legal overcrowding standards. However, it is unlawful for a landlord to restrict occupancy of an apartment to the tenant named in the lease or to that tenant and his immediate family.

When the lease names only one tenant, that tenant may share the apartment with his immediate family, one additional occupant and the occupant's dependent children, provided that the tenant or the tenant's spouse occupies the premises as his or her primary residence.

When the lease names more than one tenant, these tenants may share their apartment with immediate family, and, if one of the tenants named in the lease moves out, that tenant may be replaced with another occupant and the dependent children of the occupant. At least one of the tenants named in the lease or that tenant's spouse must occupy the shared apartment as his or her primary residence.

Tenants must inform their landlords of the name of any occupant within 30 days after the occupant has moved into the apartment or within 30 days of a landlord's request for this information.

🕸 More information on roommates in New York State is available in the *Tenant's Rights Guide*. Go to www.oag.state.ny.us and type "Tenants' Rights Guide" in the search box. See www.tenant.net/Other_Laws/ for more information.

For information in other states search the web for "tenants' rights" and the name of your state.

How Not to Get in Trouble

Owners of houses may be punished if they violate local laws. They may receive citations and will have to attend hearings. If they do not cooperate, the county may even sue them. As evidence of overcrowding, the county may use water consumption records and neighbors' testimony. If found guilty, owners have to pay fines of up to several hundred dollars for every day that regulations were violated. Prevent this from happening!

Learn your local occupancy laws. Read your rental lease to find out whether or not you are allowed to have visitors or roommates. Homeowners should call their local housing department to obtain the occupancy limits in the area. If in doubt, consult a lawyer.

Learn the definitions of basic terms. Learn what "family member" or "occasional visitor" specifically means according to the occupancy regulations in your jurisdiction. For example, in New York State, "family member" is defined as a husband, wife, son, daughter, stepson, stepdaughter, father, mother, stepfather, stepmother, brother, sister, grandfather, grandmother, grandson, granddaughter, father-in-law, mother-in-law, son-in-law or daughter-in-law of the tenant or permanent tenant. In New York State, the definition of "family member" also includes any other person(s) residing with the tenant as a primary resident who can prove emotional and financial commitment and interdependence with the tenant (unmarried partners, homosexual couples, etc., see website www.housingnyc.com/html/resources/dhcr/dhcr30.html). A "visitor" is usually someone who stays with you for up to 30 days.

Don't be afraid. The immigration status of the house occupants is of no interest to housing authorities. Be informed that housing inspectors usually are not allowed into the house to inspect the living conditions and the number of occupants. They will intervene only if the violation is clearly visible or they receive a complaint.

Don't inconvenience the neighbors. If they get annoyed, they may complain to the authorities. Make sure that your occasional visitors are not noisy and they don't use neighbors' parking spaces.

Nobody will object to your having an occasional guest. However, check your lease (if you are a renter) or local regulations (if you are a home owner) before you invite your relatives from abroad for extended periods of time. Seek a lawyer's advice before you rent out rooms in your house or apartment.

How to Rent an Apartment

Prices for apartments vary in the U.S. depending on location, size, and amenities. Water is included in the rent price; for other utilities, such as electricity and gas, you directly pay the respective companies.

Owners of small houses with few apartments may be willing to rent you an apartment without checking any information. If you seem trustworthy, provide good references, and have money for the rent, you may receive keys to your apartment without any formalities. In larger buildings, however, you must file an application and disclose your basic personal data, employer, previous addresses, family composition, and Social Security number. The landlord may check your background to ensure that you are a responsible person and you will be able to afford the rent (see section 11.5).

If you are not yet working, or you have no credit history, you may need someone to sign the rental agreement with you. This person, called a "co-signer," will have to pay the rent if you are not able to.

You sign a rental agreement or "lease" if the landlord agrees to rent to you. By doing that, you agree to pay your rent timely and stay for a specific length of time. Most leases are for one year. The lease may also list the number of people who can live in the home. In return, the landlord must keep the property safe and in good condition.

In most places, if there is no written lease, a verbal month-to-month lease applies (also called a 30-day lease). Under such a lease, you can move out any time, as long as you give at least one month's notice to the landlord. It works the other way also: the landlord can ask you to leave, but he has to give you a month's notice.

You will have to pay a security deposit, which is equal to one or two month's rent. Any damages done by you to the apartment will be paid with this money. If you leave the place like you found it (apart from regular wear and tear), the deposit should be returned to you.

It is important to pay your rent on time, as late payments may be recorded in your credit history. If you ever got evicted from an apartment, you may not be able to find a place to live because of bad tenant history (section 11.5).

After you get your Green Card, your housing rights stay the same. You may, however, qualify for government help in renting a low-income apartment or purchasing a home as a first-time home buyer.

Summary: There are limits on the number of unrelated people who can live together. Landlords will rent an apartment to you if you can prove you are a responsible person who can afford the rent.

5.2. Protect Yourself and Your Family

Health Insurance in the U.S.

The United States is the only developed country that does not provide its residents with universal health care. Medical care is expensive in the U.S., so is health insurance. You should get medical coverage for yourself and your family as soon as possible.

Most Americans get health insurance from their employers (see section 6.7). All large companies provide their workers with health coverage, but not many small companies can afford it. Some employers pay the entire monthly health insurance fee (called a premium); others pay only part of the fee and deduct the rest from the employee's paycheck.

If you are insured and go to the doctor, the bills are sent to your health insurance company, which pays for some or all of your medical services. Often you must pay a portion of your medical bills called a "co-payment."

With no health insurance, you must pay for your health care by yourself. Those who cannot afford may be able to get federal or state health-care assistance. Most states provide some type of assistance to children and pregnant women. Check with the public health department of your state or city.

If you are seriously sick or injured, you can go to the emergency room of the nearest hospital. Most hospitals are required by federal law to treat patients with a medical emergency even if the person cannot pay. You will be expected to pay the bill later, but if you are unable to, the hospital may help (see section 10.2).

Medicaid – Health Insurance for the Poor

Medicaid is a health insurance program available only to people who have limited income and meet other requirements. Each state has its own Medicaid guidelines. Potential recipients include children, pregnant women, the aged, the blind, the disabled, and people who are eligible to receive public assistance. Medicaid pays for medical services such as visits to the doctor and hospitalization.

Permanent residents who entered the U.S. before August 22, 1996 may be able to get Medicaid if they fulfill certain conditions. Permanent residents who entered the U.S. on or after August 22, 1996 may be able to get Medicaid if they have lived in the U.S. for five years or longer and meet other requirements.

🕸 You can view your state's Medicaid office contact information by visiting www.benefits.gov. In the "Benefits Quick Search" box, look for "Medicaid."

Medicare – Health Insurance for the Elderly

Medicare is a government health insurance plan that provides hospital, medical, and surgical benefits for persons age 65 and older and for people with certain disabilities. Medicare has several parts: Part A, Part B, and Part D – prescription drug coverage. Medicare Part A is free and provides basic hospital insurance. Medicare Part B, for which you pay monthly fee, covers visits to the doctor, ambulances, tests, and outpatient hospital care. Medicare Part D helps pay for medications doctors prescribe for treatment.

Permanent residents can get Medicare if they meet certain conditions. Generally, you must have worked in the U.S. for at least 10 years (or 40 quarters) over the course of your life.

For more information, read the publication *Medicare & You* available from www.medicare.gov/publications/pubs/pdf/10050.pdf.

☎ English and Spanish-speaking representatives can answer your questions at 1-800-633-4227 (1-800-MEDICARE).

State Children's Health Insurance Program

The State Children's Health Insurance Program (SCHIP) provides health coverage to uninsured children under 18 years of age whose families earn too much to qualify for Medicaid but too little to afford private coverage. All states provide immunizations and preventive care at no cost; some states may cover much more, including visits to the doctor, prescription medicines, hospital care, and other healthcare services.

Children can get free or low-cost healthcare without affecting their parents' immigration status.

⑁ More information and state SCHIP directories can be found at www.cms.hhs.gov/home/schip.asp.

Health Centers for Those Without Medical Insurance

Many government-funded clinics (medical offices) provide free or low-cost services for people with no health insurance. You pay what you can afford, based on your income. Most communities have at least one clinic.

⑁ To find a clinic or doctor near you visit http://findahealthcenter.hrsa.gov and type in your zip code.

You can also look in the yellow pages under "Social Services."

Summary: *Providing yourself and your family with health insurance is your own responsibility. Most permanent residents are ineligible for Medicaid and SCHIP during their first five years in the U.S. However, there are programs for those who cannot afford medical care.*

5.3. Education for Your Children

Immigrants have high hopes for their children's future and give them strong support for educational achievement. Their children, growing up in a bilingual, cross-cultural environment, tend to be adaptable and ambitious. For those reasons, as documented by many studies, immigrant children on average perform better at school than their American peers.

In the U.S., any child can rise to his or her full potential. But it is up to us, the parents, to ensure that they take advantage of all the opportunities. Even in a typical American public school, there are some avenues for ambitious, hard working and gifted students, starting from the first grade all the way to college.

Basics About Public Education

In the U.S., all children between ages of 5-7 and 16-18 years (depending on the state) are required to attend school. Education in public schools for grades from kindergarten through 12 is free regardless of family income or immigration status. Supported by taxes paid to the government, public schools are open to all children residing within the school district. Which public school your child attends is determined by where you live.

Some schools in the U.S. are private, operated by secular or religious organizations. They charge tuition and may have admission requirements. Some offer financial help for students who cannot pay the tuition.

In the U.S., parents may also teach their children at home. This is called homeschooling. See www.hslda.org for more information.

When you arrive to the United States, you have the obligation to register your children at school. For registration, you need proof that your children received certain vaccinations and that they live within the school district (parent's driver's license, telephone bill, light bill or any other pre-printed bill).

Your children will be placed in a class (grade) based on their age and how much previous education they have. Sometimes a school may give your child a test to decide what grade he or she should be in. In some schools, students just beginning to learn English may take an ESL (English as a Second Language) class.

Special Programs for Gifted Children

Attention: Most school districts have some kind of program for students they have identified as "gifted and talented." Find out about gifted programs in your school district; they are rarely publicized. If you overlook a note from school about the selection process, you may miss your chance.

Parents in New York should start by visiting the website http://insideschools.org. In other parts of the country, you should contact your local school district or Department of Education. Talk to teachers and other parents.

Some districts have extensive information posted online while others have next to none readily available. Remember that rules and deadlines may change. Inquire as soon as possible, because some districts test children for gifted programs as early as in kindergarten.

The special programs for the gifted and talented can give our children excellent free education. It is the duty of parents to be aware of those opportunities and ensure that their children take advantage of them.

Opportunities for Excellent Students in High School

Ambitious students have many opportunities to succeed in American high schools (grade 9 to 12), and then to move on to the best colleges. High schools provide a variety of programs: Advanced Placement (AP) courses, honors classes, independent studies, online courses (like Stanford's Education Program for Gifted Youth (EPGY), 1-650-329-9920, http://epgy.stanford.edu), various competitions, etc.

Some districts have specialized high schools for academically and artistically gifted students. To be admitted, students must pass examination in the eighth grade, sometimes earlier. For information on New York City specialized high schools see http://schools.nyc.gov.

College or University

America gives us and our children many opportunities for good college-level education, regardless of the family's financial status and even immigration status. Some public colleges, particularly community colleges, accept undocumented immigrants. Green Card holders have a broad array of choices open to them.

Students in higher education choose a specific subject to study in depth (this subject is called their "major"). Choosing a major helps prepare them for employment or further education in that field.

A college education can be expensive. Public colleges and universities cost less than private ones, especially for residents of the state where the college or university is located. However, there are many types of financial aid available for students and their families.

Table 5-1. Higher Education in the U.S.

Degree Type	Type of School	Years of Schooling
Certificate	Community College/Trade School	6 months to 2 years
Associate's degree	Community College	2 years
Bachelor's degree	4-year college or university	4 years
Master's degree	University	3 years
Doctorate degree	University	2-8 years
Professional degree	Specialized school	2-5 years

How to Pay for College

Although college education is expensive, there are many ways to minimize the costs.

Federal aid: The U.S. government provides financial help to students who qualify by their financial need, not by their grades. The federal aid includes grants (money that doesn't have to be repaid), Work Study (money earned while in school) and loans (money that you borrow and must repay later with interest).

For more information on federal financial aid programs, read the booklet *Funding Education Beyond High School: The Guide to Federal Student Aid* published by the U.S. Department of Education. Order it by calling at 1-800-433-3243 or download it from the website http://studentaid.ed.gov/students/publications/student_guide/index.html. Information is also available in Spanish.

ROTC program: Young adults can attend college free or for a low cost if they participate in the U.S. Armed Forces Reserve Officer Training Corp (ROTC), the military's college-based program for officer training. This program can offer both college financial aid assistance and a post-college career in the Army, Navy, Marines, or Air Force. No monetary payback is required.

State financial aid: All states have established their own student aid programs that can supplement federal programs. The aid programs themselves are quite varied. Contact your state commission on higher education for information on eligibility requirements. The website www.student.gov has links for all states.

College grants and scholarships do not have to be repaid. They are awarded by organizations, private companies, individuals, and the government. Searching the web for "college scholarships" will return thousands of entries. Start your research at www.student.gov. Your ethnic organizations may offer some scholarships as well.

Tuition reduction. Colleges reduce tuition for good students whom they want to attract. Some prestigious Ivy League universities, such as Harvard, Yale, and Princeton, offer free tuition to families with incomes below $60,000 and significant breaks to other middle-income families.

Your Native Language and Culture

Speak your native language at home, so your children learn the language fluently. Outside the home they will learn English to perfection, but inside the home they should communicate in your language. This will not slow down their development; to the contrary. Bilingual and multicultural environment makes children more adaptable, creative, tolerant, and confident. Speaking more that one language allows children to communicate with all members of the extended family, and later allows them greater flexibility to choose a place to live and work. Children can learn languages very quickly, and will still be able to speak English very well even if they only learn it in school.

Many ethnic communities run language and culture schools for children or religious Sunday schools in houses of worship. Your children should attend them so they can remain connected to your culture as they grow up in America.

Summary: In the U.S., exceptional, motivated students can obtain excellent education for free. There are many opportunities from grammar school all the way to college. Speak your native language at home, so your children learn your language and culture as they are raised in America.

5.4. Evaluation of Your Foreign Diploma and Continued Education

Education for You

Many immigrants need to make important decisions about improving their language and job skills. Education is always a great investment into one's future. If you decide to go back to school, you will be in good company. Americans know that learning does not have to end when you become an adult. In the U.S., people are encouraged to become "lifelong learners."

Learning English. There are many places where you can improve your language skills. English as a Second Language (ESL) classes are popular. During day or evening hours, ESL classes are conducted in community colleges, public libraries, places of worship, or at some community organizations. Private schools also give language courses on various levels. Public libraries have ESL books, tapes, CDs, and computer software.

Job training. Many community colleges and private trade schools offer adult education programs with a wide variety of employment training courses. You may enroll to prepare for a new career, or to get the latest information in your field. Employment training classes may require a fee. Visit www.careeronestop.org and click on "Education and Training" for local courses in your chosen field.

Learn about America. As you are settling in a new country, make sure to learn as much as you can about it. Along the path to achieving your goals, you must make many choices about how to navigate the U.S. financial and legal system. These choices can accelerate your economic success or slow it down. For that reason you should learn about banking, investments, money management, financial planning, taxes, insurance, credit, business, real estate, and the economy. The more you know, the easier it will be for you to build assets and financial security for yourself and your family.

Evaluation of Your Foreign Diploma

Courses, study programs, and educational systems vary considerably from one country to another. Diploma evaluation is an assessment of how your foreign education compares to a certain program in an accredited college or university in the United States.

There is no single authority in the United States for the recognition of foreign degrees and other qualifications. In the U.S., your education can be recognized by your employer, a school, or a licensing institution.

- The hiring employer can screen job applicants looking at many factors, including their education. It is up to the employer to decide whether a candidate's foreign degrees or other qualifications are sufficient. In unregulated occupations, employers don't request formal degree evaluation.

- The American college or university where you seek admission is free to evaluate the credits or degrees you earned abroad, according to its own standards.
- State licensing boards set education standards for individuals seeking to practice regulated professions in that state. If you apply for a professional license in a regulated profession, you will have to have your credentials formally assessed.

As we see, you may need to have your diploma formally evaluated when you seek employments in a regulated occupation, apply for a professional license in a regulated profession, or seek admission to an American college or university.

Upon coming to the U.S., most immigrants have no need to evaluate their foreign diplomas for employment. American employers value professional skills more than college degrees.

If you need your education evaluated, ask the requesting institution how to go about it. They will refer you to a credential evaluation service. Credential evaluation services are independent organizations that perform analyses of non-U.S. qualifications and issue recommendations as to how a particular foreign qualification compares to a similar qualification in the U.S. education system, labor market, or the professions.

If no service is recommended, then you can select a credential evaluation service yourself. Use the company affiliated with one of the following organizations: National Association of Credential Evaluation Services (NACES), www.naces.org or Association of International Credentials Evaluators (AICE), www.naeg.org (tel. 1-888-539-2804).

You can expect that different credential evaluation services may evaluate you differently according to their criteria.

Summary: *Education is the best investment, not only for your children, but also for you. Chances are that your foreign diploma will be fully respected by your employer if you work in an unregulated occupation.*

5.5. Pay Taxes that Are Due

Americans pay taxes to federal, state, and local governments in order to fund services provided by the government. There are different types of taxes, such as income tax, sales tax, estate tax, and property tax, to name a few.

The U.S. Internal Revenue Service (IRS), a division of the U.S. Treasury Department, is the federal government agency responsible for collecting federal taxes. State departments of taxation are in charge of collecting state and local taxes.

As a permanent resident of the U.S., you are obligated to pay taxes. If you don't, you may lose your resident status.

Income Taxes

Income tax is paid on "taxable income" – your wages, self-employment, tips, bank interest, etc., minus certain deductions. Most people pay income taxes by having money withheld from their paychecks. Banks usually do not withhold taxes on interest. The amount of income tax you owe depends on how much you earn. Income tax rates are lower for people who make less money.

Anyone residing in the United States who earns income over a certain amount needs to file a tax return and pay any taxes he owes, regardless of his immigration status. To "file" means to fill out and send in tax forms.

IRS Form 1040 is the most frequently used "income tax return." It should be filed by April 15 of the following year. Only those with earnings below a certain limit are exempt from filing tax returns. Many companies and individual tax preparers are ready to help you calculate your taxes and file your tax return for a moderate fee.

Social Security and Medicare Taxes

Social Security and Medicare taxes are withheld from your paycheck. You pay 7.65 percent of your wages and your employer matches this amount. This way 15.3 percent of each worker's wages are paid in Social Security taxes, up to a certain annual earnings limit. These taxes, called FICA (Federal Insurance Contributions Act) taxes are used to finance the Social Security and Medicare programs (page 49).

How to Pay Income Taxes

If you only earn salary (wages) from employment and bank interest, then filing your taxes is simple. You need the following:

Form W-2 from your employer (see page 98). Your salary and all withheld taxes are listed there.
Form 1099 from your bank stating interest paid to you (page 97).
IRS Form 1040EZ, 1040A, or 1040 plus instructions (from www.irs.gov).

Fill out the forms according to the instructions and mail them to the IRS. Make a copy of the forms to keep for your records.

If you had too much taken out of your paycheck, you will get a refund. If you did not have enough taken out of your paycheck, you must send a payment to the IRS.

The Social Security system provides benefits for certain retired and disabled workers with their families, as well as for some family members of deceased workers. Medicare taxes pay for medical services for most people over age 65. Usually, you must work a total of 10 years (or 40 quarters) over the course of your life to get Social Security retirement benefits and Medicare benefits. Younger workers need fewer than 10 years of work to get disability benefits or for their family to get survivors' benefits based on their earnings.

The Social Security Administration keeps track of your salary and paid premiums because it needs this information to determine the amount of your future benefits (see section 8.1).

Other Taxes

In the U.S., you pay many other taxes. Here are some of them.

Sales taxes are levied by state and local governments. Retail stores collect and forward sales taxes to the state or local treasury. Sales taxes help pay for services provided by state and local government such as roads, police, and firemen. Unlike in many other countries, there is no Value Added Tax (VAT) in the U.S.

Real estate tax, also called property tax, is paid by owners of real estate – houses, apartments, land, and commercial buildings. Real estate taxes – the main source of income for local governments – help support public schools, roads, local police, fire fighters, etc.

Tip: If you own real estate purchased earlier when you were a non-resident using the Individual Taxpayer Identification Number (ITIN), you may now, as a permanent resident, qualify for some real-estate tax breaks. Ask an accountant or a real-estate professional.

Estate taxes are "death" taxes applied to any property that is transferred at death. Estates below a certain limit pass to beneficiaries tax-free. This tax does not apply between spouses, who can leave any amount to one another upon death – a right known as "unlimited marital deduction."

Tip: Unlimited marital deduction does not apply when the recipient is a noncitizen spouse. For that reason, affluent couples can save a lot by assuming American citizenship. Ask your accountant for details.

What New Green Card Holders Should Know

As a permanent resident, you are required to file a tax return whether you are living in the U.S. or not, exactly as any U.S. citizen would be. You must report your worldwide income and, if necessary, pay any taxes.

If the foreign country in which you have income has a tax treaty with the United States, you can benefit from it. The U.S. has such treaties with about 60 other countries. This type of treaty would generally say that only the U.S. can tax the income you receive. However, this rule will not apply if you spend too much time (typically more than 183 days) earning income in the other country.

To learn about your country's treaty with the U.S., go to www.irs.gov and type "tax treaties" in the search box.

If you end up being taxed in both countries, you can take advantage of a "foreign tax credit" in the U.S. This means that taxes paid abroad are subtracted as a credit on your domestic tax return which prevents double taxation.

American residents working abroad may be entitled to the "foreign earned income exclusion" which could eliminate any income tax. Your accountant can explain more.

If you do not file income tax returns while living outside of the U.S. for any length of time, or if you say that you are a "non-immigrant" on your tax returns, the U.S. government may decide that you have given up your permanent resident status.

When Does Your Tax Obligation Start?

A Green Card holder becomes a U.S. resident for tax purposes (a person responsible for paying taxes on his worldwide income) on the first day in the calendar year on which he is present in the United States as a lawful permanent resident. In other words, you start paying U.S. taxes on your worldwide income starting on the first day of the year you immigrated to the U.S.

This means that if you sold your house before departure, this transaction may be taxable in the U.S. However, you can exclude up to $250,000 of the gain on the sale of your main home ($500,000 for a married couple filing jointly) if you owned the home and lived in it for at least two years in the past five years, ending on the date of the sale. The law does not differentiate whether the home is in a foreign country. It also does not consider whether you were a resident of this country during the period of ownership and use. Read IRS Publication 523, *Selling Your Home* (www.irs.gov).

Determining the date when your tax obligation would end is much more complicated. For more information, search www.irs.gov for "Residency Beginning and Ending Dates."

What if You Haven't Filed Prior U.S. Income Tax Returns?

If you lived in the United States and have not filed a U.S. income tax return for one or more years, but there is no tax liability for any of those years (you don't owe any taxes), the IRS expects you to file returns for the current year and two prior years. However, if you have not filed a U.S. income tax return for one or more years and income tax is due for any of those years, you should file returns for the current year and five previous years.

⬧ See IRS Publication 513, *Basic Tax Guide for Green Card Holders*, www.irs.gov/publications/p513/ar01.html.

Chapter 7 explains how to check your prior tax returns and how to pay back taxes.

When You Are Absent from the U.S. for a Long Period of Time

Your tax responsibilities as a Green Card holder do not change when you are absent from the U.S. for any period of time. Your tax obligation continues until you either surrender your Green Card or the Immigration authorities determine that your Green Card has been revoked or abandoned.

Therefore, even if the USCIS no longer recognizes the validity of your Green Card because it expired or you have been abroad too long, you must continue to file tax returns until there has been a final determination that your Green Card has been revoked or abandoned.

Getting Help With Your Taxes

You can get free help with your tax return at an IRS Taxpayer Assistance Center. To find the Taxpayer Assistance Center where you live, visit www.irs.gov/localcontacts/index.html. To get help by phone, call the IRS at 1-800-TAX-1040.

☞ *Your Federal Income Tax* is a free booklet that explains basics of American taxation. Order it by calling 1-800-TAX-1040 or download from www.irs.gov/publications/p17.

☞ The IRS has many free publications. See them at www.irs.gov/formspubs or call 1-800-TAX-FORM (1-800-829-3676).

> **Summary:** *It is important to pay your taxes in the United States because the failure can cost you your Green Card. You must report your income from the whole world.*

5.6. Build Your Good Reputation

Why Good Reputation Is Important

When you moved to the U.S., you left your reputation behind. It took you years to be known back home as honest, trustworthy person, but now, in the U.S., nobody knows you. How can you establish your reputation? Is it important?

Like in many other cultures, Americans judge other people according to their professional standing, financial status, level of education, or address of residence. Institutions, however, assess you by looking at the way you handle money. You are not evaluated by the size of your assets, but by the way you pay your obligations. Your money management is recorded by credit bureaus (see section 10.5) and your reputation is expressed in a form of a credit score (see section 10.1).

Your financial creditworthiness is revealed to any potential creditor, landlord, employer, or insurer who wants to do business with you.

> *You need to work in the U.S. with a stable income for several years and pay your bills on time in order to establish good creditworthiness.*

Once established, your reputation is with you to stay. You can't move to a different town and escape your financial reputation. Your credit report and your credit scores tell all – at least for 7 years.

The quality of your reputation affects various aspects of your life. It is very important to have a good credit score for the following reasons.

- A credit score affects your ability to get credit, and it influences the price you pay for credit cards, auto loans, mortgages, business loans, etc. The higher your score, the more likely you will be approved for a loan and the lower the interest you will pay.
- A credit check is a regular part of pre-employment screening. Many companies will not hire individuals who handle their finances irresponsibly (see 11.4).
- A landlord may check your credit score before renting out an apartment to you (see 11.5).
- Your credit score is checked by a telephone company when you apply for a cellular phone service or by a car dealer when you want to lease a car.
- Your scores also may determine how big a deposit you will have to pay for telephone, electricity, or natural gas service.

If you have a bad reputation (bad credit), it is likely that your application for a loan, credit card, or service will be rejected (read more on page 129 about your rights).

Building an Excellent Credit History

Building good reputation, or good credit history, takes time and patience. Financial institutions don't like lending to people who were not entrusted with financial responsibility before, so don't start by applying for major credit cards, because you may be rejected. Start small and build up slowly. Here are some suggestions:

- Open a savings and checking account. Owning a bank account does not begin your credit file but lays a foundation for your future financial dealings. If you have problems opening an account, read section 11.1.

- After you rent an apartment, put utilities (gas, electric, cell phone, etc.) in your name and pay your bills on time.
- Apply for a secured credit card – a card that is backed by your savings account. In case you default on the loan, the bank will take over your savings account. If your bank does not offer secured credit cards, visit www.bankrate.com. Click on "Credit Cards" and then on "Secured Credit Cards." On your screen, you will see a long list of the best secured credit cards in the country.
- Deposit some money into your savings account and apply for a small personal loan against your savings. Repay it early. This seems to make no sense, but it might be the only way to obtain your first loan. If you deposit the loan into your savings account, the interest earned will cut down the cost of credit.
- Apply for a department store credit card. They are easier to get than major credit cards such as MasterCard, Visa, or American Express. You could also try to get a card issued by a gas station chain.
- If you still cannot get credit on your own, ask a relative or a friend who has a good credit standing to co-sign a loan application with you. Remember, though, that it is no small matter to be a co-signer because he or she has to repay the loan if you default.

If your credit history is not what you would like it to be, read section 10.6 how to improve it.

Foreign Credit History in the U.S.

Attention new Americans: American credit bureaus don't take foreign credit history under consideration. Foreign financial institutions do not make credit payment histories available to U.S. credit bureaus, so only information provided by American institutions is seen in your credit history. Your past credit handling in other countries will not be considered. This actually may be advantageous because some foreign bureaus keep only negative information. For that reason, you have to develop your creditworthiness in the U.S. from scratch.

It can be expected that globalization and technology will contribute to development of international credit bureaus. Already some American credit bureaus have developed overseas branches. Also, some companies specialize in providing comprehensive reports of individuals' overseas credit files, primarily for employment purposes.

While seeking credit in America, you may refer to your foreign credit history on a loan application. It is up to the bank to decide whether this information will be taken under consideration. Credit grantors are usually unwilling to check credit overseas. Checking credit files in a foreign country is expensive, so sometimes it is the applicant who would have to pay for the cost of doing so.

Hint: Although a credit rating overseas generally does not influence one's credit history in the U.S., there is an exception. If your credit card (Visa, MasterCard, etc.) was issued by an American bank overseas, then American credit bureaus may have information about that account. It would be a good idea to obtain a credit card from an American bank before coming to the U.S.

Summary: *As a newcomer, you have no credit history in the U.S. You must build your reputation from scratch so you can take advantage of many financial opportunities available in America. Your credit history in another country will not be taken under consideration by American credit bureaus or lenders.*

5.7. Go Ahead to Achieve Your Dreams

From a field worker in Laos, to an office secretary in Detroit; from street peddler in China to a store owner in San Francisco; from an unemployed musician in Russia to a successful pianist in New York City; from a cab driver in Pakistan, to a computer specialist in Silicon Valley; from a housewife in India, to a college professor in Miami. We see success stories like these all around us. They inspire other immigrant jobseekers that they too can build their careers and lives in the U.S.

You also can make it in the United States. You already achieved part of your goals by getting your Green Card. You have strong determination to succeed; you are ready to work hard. Now you can achieve anything you want in this land of opportunity, where you will not be judged by the color of your skin, by your religious beliefs, or political views. Your rights and chances are equal, the playing field is leveled. The next chapters will help.

Whether you would like to build your own business, launch a successful professional career, or establish financial security for your family – set your goals high and go for them! The New American Guides series is with you to help.

6. FIND GOOD LEGAL EMPLOYMENT

After getting a Green Card, a priority for many immigrants is securing a job that they might not have had the opportunity to obtain while without papers. While appreciative of the first job they had when they arrived in the U.S., immigrants are eager to move on to a better paying position with better prospects for the future.

6.1. Your Legal Status Is Just the Beginning

With a Green Card, all opportunities are open and you can compete with other Americans on equal footing. However, even with a Green Card, newcomers face severe disadvantages in the job market. Some of them are:

- language barrier
- lack of demand for the profession learned in one's native country
- non-acceptance of foreign licenses for certain professions such as doctors, dentists, nurses, plumbers, electricians, etc.
- American citizenship requirements for some industries such as national defense
- over-qualification for a given position (too much education and experience for a job may be even more disqualifying than a lack thereof; employers know that a highly skilled person will get frustrated with a menial job and will leave as soon as he or she finds a better opportunity)
- lack of American job experience.

In this chapter, we concentrate on the issues that are problematic for job seekers from abroad.

For immigrants, finding a good job in the U.S. is more difficult than it is for Americans. There is a lot to learn about the job-hunting process.

6.2. Employment Background Check

Before you apply for a job in the U.S., you should know everything about the background check, especially if there is something in your past that you would not like your employer to find out.

Who May Check Your Record and Why

Most American employers are trusting – they tend to believe in anything you put on your employment application and won't ask for copies of college diplomas or statements from former employers. Beware, however, that employers may check your past before they hire you. They may use the services of screening companies that have online access to public records and commercial databases. These companies (specialized consumer reporting agencies, see 9.1) can gather and sell information about anyone, and many of them specialize in pre-employment screening.

In section 11.4, we explain how pre-employment screening (background check) is conducted and what laws protect you.

The thoroughness of pre-employment screening depends on the job requirements and on the price the employer is willing to pay for it. The simplest screening will yield only your credit report, while a more thorough screening may reveal much of your past.

Pre-employment background checking is required in many industries, including financial services, security, medicine, and education. Domestic employers often carefully check their babysitters, nannies, and housekeepers before they allow them to become a part of their household and care for their children.

In military, telecommunication, defense-related industries, and other sensitive areas, a government security clearance might be mandatory. A security clearance is a license issued by a federal government agency. It authorizes a worker to handle classified information, which is information deemed confidential or secret by the U.S. government. It is not easy for foreigners to obtain a security clearance.

Sometimes the job is not sensitive, but an employer simply wants to find out whether or not you have told the truth on your application or in an interview (a meeting with your potential employer).

If You Have Criminal Record

A check on your background will probably also include a search for a criminal record, which will reveal any arrests or convictions you might have had (see chapter 15). It is very difficult to get a good job if you have ever been convicted of criminal charges, and you should try to have your records sealed. Regulations vary from state to state regarding whether an employer may deny employment because of an arrest or conviction.

You may have a criminal record through no fault of your own. You might have merely been in the wrong place at the wrong time, or you might have been trying to help a friend. Being released without appearing before a judge will work in your favor. If the plaintiff or prosecutor fails to press charges, that information will influence the employer to look on the incident favorably. It will also help if you were issued a not-guilty verdict. Although arrest without conviction is removed from public records in some jurisdictions (section 15.4), you need to be prepared to explain the circumstances of the arrest.

A potential employer cannot order a criminal background check without your permission. However, you usually consent to that by signing your job application, so be sure to read the document carefully! If the application asks whether or not you've ever been convicted of a felony, you may honestly answer "no" if you were only convicted of a misdemeanor. The Fair Credit Reporting Act requires that no information more than 7 years old is reported on a credit report unless the job being sought pays $75,000 or more annually. Criminal records, on the other hand, show all arrests and convictions regardless of the date.

Summary: *Be truthful on your job application, because your employer may verify the information by checking your consumer report, which includes credit, criminal, academic and other information. Some sensitive jobs require a security clearance: permission to handle classified documents or accessing restricted information, which necessitates a thorough background check. The FCRA protects your rights in case you are rejected for employment due to incorrect information in your credit or consumer report.*

6.3. Get American Job Experience

Before you begin a job search, realize that the biggest barrier facing immigrants (as well as new graduates) is lack of American work experience. Employers want people who have experience in a certain field, preferably in the United States. They are unwilling to waste time on training, which in some professions takes months or years.

Table 6-1. Who Earns the Most – Median Wages

	Occupation	Hourly Wages	Annual Wages
1	Anesthesiologists	$70.01+	$145,600+
2	Internists, General	$70.01+	$145,600+
3	Obstetricians and Gynecologists	$70.01+	$145,600+
4	Surgeons	$70.01+	$145,600+
5	Family and General Practitioners	$66.19	$137,700
6	Pediatricians, General	$65.62	$136,500
7	Chief Executives	$65.58	$136,400
8	Psychiatrists	$65.12	$135,400
9	Airline Pilots, Copilots, and Flight Engineers	N/A	$128,100
10	Dentists	$57.90	$120,400
11	Air Traffic Controllers	$46.64	$97,000
12	Engineering Managers	$45.98	$95,600
13	Podiatrists	$45.94	$95,600
14	Lawyers	$44.58	$92,700
15	Judges, Magistrate Judges, and Magistrates	$43.86	$91,200
16	Computer and Information Systems Managers	$43.51	$90,500
17	Optometrists	$41.99	$87,300
18	Natural Sciences Managers	$41.78	$86,900
19	Law Teachers, Postsecondary	N/A	$86,400
20	Astronomers	$41.30	$85,900
21	Marketing Managers	$40.97	$85,200
22	Petroleum Engineers	$40.73	$84,700
23	Physicists	$40.18	$83,600
24	Nuclear Engineers	$40.03	$83,300
25	Computer and Information Scientists	$39.81	$82,800

Source: Occupational Outlook Handbook, U.S Department of Labor, www.bls.gov/oco

Employers' dislike for beginners can even be observed in newspaper ads, which frequently stress: "no entry position." Companies do not wish to be flooded with undesired job applications. Novices often search for jobs for a long time. They are unable to find a job because they lack experience, but they lack experience because they cannot find a job.

Long before you start to look for your first job in your profession, even while still waiting for your Green Card, you must try to get some practical training in your field. This effort will not only make you familiar with your industry, but it will also look good on your résumé. How can this be accomplished?

Become a Volunteer

If you really want to do something, but no one is willing to pay you for it (at least not yet), then do it for free. If it is hard to find a volunteering position in your field, then look elsewhere.

American employers value the virtues of volunteer work – performed of your own free will and without payment. Companies recognize volunteering as evidence of motivation and entrepreneurship, and a way of developing teamwork and problem solving skills. Many American corporations accept volunteer service or free internships as part of work history on the applicant's résumé. A person with a history of community service, fundraising, and other volunteer service stands out from the crowd of other job applicants as someone having broad interests, energy, and willingness to contribute to society. Employers know that such people make excellent employees.

Start volunteering at your house of worship, your child's school, or at an ethnic organization. They all can use help.

In the United States, there are hundreds of companies or institutions which can put you in contact with organizations looking for volunteers. You can find them in the White Pages under "Voluntary Action Center," "Volunteer Information and Referral," or in the Yellow Pages under "Social Services," or "Community Organizations."

🏛 Online check http://my.charityfocus.org or www.nycares.org.

Freelancing

Freelancing is an excellent way to get the necessary American experience. A freelancer is a self-employed professional. For example, a computer programmer can establish contact with a consulting firm and write programs for the firm from home. He could also instruct clients on how to use popular computer software and fix small problems. A future accountant can keep the books of small businesses or prepare tax returns for individual clients. This experience will not necessarily qualify him for a position of head accountant but will definitely help in launching his career.

The point here is not just to make an immediate profit but to learn skills, meet people, and gain familiarity with your profession.

◈ Visit www.elance.com, a website where companies and individuals meet service providers specializing in various areas. If you have marketable skills, you can sell them on Elance.com.

Internships and Work Study Programs

If you are attending an American college, take advantage of any work on campus. Although academic work is preferable, any employment is better than none. Universities need assistants to work in scientific laboratories, computer rooms and libraries, as well as cafeterias and dormitories. Many colleges arrange for internships with nearby companies. Many students find internships by themselves. A chemical engineer who worked in a laboratory over the summer will have an advantage over less experienced job candidates.

Why do employers consider college work experience important? Because it shows that a person is enterprising, responsible, and can combine full time studies and employment. These traits are essential in a workplace.

Upon completion of your internship, work study, or volunteering job, ask your boss for recommendations.

Summary: Employers like to hire people with American work experience. Become a volunteer, a freelancer, or an intern. You will meet interesting people, sharpen your skills, and get valuable experience.

6.4.   How to Increase Your Chances for Employment

Learn the process of job search in the United States, so you don't miss any opportunities. For example, if you do not prepare the résumé in accordance with commonly accepted rules, it may be rejected despite your good qualifications. If you are too quiet and passive during the interview, your future boss may think that you have no initiative or leadership skills.

Chapter 6.5 will explain the process of job search in the U.S.

Get References and Letters of Recommendation

As a newcomer to the U.S., you might not know many people willing to recommend you for a job, so providing references to your employer may be a problem.

Definition: A reference is a formal recommendation, usually written by a former employer to a potential future employer, describing the person's qualifications and dependability (letter of recommendation). A person providing that recommendation also is called a reference.

In the U.S., unlike in other countries, it is not customary to get references in writing upon leaving the company. Instead, you should be ready to provide phone numbers of your former superiors at request.

There are three types of references.

- **Employment references** are the most important, because your prospective boss wants to know how you performed in your previous job. The best reference is your former boss, but you can include coworkers, members of professional organizations, or customers you serviced.

- **Academic references.** If you are a recent graduate, provide academic references from professors or instructors who can speak positively about you. If you belonged to a sports team, your coach could attest to your character and leadership.

- **Personal references** are not really useful in a job search. Rely on these only if you cannot provide other references at all. Ask a religious leader or an organization where you volunteered for a letter of recommendation that would describe your skills, attitude and character. Never use your relatives.

Be prepared to provide the person's name, occupation, phone number, length of time you have known each other, and the nature of your relationship.

Choose your references carefully. When selecting a reference, consider his status or position as well as how well the person knows you and how objectively he can speak. Avoid people who live abroad, those who may not be dependable, or those who would feel a conflict of interest. Avoid references that may be controversial or may concern the employer such as a business competitor, clergy of different denomination, etc.

When using someone as a reference, always get his permission first. Find out the best time and place to reach him. Give him your up-to-date résumé. Describe the job you are seeking and explain why you are the best candidate. Before your interview, call your reference and remind him that somebody from the company may call him.

Personnel departments in larger companies often check references to avoid any future liability. They will look for inconsistencies between information obtained from you, from your references, and from your background check (see section 6.2). However, bosses who make hiring decisions rarely rely on references as they know that former employers may choose not to speak negatively about bad employees in order to avoid lawsuits.

In addition to preparing a list of references, you may obtain letters of recommendation from former bosses, coworkers, team members, etc. Copies of written performance evaluations from current or past employers may also be helpful.

Be Ready to Demontrate Your Past Achievements

Tip: Create a portfolio showing your professional accomplishments.

A portfolio is a set of pieces of creative work collected to be shown to potential customers or employers. Preparing a portfolio is typical for artists, architects, and designers, but other professionals can also present work samples to demonstrate their skills. For example, a construction worker can show pictures of buildings and close-ups of structures he worked on. An office employee can bring brochures he helped to create, reports he wrote, pictures of events he helped to organize, etc. A seamstress can wear a dress she made.

Table 6-2. Fastest Growing Occupations

#	Occupation	Employ-ment 2004	Projected employ-ment 2012	% Change
1	Medical assistants	364,600	579,400	59%
2	Network systems and data communications analysts	186,000	292,000	57%
3	Physician assistants	63,000	93,800	49%
4	Social and human service assistants	305,200	453,900	49%
5	Home health aides	579,700	858,700	48%
6	Medical records and health information technicians	146,900	215,600	47%
7	Physical therapist aides	37,000	54,100	46%
8	Computer software engineers, applications	394,100	573,400	46%
9	Computer software engineers, systems software	281,100	408,900	45%
10	Physical therapist assistants	50,200	72,600	45%
11	Fitness trainers and aerobics instructors	182,700	263,900	44%
12	Database administrators	110,000	158,600	44%
13	Veterinary technologists and technicians	52,700	75,900	44%
14	Hazardous materials removal workers	37,600	53,800	43%
15	Dental hygienists	148,000	211,700	43%
16	Occupational therapist aides	8,300	11,800	43%
17	Dental assistants	266,000	379,000	42%
18	Personal and home care aides	607,600	853,500	40%
19	Self-enrichment education teachers	200,400	280,800	40%
20	Computer systems analysts	468,300	652,700	39%
21	Occupational therapist assistants	18,500	25,700	39%
22	Environmental engineers	47,100	65,100	38%
23	Postsecondary teachers (college professors)	1,581,200	2,184,000	38%
24	Network and computer systems administrators	251,400	345,300	37%
25	Environmental science and protection technicians, including health	27,600	37,700	37%

Source: Occupational Outlook Handbook, U.S Department for Labor, www.bls.gov/oco

If there was ever an article written about your achievements or about your company's activities to which you were instrumental, include a copy. If it is in a foreign language, enclose a translation. Put everything in an attractive folder and show it to your interviewer when he asks about your past accomplishments. This will help you stand out from the crowd. Your employer will remember you better if you leave the folder with him.

Since English is probably your second language, the portfolio will eliminate the need for a lengthy monologue and will strengthen your confidence.

Learn About the Company

Americans are familiar with most large companies in the U.S., but as a newcomer you are probably not. Be sure to familiarize yourself with major names and acronyms in your industry such as HP, A&P, H&M, IBM, etc.

It is important to research the company where you are trying to get hired. You may even be asked what you know about the company in the interview. While talking to your prospective boss, you may inquire about the mission of the company, its philosophy, and its plans, but never ask "What are you actually producing?" Your ignorance indicates that you are not seriously interested in the position.

All corporations have websites where you can find a lot of information. Also, search the news for the company name (go online to www. google.com, click on "News," and type in the company name).

Dan & Bradstreet (www.dnb.com/us) can help you locate any American business. For a moderate fee, you may purchase the company profile with company's key sales and contact information. More detailed reports cost more.

Do Not Be Too Humble

In your culture, good manners may require humility. It pays to be modest in the U.S. also, but not at a job interview. You have to sell yourself! However, if you worked on a team project in the past, do not assign all the credit to yourself, but emphasize that you played an important role.

You should be straightforward and precise about your accomplishments. Be ready to give concrete examples of how you improved productivity, satisfied important customers, gained new clients, or otherwise made your mark at previous jobs. Describe your achievements in numbers, whenever possible. For example, you increased sales by 20 percent, or helped to complete a project one month before the deadline, thus saving the company a certain amount of money.

The interviewer may ask you about your weaknesses. Nobody is perfect, so it is fine to admit your shortcomings, but do so in a positive way. Respond honestly and show how you are improving your weak points. For example, your short American experience can be your drawback. However, you can point to a related experience in your country and to your quick learning ability.

Summary: *To get your first good job, you should have some American experience. Get it by freelancing or volunteering. Also, prepare references, a list of your past achievements, and learn about your potential employer before you have an interview.*

6.5. Job Searching in America

American customs related to job searching may be different from those in your country. You should get acquainted with these customs and proceed accordingly.

Your Résumé

When searching for a serious position, you are required to submit a résumé (in other countries called curriculum vitae).

Definition: A résumé is a summary of education and work experience. Only some blue collar workers and domestic helpers apply for a job without having a résumé on hand. It is not an exaggeration to say that a good résumé accounts for half of your success. Approximately 95 percent of employees introduce themselves to a company by their résumé. They would not be hired if their résumé was poorly written. Sometimes people who would have been perfect for the job do not get hired simply because their résumé was not well written.

📖 There are many comprehensive books about the art of writing a good résumé. Visit a library, a bookstore, or www.amazon.com.

🕸 Also, hundreds of websites show sample résumés for many professions, for example www.freeresumesamples.org or www.best-sampleresume.com. CareerOneStop has Résumé Tutorial at www.acinet.org, a module that helps write résumés and cover letters.

Cover Letter

A cover letter is a short introductory letter sent along with a résumé. It should be one page long and include the recipient's name and department. The content depends on the situation.

It is helpful to mention the ad you are responding to or the name of a person who recommended the company to you. You should state the position you are applying for and stress that your education and professional experience make you a perfect candidate for this job. Show your interest in the company and eagerness to come for an interview.

A sample cover letter is shown below.

If you need help writing your résumé or cover letter, search the web for "sample résumé" or "sample cover letter."

🕸 The website www.quintcareers.com/cover_letter_samples.html has more than 40 samples of cover letters.

Sample Format of a Cover Letter

Individual's name and title

Name of organization

Dear Mr./Ms. _____:

First paragraph: Explain the reason for writing and how you learned of the opening in the company. Name the specific position or type of work for which you are applying.

Second paragraph: Explain why you are perfect for the position. Be brief; do not repeat the information on your résumé – one or two qualifications will be enough. Tell why you are interested in the position (location, type of work).

Third paragraph: Express your desire to meet with the employer. Indicate when you are available; show your flexibility to the time and place. Include day and evening contact information. Be sure to communicate your plan to follow up. Never leave it up to the employer to get in touch with you. Refer the employer to the enclosed résumé. Thank him for his time.

Sincerely,

Your signature

Your name, street address, city, state, zip code, phone number

Job Interview

If the company likes your résumé and considers hiring you, it will invite you for an interview. A job interview is a meeting with your potential employer or supervisor at which you are evaluated for prospective employment.

You have to be well prepared for the interview to properly respond to anything you are asked, to pose right questions yourself, and to project the image that you are perfect for the job.

You have to keep in mind that an interview is a conversation where both parties, you and your potential boss, want to learn about each other as much as they can. Although your employer plays an active role during the interview, you should also show some initiative to prove your interest in the position. Get prepared to ask questions about the position and the company. Practice speaking in English if professional terminology may pose a problem.

Large companies use a multilevel selection process. First, you are interviewed by a person from the personnel department and then by your potential manager. If you are a professional (e.g. computer analyst) and the manager is not familiar with the technical side of the position, you will also be interviewed by a specialist who will evaluate your technical skills. The manager may also ask you to meet with your prospective coworkers, and in the end he may arrange a meeting between you and his supervisor.

Some job candidates have to go through a series of up to five interviews. Large corporations are very careful when selecting workers, because they do not like to lay off employees. But once you are hired, the company provides job stability, good benefits, a steady income, and more career opportunities.

During the interview you should convince the interviewer that:

- you are perfect for the job
- you fit into the company's corporate culture and will get along with coworkers
- you would love to be hired for the position.

Questions Asked at an Interview

The interviewer will ask you a lot of questions to determine whether you are suitable for the position. Your previous employment will be the topic of most interest. Companies prefer experienced employees who are productive from the start. Be prepared to answer specific questions about your previous jobs and reason for leaving your former place.

The following list contains questions most commonly asked during interviews:

- Could you tell us about yourself?
- Why did you leave your last job?
- What do you expect from our company?
- What kind of work interests you the most?
- Tell us more about your professional experiences.
- Why do you want to work for us?
- Why do you think you are suitable for this job?
- What do you know about our company? What do you know about this position?
- What is your strongest/weakest point?
- Why should we hire you?
- How important is team work to you?
- How would you define a good supervisor?
- If you could choose any position, which would it be?
- Where do you see yourself in five years?
- What was your biggest defeat/achievement?
- Are you willing to go on business trips?
- Are you willing to relocate if the company asks you to?
- Can you work overtime?
- Do you like to manage other people?
- What were your achievements at your previous job and how did the company benefit from them?

Thank-You Letters

After the interview, it is appropriate to write to the person you spoke with to thank him for his time and consideration. Send a thank-you letter to display courtesy and to confirm your interest in the position.

A sample thank-you letter is shown on the next page.

Summary: Send a résumé to your potential employer together with a cover letter. If the employer is interested in you, he will invite you to an interview. Be prepared to answer typical questions. After the interview, send a thank-you letter.

6.6. Places to Look for a Job

While immigrants without employment authorization are confined to looking for jobs in ethnic newspapers and through local ethnic employment agencies, permanent residents can use many other resources. In addition to classified ads in Help Wanted sections of main-stream newspapers and private employment agencies (also called career consultants), you may use many official government sources of job information.

State Job Service

The State Job Service works with the U.S. Department of Labor's Employment and Training Administration to maintain a national database of job listings, educational and training requirements, as well as local career resource centers.

> **Post-Interview Thank-You Letter**
>
> Ms. Jane Smith, Title
> Company, Address
>
> **First paragraph.** Express appreciation for the opportunity to be interviewed. Refer to the date of the interview and to the position for which you were applying.
>
> **Second paragraph.** Indicate particularly interesting areas discussed in the interview. Briefly reiterate some of your qualifications that will enable you to perform the job. Add relevant experience that you may have omitted during the interview.
>
> **Third paragraph.** Confirm your interest in the position. Indicate that you are looking forward to the results of the interview.
>
> Sincerely,
>
> Your signature

A database known as Career OneStop can be accessed through the Internet at www.careeronestop.org. You may also call at 1-877-348-0502.

At One-Stop Career Centers all around the country, you can use a computer to search for job listings, post your own résumé, explore wages and occupational trends, learn about job training, as well as locate potential employers. It is a free service, but you must register to post your résumé.

A One-Stop Career Center can be also found through America's Service Locator at www.servicelocator.org or call 1-877-US-2JOBS.

Some parts of the CareerOneStop website are translated into several languages: Spanish, Italian, French, German, Brazilian Portuguese, simplified and traditional Chinese, Japanese, and Korean.

America's Job Exchange

America's Job Exchange connects job seekers to job openings throughout the country. It allows you to search through a database of over a million jobs nationwide, create and post your résumé online, in addition to setting up an automated job search. The database contains a wide range of mostly full-time private sector jobs that are available all over the country.

Using America's Job Exchange database is simple. First you select a job category from the menu or enter a keyword that describes the job you would like to find. Then you choose the area of the country by entering a U.S. city or zip code. The computer will display job offers within a 50 mile radius.

🖉 Job seekers can access America's Job Exchange at www.americas-jobexchange.org.

America's Career InfoNet

America's Career InfoNet is a website sponsored by the U.S. Department of Labor. It offers career resources and workforce information to job seekers and businesses.

America's Career InfoNet provides information on educational, licensing, and certification requirements for different occupations by state. It also provides information on wages, cost of living, and employment trends, and helps job seekers identify their skills and write résumés and cover letters.

🖉 America's Career InfoNet has its website at www.acinet.org.

Federal Government

Information on obtaining a position with the Federal Government is available from the U.S. Office of Personnel Management (OPM) (www.opm.gov, 1900 E Street NW, Washington, DC 20415, tel. 1-202-606-1800).

Federal job offers are available from the OPM at www.usajobs.com. About 20,000 jobs posted there by the federal government can be searched by various categories and locations.

Private Websites

There is a multitude of private Internet sites helping jobseekers and employers. The biggest of them are: www.monster.com, www.hotjobs.yahoo.com, www.jobweb.com, www.job-hunt.com, and many others.

They post not only job offers, but also useful advice about résumés, interviews, and more.

Summary: *As a permanent resident, you qualify for various federal and state government sources of employment information. Take advantage of them in addition to looking through newspapers, websites, and private employment agencies.*

6.7. Benefits of Legal Employment

Unlike jobs off the book or work for small companies, legal employment for larger companies gives you many benefits that can substantially add to the value of your compensation.

Health Insurance

The United States is the only developed country that does not provide its citizens with a national health insurance plan. For that reason, health insurance is the most valuable of all job benefits. It protects you and your family from the high cost of medical treatment and hospitalization. Some companies provide one type of medical insurance, while others offer a whole package of benefits called Flex Program that allows employees to tailor the benefits package to fit their needs. It may include medical plan options, dental plan options, life insurance coverage for the employee and dependent spouse and children, vision care options, long-term disability, long-term care, as well as flexible spending accounts for health care and dependent care.

Usually, you contribute some money to pay for your benefits. The more you contribute, the more comprehensive the program you can chose.

Unemployment Benefits

The unemployment insurance program is intended to provide temporary financial assistance to workers who lost their jobs through no fault of their own and who meet the requirements of state law. Regulations are more stringent for aliens.

Attention new Americans: To collect unemployment insurance benefits, an alien must establish that he was in satisfactory immigration status while he earned the wages in addition to being lawfully present and authorized to work now, when he claims the benefits.

According to the Federal Unemployment Tax Act (FUTA, Section 3304(a) (14)(A)), only those periods of employment are considered for calculation of unemployment compensation when the following conditions were met:

- the alien had a Green Card at the time the services were performed
- the alien was lawfully present for the purposes of performing the services, or
- the alien was in the United States "permanently residing under color of law" (PRUCOL) at the time these services were performed. *The American Guide to Surviving in the U.S. While Waiting for Your Green Card* explains PRUCOL status in detail (see the Appendix on page 262).

This means that if you have earned the wages while not being legally entitled to employment, these wages will not be tallied by the unemployment office. You also must be legally authorized to work in the United States when you claim the benefits. If one's legal status or work authorization expired, he will not receive the benefits.

Pension Plan

A pension plan is a program that provides a retirement income to workers who meet certain age and service requirements when they leave the company. The benefits are based on length of service and average earnings for a stated period of time before retirement. The plan may also provide income for a spouse if an employee dies before retirement. Company pensions are separate from Social Security retirement benefits.

Many companies pay the full cost of this benefit, and participation is automatic. At some companies the plan is contributory, meaning financed by both the employer and the employees.

Pension plans are very expensive, so companies are increasingly switching to savings programs such as 401(k) described below.

Investment Savings Plan 401(k)

Your company can help you save for retirement. A plan called 401(k) is the most popular. Its name comes from a paragraph in the tax code. It is a savings plan established by your employer that lets you set aside a percentage of your wages, up to $15,000 annually (adjusted occasionally for inflation). If you are age 50 or older, you are allowed to contribute an extra $5,000 annually. Your employer may contribute up to a dollar for every dollar you deposit into your 401(k) account, and the company's contributions become yours gradually over five years (which is called vesting).

Like an Individual Retirement Account (IRA), a 401(k) plan is used to save for retirement. You don't pay taxes on the amounts deposited. Earnings in your 401(k) account are tax-deferred, which means that you will not pay taxes on them until you withdraw the money. Once money is in your 401(k) account, you cannot make withdrawals before age 59 ½, except for special circumstances.

You can make your own investment choices from several mutual funds professionally managed by an investment company chosen by your employer. Usually, the plan permits participants to borrow against their vested benefit without incurring current tax.

Employees' Stock Purchase Plan

Offered by some companies, an employee stock purchase plan is another version of a savings plan. It allows employees to buy company stock at a discount price. Eligible employees can designate a certain percentage of their income to purchase stock through a payroll deduction plan at a below-market price.

Investing your retirement savings in the stocks of only one corporation can be risky. For example, due to Enron's bankruptcy, its 20,000 employees lost not only their jobs but their retirement savings too.

Other Benefits

Large companies offer many other benefits. They may include generous vacation days, sick days, reimbursement for educational expenses, matching gifts program, parking privileges, and merit-based scholarship programs for children of employees. In some large companies, the benefit package even includes benefits for part-time employees and for same-sex domestic partners.

Where to Learn More

🏛 At www.bls.gov/ebs, Bureau of Labor Statistics, a part of the U.S. Department of Labor, has comparative lists of compensation and benefits in private companies.

📖 *Your Rights in the Workplace* by Barbara Kate Repa, Nolo Press, www.nolo.com, tel. 1-800-728-3555, 950 Parker Street, Berkeley, CA 94710-2524.

Summary: There are many benefits to legal employment in the U.S. Businesses provide employee benefits in order to attract, reward, and retain talented individuals. Health insurance and a retirement plan are the most important benefits.

Part II

Clean up Your Past

7. SETTLE YOUR SCORE WITH THE IRS

The Internal Revenue Service (IRS – the U.S. federal tax agency) and the Social Security Administration (SSA – an agency that manages retirement and disability programs) are the first institutions newcomers come in contact with. The importance of paying income and Social Security taxes was explained in chapter 5.5. However, immigrants often neglect to pay taxes because they try to keep a low profile or are not aware of regulations. When they settle down and try to start a new life, they must ensure that their taxes are up to date with the IRS and SSA. This book gives detailed explanations how to proceed.

7.1. The Tax and Social Security Mess

Many immigrants come to the U.S. only to work for a couple of years and then return to their native countries. Later on, some of them manage to obtain a Green Card and come back to the U.S. As new permanent residents, the immigrants may face problems caused by the unfinished business they left behind the first time they were here. Most of their troubles involve the IRS and the SSA.

Real-Life Examples

John arrived to the U.S. many years ago. Although he only had a tourist visa, he received a proper Social Security number (SSN), which was easy back then. He worked and received his paychecks for a couple of years. Now he doesn't even remember whether or not he filed his tax returns every year, which he was supposed to do.

While in the U.S., Melinda worked legally and had her taxes prepared. Her last tax return resulted in a tax deficiency of $1,100. Melinda did not pay this amount because she decided to return to her native country, never thinking she would come back to the U.S. But her plans changed. Now Melinda got a Green Card, returned to the U.S. and is afraid that the IRS will arrest her for nonpayment of taxes.

Barbara thinks she got cheated by her employer. She agreed to work legally, on the books, as a housekeeper for $400 a week after taxes, and she received weekly checks for that amount. But when tax time came around, and she asked her employer for a W-2 form with the summary of her earnings and withheld taxes, she was told that taxes are her responsibility. Barbara thinks that her employer never paid any of her employment taxes to the government, although he promised to.

Before leaving the U.S., Mark gave his Social Security card to his cousin to use for employment. No one knows how long his cousin has worked using the Social Security number or if anybody else has used it as well. It is possible that Mark's identity was misused.

Rajiv held many jobs in the past years. Now he would like to make sure that his employment is properly credited by the Social Security Administration towards his retirement.

Immigrants like these need to clean up the disarray in their tax records. If you are one of them, here is what you need to find out.

- How long were you legally employed? Did your employer forward your taxes to the government?
- For which tax years did you file your tax returns and for which you did not?
- Did anyone use your Social Security number for employment; if so, for how long?
- How many Social Security credits did you earn?
- How much do you owe to the IRS?
- Are any tax delinquencies reflected in your credit history?

This chapter will help you find answers to these questions.

Who Knows About Your Employment

You should know that several government agencies receive and track information about workers. You can check your records in their archives and correct them, if necessary. Let's see who receives your employment information and why.

The Internal Revenue Service (IRS). Your employer is required by law to withhold the income taxes from your paycheck to pay the IRS. He reports all wages to the IRS on Form 941, *Employer's Quarterly Federal Tax Return,* Form 942, *Employer's Quarterly Tax Return for Household Employees,* or Form 943, *Employer's Annual Tax Return for Agricul-*

tural Employees. These forms show gross wages and taxes for the employer's payroll for the quarter. The same information is sent to the SSA (see below). If you fail to file your tax return for the given year, you will not remain anonymous because the IRS already knows about you.

The Social Security Administration. Social Security tax, called FICA tax (short for Federal Insurance Contributions Act), is withheld from every worker's paycheck at the rate of 7.65 percent. The employer matches this amount, which means he pays the same amount. In total, an amount equal to 15.3 percent of your wages is forwarded to the Social Security Administration (SSA), so that you will have health insurance (Medicare, page 49) and a small but guaranteed retirement pension in the future. The employer reports your annual wages and the taxes you paid in a calendar year to the SSA on Form W-2, *Wage and Tax Statement.* He conveys his company's total payroll numbers on Form W-3, *Transmittal of Wage and Tax Statement.* This reporting enables the SSA to keep track of the wages of all workers in the U.S.

Other government institutions. Other institutions are notified about employed workers. Among them are the State and the City Departments of Taxation as well as other offices, which provide employers with insurance as required by law.

Summary: During the years when you were waiting for your Green Card, you may have neglected filing your tax returns. However, if you were on a company's payroll, the Internal Revenue Service already received the taxes that were withheld by your employer, and the Social Security Administration received information about your earnings.

7.2. How to Get Your Tax Information from the IRS

Get Information About Your Past Tax Returns

To make sure all your taxes are in order, first check your tax payment history. The IRS meticulously tracks tax payments of all taxpayers. If you know how, you may request information from the IRS which will tell you:

- what returns have been filed already – either by you, the IRS, or a person who could have used your name

- how much taxes you owe
- which refunds (if any) have been applied to delinquent taxes.

To find out this information, order a transcript of your return for all years in question.

Transcript of a Return

A transcript – an official record of your tax return – is available free of charge. To get it, use Form 4506-T, *Request for Transcript of Tax Return*. The form gives you several options, which you choose by marking the appropriate box.

Return transcript will give you a line by line listing of the tax form (1040, 1040A or 1040EZ) for the year requested, including accompanying schedules and attachments. Return transcripts are available for the current year and returns processed within the past three years. You should receive the return transcript in 7 to 10 work days after the IRS receives your request.

Account transcript (also called "account information") shows the financial status of your account, including information such as your tax liability (income taxes you may owe), payments made by you, penalties assessed by the IRS, any later adjustments made either by you or by the IRS. Account transcripts are available for most returns, so if you need your old tax information, this is what you should request. Allow about 30 days for delivery.

Record of account is a combination of the above. It contains line item information and later adjustments to the account. You may want to choose this option to have complete data. A record of account is available for the current year and three prior tax years. Most requests will be processed within 30 calendar days.

Verification of no filing will give you proof that you did not file a return for a certain year. The IRS will reply to you in about 10 days.

Transcript of specific forms is available for up to 10 years back. For example, you can order a copy of your W-2 (showing your earned income and withheld taxes), 1099 (showing your investment income), 1098 (with deductible interest that you paid to a bank) or 5498 (IRA contribution information). Current year W-2 information might not be available until the year after it is filed with the IRS. For example, W-2 information for 2007, filed in 2008, will not be available from the IRS until 2009. Most requests will be processed within 45 days.

To request either version of transcript, call 1-800-829-1040 and follow the prompts in the recorded message. You may also download IRS Form 4506-T, *Request for Transcript of Tax Return* from www.irs.gov/pub/irs-pdf/f4506t.pdf. Complete it and mail to the IRS office in your region, according to instructions on the form. Transcripts are free and available for the current and three prior calendar years.

Photocopy of Your Tax Return

For a small fee, you can request a photocopy of the actual tax return and attachments – W-2 and schedules. For that, you need IRS Form 4506, *Request for Copy of Tax Return*. Download it from www.irs.gov/pub/irs-pdf/f4506.pdf or call 1-800-829-1040. Complete the form, sign it, and send it to the address provided on the form.

By checking the box on line 6, you may also request that the IRS sends you certified copies (attested to be true by the IRS) which would meet court or other administrative proceeding requirements. If the Social Security Administration needs your tax return for correcting your earnings record, be sure to order a certified copy from the IRS.

You can order copies of your tax return for up to the 6 past years; older returns are not available for making copies. There is a fee for each tax period requested. It can take up to two months to get a copy of a tax return with all schedules and W-2s attached.

Check for Tax Liens In Your Credit History

If you neglected to pay your taxes, the IRS may have issued a federal tax lien against you or your property. A tax lien is a government claim for unpaid taxes, which can cause your property to be seized.

Once the lien is filed, it is noted in your credit history and your credit rating is harmed (see chapter 10 for more information). You may not be able to get a loan to buy a house or a car, get a new credit card, or sign a lease. Therefore it is important that you work to resolve your tax liability as quickly as possible, before lien filing becomes necessary.

To check for a tax lien, request a copy of your credit file from any of the three major credit bureaus (see chapter 10.5).

Summary: *There are several ways of obtaining the information that the IRS has about your filed and unfiled tax returns. To find out what you owe the IRS, get transcripts of your tax returns for the past years. Transcripts are for free; there is a small fee for the copies of your actual tax return.*

7.3. Consequences of Failure to Pay Taxes

Can You Go to Jail for Nonpayment of Taxes?

Failing to pay federal taxes is a misdemeanor, for which you may be punished with a fine of up to $25,000 for each delinquent year or by up to a year in jail. In reality, however, the IRS very rarely puts unwilling taxpayers to jail; it much prefers them to pay up. That's why the agency does not prosecute anyone who voluntarily comes forward to correct the situation.

The IRS will charge penalties and interest. The penalty for the failure to file taxes is up to 25 percent of the tax due for every tax return. On top of penalties, the agency applies interest, which can add up quickly on taxes several years overdue. Quite often, penalties and interest exceed the taxes – on returns 10 years overdue, total penalties and interest may exceed taxes several times.

You will most likely not go to jail for nonpayment of taxes, but you will have to pay delinquent taxes and more. The combined charges for interest and penalties may exceed the original tax debt.

Only in certain circumstances may the IRS remove the penalty charges. These are: death or serious health condition suffered by the taxpayer or his family member, a drug or alcohol problem, bad advice from an accountant, and extended military service.

Can You Lose Your Green Card?

Yes, in some circumstances you can lose your Green Card for nonpayment of taxes. If you, a permanent resident, are living outside the U.S. for an extended period of time, and you do not file income tax returns, or you filed forms as if you were a nonresident (1040NR), the government may perceive that you have given up your permanent residency.

Substitute for Tax Return: When the IRS Files a Tax Return for You

If you haven't filed your tax returns in the past years, it is possible that the IRS filed them for you.

The law allows the IRS to take any income reported to the IRS on your Social Security number, and file a tax return called a Substitute for Return (SFR) in your name. This is not a good thing, because the IRS calculates your taxes at the highest rate – as if you were single, even though you may qualify for a lower rate as "married filing jointly" or "head of household." The IRS gives you no dependents or itemized deductions. Self-employed individuals don't get any business deductions. Therefore, the tax calculated by the IRS may be much higher than it should be.

The IRS mails an official notice of this action to your last known address. If you moved out, you may not be aware of the letter. Should you owe taxes, the amount of interest and penalties will continue to grow. However, if a sufficient amount of income taxes was withdrawn from your paycheck, you have nothing to worry about.

Once you discover that the IRS filed the SFR for you in the past, you should file the return for that year by yourself to lower the tax burden. Once the agency accepts the return, the tax is reduced but the penalties and interest remain. However, if the tax is lowered, your penalties and interest can also be decreased. For that reason, you should always apply for reduction of penalties and interest. If a tax professional told you that you should not file your tax return because of your illegal immigration status, the IRS may waive the penalties for non-filing of taxes.

If a tax delinquency was small, the chances are that your case will be disregarded, but it will still stay in IRS computers. On the other hand, if the liability is higher, then the IRS will place a tax lien against you and will report you to a credit bureau. A tax lien stays on your credit history for a long time, and prevents you from obtaining a credit card, a loan, or a mortgage.

Summary: *You will most likely not go to jail for nonpayment of taxes. However, penalties and interest may be severe. The IRS may file the tax return for you, assuming the highest tax rates.*

7.4. Pay Your Back Income Taxes

Why Pay Your Back Taxes

There are many reasons to settle your score with the IRS. First of all, you have to show your tax returns in many situations, for example at the U.S. Citizenship and Immigration Service (USCIS) when getting your Green Card, or at a bank when applying for a loan. Furthermore, by paying back taxes, you will stop penalties and interest from accumulating. Over the years, those charges can exceed the taxes many times over.

Another reason to file is to obtain tax refunds from prior years. A tax refund is an amount of money that the government returns to a taxpayer who has paid more taxes than were due. No refunds can be claimed after three years if a tax return was not filed. By not filing, the money that is rightfully yours will go to the U.S. Treasury. File as soon as possible to preserve that statute of limitation.

Finally, many people are compelled to pay delinquent taxes in order to earn Social Security credits (one quarter of covered employment is equal to one credit; a person needs at least 40 credits to qualify for Social Security retirement benefits).

Back Income Taxes of an Employee

In order to file your tax return for a previous year (or years), you need a copy of Form W-2, *Wage and Tax Statement,* from your employer. This form is sent by employers to their employees by January 31 the year following the one for which taxes are being paid. Form W-2 tells you not only how much you earned that year but also how much federal, state, and Social Security tax was withheld from your pay. Without this form, the IRS will assume that no taxes were withheld. This means that you will have to pay double: the tax you have already paid in the past, and now the tax that will be assessed a second time.

In the following section, you will find out how to recover your old W-2 forms.

For taxpayers with only employment income (plus some bank interest), preparing a tax return is simple. Fill out a simplified IRS Form 1040EZ or 1040A for a given year. Remember to use the tax tables for the correct year. You will find them in the instructions.

Income taxes for most people are quite moderate. Amounts equal to the standard deduction and personal exemption for every family member are free of tax, and the tax rate in the lowest bracket is only 10 percent. Therefore, your back income tax can be lower than you think, and it is possible for penalties to be waived. Ask a tax specialist for assistance.

🖎 Tax forms and instructions for previous years can be ordered from the IRS or downloaded from www.irs.gov/formspubs/index.html. Click on "Previous years."

Back Income Taxes of a Self-Employed Person

The procedure of paying overdue taxes is different for someone who is self-employed. Self-employed persons, also called independent contractors or free-lancers, are in business for themselves and do not get W-2 forms.

If you made more than $400 working for yourself, the IRS wants you to pay self-employment tax, which consists of both Social Security and Medicare tax as calculated on Schedule SE, *Self-Employment Tax*.

A business that paid you $600 or more in a year for your services must report the payment to the IRS on Form 1099-MISC (short for miscellaneous), and give you a copy. You should report this income on your tax return. To get information about 1099 forms issued for you in the past, follow the instructions in section 7.5 of this book.

Being an undocumented alien, you probably worked off the books for cash, so nobody reported your earnings to the IRS. Thus, you now have no proof of your earnings, but don't let this worry you. You should reconstruct your past earnings to the best of your knowledge and file your tax return using the following forms:

IRS Form 1040, *U.S. Individual Income Tax Return*. This is the primary tax form used to declare income from employment, bank interest, and other sources. You cannot pay Social Security tax (FICA) without simultaneously paying income tax. If the source of income was your own business, you write the amount in the line "Business Income or Loss." You get this figure by completing Schedule C.

Schedule C, *Profit or Loss from Business*. Part I of this form is for your income and Part II is for your business expenses. Your business expenses must pertain to the business activities and must be documented. Don't send supporting documents (receipts) to the IRS, but keep them in case of an IRS audit. The difference between income and expenses is net profit, which is taxable.

Schedule SE, *Self-Employment Tax,* is used for calculation of Social Security and Medicare taxes for the given year. Half of self-employment tax goes on your Form 1040 as a tax deduction.

State tax return. You will have to use the Resident Income Tax Return for the state you live in. Some states, such as Florida, Nevada, and Alaska, do not levy state income taxes.

> *Summary: If you start a new life in the U.S., you should pay the back taxes that you owe. The sooner you pay the better. The tax return of an employee differs from that of a self-employed person. Ask a tax specialist for assistance.*

7.5. Missing W-2 and 1099 Forms

Employment Income vs. Self-Employment Income

Definition: Forms W-2, *Wage and Tax Statement,* are used by employers for annually reporting their employees' income and withheld taxes to the SSA. When you are legitimately employed, your employer automatically withholds and pays all of the necessary employee taxes: federal income tax, FICA (Social Security and Medicare tax), as well as state and local taxes. All your annual earnings and withheld taxes are summarized on your Form W-2, which your employer sends to you at the end of every January. Employers report your whole payroll for the quarter to the IRS on Forms 941, *Employer's Quarterly Federal Tax Return.*

Businesses use forms **1099-MISC** to report payments made to self-employed individuals. Taxes are not withheld from that income, so it is the self-employed person's responsibility to pay the taxes owed to federal, state, and local governments.

Banks and other financial institutions use other versions of forms 1099 (**1099-INT or 1099-DIV**) to report interest or dividends paid to their customers.

Figure 7-1. Sample Form W-2, Wage and Tax Statement

a Control number	22222	Void ☐	For Official Use Only ▶ OMB No. 1545-0008			
b Employer identification number (EIN) 10-2255412				1 Wages, tips, other compensation 48215.00	2 Federal income tax withheld 4904.00	
c Employer's name, address, and ZIP code Financial Planners Inc. 12 Center Circle Anytown, US 10123				3 Social security wages 48215.00	4 Social security tax withheld 2989.33	
				5 Medicare wages and tips 48215.00	6 Medicare tax withheld 699.12	
				7 Social security tips	8 Allocated tips	
d Employee's social security number 222-00-1287				9 Advance EIC payment	10 Dependent care benefits	
e Employee's first name and initial Albert W. Last name Wentworth Suff.				11 Nonqualified plans	12a See instructions for box 12	
2 Shady Tree Lane Anytown, US 10111				13 Statutory employee ☐ Retirement plan ☐ Third-party sick pay ☐	12b	
				14 Other	12c	
					12d	
f Employee's address and ZIP code						

15 State	Employer's state ID number	16 State wages, tips, etc.	17 State income tax	18 Local wages, tips, etc.	19 Local income tax	20 Locality name
UT	Y11111	48215.00	4904.00			

Form **W-2** Wage and Tax Statement   **2006**   Department of the Treasury—Internal Revenue Service

For Privacy Act and Paperwork Reduction Act Notice, see back of Copy D.

Copy A For Social Security Administration — Send this entire page with Form W-3 to the Social Security Administration; photocopies are not acceptable.

Cat. No. 10134D

Do Not Cut, Fold, or Staple Forms on This Page — Do Not Cut, Fold, or Staple Forms on This Page

> *If you were an employee on a payroll, your income taxes and FICA taxes have been withheld and paid to the government. Even if you neglected filing the return, part of your taxes has already been paid!*

As a self-employed person, however, you did not have taxes withheld and paid by anybody. It was solely your responsibility. Therefore now, when you want to pay your back taxes as a self-employed person, you may owe the full amount of income and FICA taxes.

How to Get Your Old W-2 and 1099 Forms

There are several ways to obtain your W-2 (and 1099) information for previous years.

The quickest way to obtain a copy of your old W-2 is through your employer. If the employer refuses to cooperate or has gone out of business, contact the IRS.

📖 Order a transcript of your tax return for free using IRS Form 4506-T, *Request for Transcript of Tax Return* from www.irs.gov/pub/irs-pdf/f4506t.pdf. Mark box 8 – "Form W-2." The IRS can provide W-2 information for the past 10 years.

To get a copy of the actual Form W-2 or 1099 filed with your return (if you filed it), use Form 4506 and request a copy of your return with all attachments. You have to pay for this service.

If you need W-2 information for retirement purposes, get it from the Social Security Administration. For that, complete the Form SSA-7050-F4, *Request for Social Security Earnings Information*, as explained in section 8.2.

Late W-2 Forms

Let's say that you want to file your tax return for the last tax year, but your W-2 form did not arrive yet, although it is already past January 31. In this situation, contact the employer and ask for a replacement form. If you still do not receive it by February 15th, contact the IRS tax help line for assistance at 1-800-829-1040. Do the same if your employer refuses to give you your W-2 form.

When you call the IRS, have your last pay stub in front of you. You will need all information shown there: the employer's name, address, identification number (if known), and telephone number. An IRS representative will ask you for your wages, Social Security and income taxes withheld. You may as well send all that information to the IRS on Form 4852, *Substitute for Form W-2, Wage and Tax Statement*. However, shortly before the April 15 tax filing deadline, you may not have enough time.

If the employer paid you in cash or personal checks, and you don't have pay stubs, calculate the amount of your earnings by yourself.

The IRS will send your employer a note that you did not receive your W-2 form. You will get a copy of this notice from the IRS as well as Form 4852, *Substitute for Form W-2, Wage and Tax Statement* with the information you provided.

If your employer still does not send you a replacement wage statement, you may file using Form 4852 in place of the missing W-2.

Incorrect W-2 Forms

In the event that your employer issued erroneous W-2 information, he is obliged to issue a corrected statement called W-2c, *Statement of Corrected Income and Tax Amounts*. If you have already filed your income tax return for the year shown in box A, you may have to file an amended return. Compare amounts on the new W-2 statement with those reported on your income tax return. If the corrected amounts change your U.S. income tax, file Form 1040X, *Amended U.S. Individual Income Tax Return*, with Copy B of this W-2c form to amend the return you already filed.

If you have not filed your return for that year, attach Copy B of the original Form W-2 you received from your employer and Copy B of this Form W-2c to your return when you file it. For more information, contact your nearest IRS office.

If Your Employer Refuses to Issue a W-2 Form

Warning: Some employers try to take advantage of their immigrant workers by paying them in cash or non-payroll checks without paying employment taxes to the government. Some issue Form 1099 instead of W-2, as if the worker was an independent contractor, not an employee. Sometimes the employer states a different salary on the form than what the worker actually received. Some employers don't issue any forms at all, keeping the employment off the books. What should you do then?

First of all, contact your boss and ask whether a W-2 form was submitted. It is possible that a mistake was made or the form was sent to wrong address. After contacting your employer, allow a reasonable amount of time for him to resend or to issue the W-2. If you still do not receive your W-2 by February 15th, contact the IRS tax help line for assistance at 1-800-829-1040. When you call, have the following information ready:

- your employer's name, address, city, and state, including zip code
- your name, address, city and state, including zip code, and your Social Security number.

You still must file your tax return on time even if you do not receive your Form W-2. If you do not receive the missing information in time to file, you may file you may use Form 4852, *Substitute for Form W-2, Wage and Tax Statement* (see below). Attach Form 4852 to the return, estimating income and withholding taxes as accurately as possible. There may be a delay in any refund due while the information is verified.

In addition, you may file a complaint at your state labor department.

Form 4852, Substitute W-2

If your boss did not give you your W-2 form with the summary of earnings and taxes paid, you may recreate that form using IRS Form 4852, *Substitute for Form W-2, Wage and Tax Statement*. You may use old pay stubs, paycheck, bank records, and prior year forms to reconstruct the numbers. Make sure to identify your employer properly by providing the company name, address and the Employer Identification Number, if you have it. If not, get it from the previous year's W-2 or ask your former coworkers.

Important: In line 7(A)(a), enter the sum of your cash wages and Social Security and Medicare taxes due from your employer (7.65 percent of your wages). For example, you were paid $500 a week for 36 weeks, which amounts to total of $18,000. The employer's portion of the Social Security and Medicare is 7.65 percent of the gross wages, which means $1,377. Therefore the amount in line 7(A)(a) is $19,377 ($18,000 + 1,377) and the amount in line 7(A)(b) is $18,000.

When filling out Form 4852, the answer to line 8 should be following: *"7(A)(a) is the sum of cash wages and employee Social Security and Medicare paid by employer. 7(A)(b) is cash wages alone."*

In line 9, the IRS wants you to explain your efforts to obtain Form W-2. Here is a sample of a brief, simple statement: *"I worked as a full-time secretary from February 1 to October 23, 20XX. I was paid $500 per week. I called my employer twice and requested my W-2 form. He promised to send it to me, but never did."*

If later you receive the correct W-2 form, which will change your tax amount, you should file an amended tax return on IRS Form 1040X. Check your Social Security statement a year later to make sure that the SSA properly credited your earnings.

❧ Forms 4852 and 1040X, as well as instructions on how to fill them out, are available on the IRS website, www.irs.gov. You may also order them by calling 1-800-TAX-FORM (1-800-829-3676).

Amended Tax Return

If you filed a return but made a mistake, you are allowed to correct it.

The IRS will correct for you mathematical errors or will write to you asking for missing information. However, if you forgot to include certain income or deductions, if you used wrong filing status or entered incorrect information, you should file Form 1040X, *Amended U.S. Individual Income Tax Return.*

You can file 1040X any time of the year. Attach copies of any schedules that have been changed or any W-2 forms that you did not include. Enter information that got changed on the form.

You may amend a return within three years of the date on which you filed your original return or within two years after the date on which you paid the tax on that return – whichever is later. For example, a 2006 return that you filed on February 2, 2007, can be amended until April 15, 2010.

❧ Download Form 1040X from www.irs.gov/pub/irs-pdf/ f1040x.pdf.

Summary: In order to pay your overdue taxes, you need to know the amount of your earnings and withheld taxes that were reported to the government by your employers. Typically, you get this information from the W-2 form provided to you by your employer. If your employer did not give you the W-2 form although he should have, you can report this to the IRS or use a substitute W-2 form. Self-employed people must calculate their annual earnings and pay full income taxes as well as full Social Security tax by themselves.

7.6. How to Mitigate the Consequences of Nonpayment of Taxes

A Real-Life Example

While temporarily residing in the U.S., Mark declared three children on his tax return as his dependents in order to save on taxes. The IRS discovered that the children's Social Security numbers were incorrect, disallowed deductions, and demanded an additional $2,000 in taxes from Mark. However, Mark disregarded all letters from the IRS and returned to his country one year later. After some time, his plans changed. He obtained a Green Card, came back to the U.S., and decided to purchase a truck to earn a living as a truck driver. The truck dealer was ready to sell the vehicle to Mark on credit, but changed his mind when he saw Mark's credit report. The report showed an unpaid amount of $10,000 which Mark owed to the IRS. This was the balance of all the unpaid taxes, interest rates, and penalties that had accumulated over the years. That is how Mark's dreams of having his own business were shattered.

> *Past due taxes, penalties and interest may add up to huge amounts! The sooner you settle your affairs with the IRS, the better.*

If you find yourself in a similar situation, seek the help of an experienced accountant who will negotiate a partial reduction of your tax debt. Taxpayers without any savings stand a better chance of having their debt reduced.

Be informed that tax evasion where the loss to the government exceeds $10,000 is considered an aggravated felony (a serious crime) and therefore constitutes a ground for deportation.

Apply for Reduction of Interest and Penalties

When you have a reasonable explanation of why you got into trouble with the IRS, you should apply for tax abatement, which is a reduction of rates and late fees. The reasons accepted by the agency may be the following:

- failure to file a tax return due to a serious illness
- death in the family
- the loss of important tax documents resulted from matters beyond the taxpayer's power (e.g. flood, fire)
- incorrect tax advice of a tax professional.

The IRS is sometimes lenient towards an immigrant who did not file a tax return because of the fear that his immigration status would be revealed. The IRS does not accept such reasons as lack of knowledge about regulations, negligence, or change of address.

Take out a Loan to Pay Back Your Taxes

The IRS expects you to pay delinquent taxes. Perhaps you will have to use your savings, sell some stocks, mutual funds, or a car to do so. Sometimes it is a good idea to take out a loan. You can charge smaller amounts to your credit card. A home equity loan will help to pay off a large debt. The good thing about home equity loans is that the interest you pay is tax deductible.

Pay Taxes in Installments

Another solution is to pay off your tax debt in installments.

If you owe less than $10,000, you may request installment payments. You need to fill out IRS Form 9465, *Installment Agreement Request*, and offer a repayment period. Remember that the debt, interest rates, and penalties must be remitted within three years only. The IRS will send you an answer if your request was granted.

If your debt exceeds $25,000, you should try to negotiate different payment options with the IRS. If the agency knows about any other assets you own which are not crucial for your family financial support, it will ask you to sell them and will deny your request for installment payments.

Where to Learn More

- 🕸 The Internal Revenue Service has a lot of useful information on its website at www.irs.gov. Click on "Individuals."

- 📖 *Stand up to the IRS*, author: Frederick W. Daily, Nolo Press, www.Nolo.com, phone: 1-800-728-3555, address: 950 Parker Street, Berkeley, CA 94710-2524.

- 📖 *Surviving in the U.S. While Waiting for Your Green Card*; the book explains taxation issues pertaining to undocumented immigrants. See the Appendix on page 262.

Summary: *Penalties for nonpayment of taxes can be severe, and together with accrued interest they can add to the tax burden. The sooner you file your taxes, the sooner those charges will stop accruing. As a former illegal alien who was ill advised, you can try to have the penalties waived. You may apply to pay your tax delinquency in installments.*

8. CLEAN UP YOUR SOCIAL SECURITY ACCOUNT

At the beginning of your life with legal status in America, you should get your affairs in order with the Social Security Administration. Many illegal immigrants earn a living off the books by working on a Social Security number not good for employment, using somebody else's Social Security card, or getting wages in cash only and not paying taxes at all. Some immigrants are cheated by employers who withhold their taxes but never forward them to the government. Other newcomers work legally for some time, but move frequently and lose all documents.

Regardless of your previous situation, as a permanent resident now you may want to check your Social Security record, fix mistakes and fill gaps in your earning history. Remember: every calendar quarter of legitimate employment counts toward your future Social Security retirement or disability benefits.

8.1. How Earnings Are Posted

SSN, Non-Work SSN, and ITIN

The Social Security Administration (SSA) maintains records of wages employers pay to individuals. The way the SSA handles and stores the wage information depends on the way the wages are identified (by Social Security number, non-work SSN, or Individual Taxpayer Identification Number), and their accuracy.

Each year, employers and self-employed individuals report earnings information to the SSA using a unique 9-digit identifier called a Social Security number (SSN). This information is used to determine:

- whether an individual is eligible for retirement or disability benefits and
- the size of the benefit payment.

Regular **Social Security number.** The SSN is a worker's identifier. The SSN is the main identification number of individuals in the United States. Earnings posted on a regular (unrestricted) Social Security number are verified and placed in the **Master Earnings File** (MEF). If the SSA cannot match information (names and SSNs) on employer reports with information in its system, earnings are placed in the **Earnings Suspense File** (ESF). Currently, the ESF contains over 250 million records, and this number keeps growing.

The non-work Social Security number is assigned to an alien who does not have rights to work in the U.S. Earnings reported on non-work SSNs go to the **Non-Work Alien File** (NAF) which contains information posted to SSNs issued for non-work purposes (such as paying income taxes or receiving certain government benefits). The NAF contains annual earnings amounts, worker names and addresses, and employer names and addresses. Close to 8 million non-work SSNs have been assigned to date, of which half a million show up in this file. The NAF is not available to the Department of Homeland Security (DHS) because tax records are confidential in the U.S. Furthermore, the data is largely inaccurate, because names of immigrants who obtained work authorization are not always removed from this file.

Individual Taxpayer Identification Number (ITIN) is issued by the IRS for tax purposes, not by the SSA. It happens to have 9 digits, just like the SSN, and is frequently used by aliens for employment. Yet when employers report wages to the Social Security Administration using the ITIN rather than the individual's SSN, the agency is unable to post these earnings to the wage earner's record, because the record does not exist. For that reason, such earnings are posted in the Earnings Suspense File (ESF), the agency's repository for mismatched earnings.

How Earnings Are Reported

Employers report their employees' wages to two institutions: the Internal Revenue Service and the Social Security Administration.

- Quarterly, employers send to the IRS Form 941, *Employer's Quarterly Federal Tax Return,* Form 942, *Employer's Quarterly Tax Return for Household Employees,* or Form 943, *Employer's Annual Tax Return for Agricultural Employees.* These forms show gross wages and total taxes for the employer's payroll for the quarter.

- At the end of the calendar year, employers send reports to the SSA and to employees. Form W-3, *Transmittal of Wage and Tax Statement,* is used to summarize the total salaries and taxes; Form W-2, *Wage and Tax Statement,* sent to individual workers, shows their annual earnings and taxes. Employees send one copy of their W-2 to the IRS with their tax returns.

At the Social Security Administration, paper reports are scanned and converted into electronic form. Unreadable reports are rejected and the employer is asked to provide legible copies. Reports that are received late are identified and sent back with possible penalty assessments. The rest of the reports are processed for employee name and SSN verification.

When Earnings Don't Match

Reported earnings must be verified and credited to the workers accounts. About 10 percent of the W-2s received by SSA have invalid name/SSN combinations when they first arrive. Over twenty automated processes are used to match the earnings with their owners. When a worker's name and SSN match is found, the earnings information from the W-2 form is placed in the **Master Earnings File,** the main computer data file where the Social Security Administration records earnings for individuals. Earnings reported on non-work numbers are placed in the **Non-Work Alien File**. About 4 percent of all earnings reports remain unmatched and are electronically placed in the **Earnings Suspense File** (ESF), where the SSA uses additional automated and manual processes to continue to identify valid records. An approximate total of 250 million wage items so far could not be matched to the appropriate earnings records, resulting in the accumulation of over $422 billion in wages in the ESF.

Reports that do not match are identified and the employee is asked to provide corrected name and number information so the SSA can post the reported earnings to the correct record. If the wage report does not show a usable address for the employee or the letter cannot be delivered, the employer is contacted and asked for the correct information.

> *Earnings reported using ITIN do not match the SSA records and are captured in the Earnings Suspense File. The employer reporting these earnings is contacted for explanations.*

Warning: Mismatch of wage information occurs most frequently with immigrants. Because having a Social Security number is important for legal and financial assimilation in the USA, criminals obtain SSNs in various ways and sell them to unwary immigrants. Crooks improperly obtain SSNs by:

- presenting false documentation
- stealing another person's SSN
- purchasing an SSN on the black market
- using the SSN of a deceased individual, or
- making up an arbitrary 9-digit number.

The Social Security Administration actively combats SSN misuse.

Earnings Reconciliation Between the SSA and IRS

After posting reported wages to the right accounts, the SSA and the IRS try to verify the integrity of the earnings amount using a process called earnings reconciliation. Employer total annual wage reports (W-3, *Transmittal of Wage and Tax Statement*) are compared with the totals from the IRS employment tax records compiled from Forms 941, 942, or 943.

When more wages were reported to the IRS than to the SSA, then the SSA becomes concerned that employees' earnings are not being credited correctly to SSA records. The SSA examines some of these cases and makes an effort to resolve the difference without contacting the employer. When that effort is unsuccessful, the SSA sends a notice to the employer requesting information needed to resolve the case. If the SSA does not receive a response after 120 days, a second notice is sent to the employer. When no response is received after the second notice, the IRS is responsible for contacting the employer, and it may impose penalties.

When more wages are reported to the SSA than to the IRS, the IRS becomes concerned that employees did not pay all of their taxes, and the agency contacts the employer.

Employer reporting is described in detail at www.ssa.gov/employer.

> *Summary: Earnings reports sent by employers are scanned, validated and entered into computerized databases of the IRS and the SSA. Both agencies implement various processes that verify the information and check its integrity. The SSA matches reported earnings to workers' accounts.*

8.2. Check Wages Reported Using Your SSN

The SSA maintains records of the reported earnings of individuals. The reported earnings that match an individual's name and Social Security number are posted to the individual's record and are used to determine an employee's eligibility for retirement, survivors, and disability benefits.

Get Your Total Annual Earnings

If you want to check your annual earnings recorded by the SSA, you may order your Social Security Statement.

A Social Security Statement includes your reported income year by year, the amount of Social Security taxes paid by you

---

Social Security Credits

Social Security work credits (sometimes called **work quarters**) are quarters of coverage you earn while working and paying taxes. As you work, you earn one credit toward Social Security benefits for every $1,090 of your salary (up to 4 credits annually).

You need 40 credits to qualify for retirement benefits. As you can see, you need to work 10 years earning at least $4,360 annually (as of 2009) to be fully insured and to qualify for Social Security retirement. The minimum amount of wages is annually indexed for inflation.

---

and your employer, as well as estimated benefits you and your family may be eligible for now and in the future. Normally, this is all the information that is needed to determine your Social Security eligibility and benefits.

You may ask for your Social Security Statement online at www. ssa.gov or by using Form 7004, *Request for Earnings and Benefit Estimate Statement.* You may order the form by mail (1-800-772-1213) or download it from www.ssa.gov/online/ssa-7004. html. More information is available at www.ssa.gov/statement.

On the form, you need to write your name as shown on your Social Security card, your Social Security number, your date of birth, your place of birth and your mother's maiden name.

Within few weeks, you will receive statement SSA-7005, *Personal Earnings and Benefit Estimate Statement,* showing your reported income and paid premiums year by year. This way you can see employment gaps and find out whether anyone worked using your name and SSN.

Once a year, the Social Security Administration mails out statements to each worker to the last address reported at the SSA by the employer.

Get Your Detailed Earnings Information

To obtain a detailed statement of your employment history, you need to complete Form SSA-7050-F4, *Request for Social Security Earnings Information.* For every year you request, you will receive names and addresses of your employers and a statement of how much you earned working there.

It takes more time to prepare detailed earnings information. Unlike the electronically available annual earnings information used to compute Social Security benefits, detailed earnings must be extracted manually from microfilmed records and visually examined before a statement can be produced.

There is a small charge for this information. You pay extra for certification of the information, which you normally do not need unless you intend to use the information in court.

The SSA does not charge for providing more detailed earnings information when it is needed for correcting a Social Security record or for establishing entitlement to Social Security benefits.

   Get Form SSA-7050-F4 with the fee schedule from the SSA website at www.ssa.gov/online/ssa-7050.pdf. You may order it by mail by calling the SSA at 1-800-772-1213.

Can You Get Someone Else's Statement?

Let's say that you are divorced and you want to retire on your exhusband's/wife's record. (You can get Social Security retirement benefits on your ex-spouse record if you meet certain requirements; visit www.ssa.gov for more information). Can you get his/her earnings information?

The answer is no. For information about potential benefits on someone else's record, you should call or visit your local Social Security office. If your former spouse is still living, privacy rules prohibit the SSA from revealing his or her earnings record. However, an SSA representative can tell you what benefits you may be entitled to, after he has established your former marital relationship to your ex-spouse.

If your spouse died sometime in the past, an old statement won't give you the up-to-date estimate of benefits you might receive. Contact the SSA and get the correct numbers.

Under certain circumstances, a legal guardian of a mentally incompetent adult or the parent of a minor (child) may sign a consent form to authorize release of records about a number holder.

 Summary: *All your recorded earnings information is available from the Social Security Administration. The SSA does not charge a fee for providing individuals with a statement showing yearly totals of earnings and the amount of Social Security taxes paid. If you need detailed earnings information, you may have to pay a moderate fee.*

8.3. How to Pay Back Your FICA Tax

Many immigrants work in the United States illegally and do not always pay income taxes or participate in the Social Security program. Young people hardly lose sleep over this situation. The trouble starts for older newcomers who after obtaining their Green Cards would like to get Social Security credits for the years they worked illegally.

You Must Pay Back Income Taxes

If you want to earn back Social Security credits, you must pay all your overdue taxes for the years in question. Here is the list of taxes you must pay:

- **FICA tax** (short for Federal Insurance Contributions Act) consists of Social Security and Medicare tax, totaling 15.3 percent of your wages. The rate consists of two parts: 12.4 percent for Social Security (old-age, survivors, and disability insurance) and 2.9 percent for Medicare (hospital insurance). Above a certain limit ($106,800 in 2009) you pay only 2.9 percent for Medicare. FICA taxes are paid half by the employee and half by the employer. However, if you are filing your tax returns retroactively for years when no employer withheld your FICA taxes, you may have to pay the whole amount by yourself.

- **Federal income tax.** The rate can be 10, 15, 25, 33 or 35 percent depending on the level of your income in a given year. The more money you make, the higher your tax rate. However, the first several thousand dollars equal to the sum of standard deduction and personal exemption for the given year are tax free: from about $9,000 to over $20,000 depending on the filing status, age, and number of dependents. The numbers are adjusted for inflation every year, so see www.irs.gov for details.

- **State and city income taxes** range from zero in some states (such as Florida, Wyoming, Nevada, and Texas) to over 14 percent in the most expensive states (New York, Connecticut, Maine, and California). For people with low income they may be very low or non-existent.

When you add FICA, federal, state, and local taxes, you will see that paying them can be expensive, especially for people with large incomes. Some tax deductions may help. Remember that FICA tax (15.3 percent) applies to your earned income, but not to your passive income such as bank interest or dividends.

Attention new Americans: Do not think that you can pay back 10 years worth of taxes and then collect Social Security retirement benefits for the rest of your life. Whereas the IRS will take your money for any number of past years, the SSA will only issue you Social Security credits for up to three years, three months, and 15 days after the year in which wages were paid.

Paying Back Taxes as an Employee

The way to pay back Social Security taxes depends on your situation. It is different for employees and for the self-employed.

As you already know, the Social Security Administration learns about your earnings from your employer, who each year sends Copy A of all W-2 forms to the SSA. The agency matches the name and the Social

Security number (SSN) on each W-2 with its database indexed by Social Security numbers. When a match is found, the earnings information from the W-2 is recorded in your earnings history. Your lifelong earnings history is the basis for determining your future eligibility and benefit amount for Social Security retirement, disability, and survivors programs. That's why it is critical that the year-end Form W-2 contains your correct name and SSN, exactly as shown on your Social Security card.

What to do now: If you want to get Social Security credits for the past three years, file back income tax returns. See section 7.4 for information on how to do this.

Paying Back Taxes as a Self-Employed Person

Having been self-employed, you must do all reporting to the IRS and the SSA by yourself.

Self-employed individuals pay self-employment tax (SE tax), which consists only of Social Security and Medicare tax. You calculate SE tax yourself using Schedule SE, which is an attachment to the main tax form 1040). The self-employment tax rate is 15.3 percent on the first $106,800 of wages (as of 2009) and 2.9 percent on wages above that limit.

As a self-employed person, you must pay the government estimated income taxes if you expect to owe $1,000 or more. You report and pay your estimated quarterly taxes on Form 1040-ES, *Estimated Tax for Individuals* by April 15, June 15, September 15, and January 15 of every year. The Social Security Administration posts your earnings in your Social Security file.

By the 15th of April following any year in which you have net self-employment earnings of $400 or more, you must complete the following federal tax forms:

- Form 1040, U.S. Individual Income Tax Return
- Schedule C, Profit or Loss from Business
- Schedule SE, Self-Employment Tax.

What to do now: In order to get Social Security credits for the past three years in which you worked off the books, you must pay back your income taxes and your self-employment tax, as explained in

Chapter 7.4. If you do not owe any income tax, you still must complete Form 1040 and Schedule SE to pay self-employment Social Security tax.

Minimum Benefits You May Receive

If you pay taxes on net earnings of at least $4,400 annually (the minimum amount that gives you four credits annually – one credit for each $1,090 of earnings, as of 2009) for only 10 years, you will qualify for Social Security benefits, but your retirement check will not measure up to your expectations.

Example: Fernando came to the United States in his fifties. Although he worked illegally for several years before he got his Green Card, his earnings were substantial. Because of age, he decided to pay back taxes on some of his income to make up for lost time. A tax specialist agreed to take care of everything for $300 fee. An annual income of only $4,000 plus bank interest was declared for the last 4 years. The taxes cost Fernando $2,500 but the expectation of a nice pension made it easier to part with the cash.

The IRS gladly accepted the tax returns along with Fernando's money, but imposed penalties and interest. Taking the tax specialist's advice, Fernando asked the IRS to waive the penalties due to his inability to pay taxes as an illegal worker. The IRS agreed but still wanted interest of several hundred dollars.

Fernando was surprised when he learned the results of his efforts. *The Personal Earnings and Benefit Estimate Statement* from the SSA indicated that Fernando will receive an early retirement benefit of only $30 a month assuming he will keep earning in the future at the same pace (i.e. about $4,500 per year). If he works until his 65th birthday, his retirement check will be $56 and only $23 in case of disability. Fernando also learned that even if he continues working 7 more years to qualify for retirement and declares an income three times higher, his retirement benefits will be still very small.

Summary: It is important to pay your taxes so you can get Social Security benefits in the future. To be eligible for Social Security retirement benefits you need at least 10 years of work (40 credits) on record. If you declare only a minimum amount of income, your retirement benefits may be very small.

8.4. Earnings Errors

Let's say that you requested your *Personal Earnings and Benefit Estimate Statement* from the SSA, as described in section 8.2. When you received it, you discovered gaps in your employment or incorrect earnings. Various problems could have occurred.

How Errors Occur

In order for wages to be credited to the correct worker, the worker's name and SSN on the W-2 form (sent by the employer) must match the name and SSN recorded on the SSA's Master Earnings File that contains all Social Security numbers issued. The Social Security Administration receives more than 240 million W-2 reports annually. About 10 percent of them have an invalid name/SSN combination.

An error in your earnings report may result from:

- failure of your employer (or you as a self-employed individual) to file the required reports with the SSA and IRS
- errors in reports filed by your employer (or you as a self-employed person), for example, an incorrect or missing SSN, misspelled name, or incorrect dollar amount
- filer's neglect to register his/her name change with the Social Security Administration, for example a newlywed
- identity fraud (see chapter 12)
- errors made by the SSA staff in transcribing received reports into the SSA database.

Problems for immigrants are commonly caused by:

- nonpayment of taxes
- working on somebody else's Social Security number
- working on an Individual Tax Identification Number (ITIN)
- using a fake or purchased Social Security number.

Where Mismatched Earnings Go

What happens to the money collected by the SSA for which owners cannot be found?

When the name and SSN on a W-2 statement do not match the SSA's records, the earnings are placed into the Earnings Suspense File (ESF).

The ESF is an electronic holding file for W-2s that cannot be matched to the earnings records of individual workers. If the SSA later obtains the correct name or SSN for a worker, the wages are credited to that person's record. Since 1937, the ESF has grown to nearly 300 million reports of individual earnings with a value of almost $520 billion. About $6 billion is being added to this unclaimed stash every year.

All W-2 reports received by the SSA that have an Individual Tax Identification Number (ITIN) in the SSN field, instead of a valid SSN, are sent to the suspense file. An ITIN is a 9-digit number issued by the IRS to noncitizens who need tax identification numbers for tax purposes and who otherwise do not qualify for an SSN. When an ITIN shows up on the W-2 report, this W-2 is being posted to the suspense file because an ITIN is not a valid SSN.

Will Your Earnings Be Credited?

If you were assigned **a work SSN after January 1, 2004**, then all your covered earnings will be recognized regardless of your prior immigration status or former lack of work authorization. Of course, you must have legal immigration status in order to get a work SSN.

If you were assigned **any type of valid SSN before January 1, 2004** (even a non-work number), your previous years of earnings will be credited based on standard rules, even if you are currently not a lawful alien. These rules state that the undocumented aliens are entitled to collect Social Security retirement benefits only abroad.

If you worked in the past using a **fake SSN**, a number that belonged to another person, or your Taxpayer Identification Number, those earnings will not be credited to you until you legitimize your immigration status and obtain a Social Security number valid for employment.

The time limit in which earnings can be corrected is 3 years, 3 months, and 15 days after the year in which wages were paid or self-employment income was derived. However, there are many exceptions from this rule: apparent error, fraud, conforming to tax returns, error in earnings allocation, no entry or incomplete entry of earnings, etc.

Summary: *For various reasons, the Social Security Administration is not able to correctly match several percent of all wage reports. Mismatched earnings are posted in the Earnings Suspense File (ESF) and may be reclaimed by workers who present appropriate documentation.*

8.5. How to Correct Your Earnings Record

Procedure for Correcting Your Earnings Record

The Social Security Administration is responsible for establishing and maintaining accurate and complete earnings records of all taxpayers. Therefore, if you discovered an earnings discrepancy, contact the Social Security Administration because the agency is obligated to assist you in resolving any earnings issues.

☎ You may download SSA Form 7008, *Request for Correction of Earnings Record* from www.ssa.gov/online/ssa-7008.pdf or order it by calling 1-800-772-1213.

Fill out the form according to instructions. If you prefer, go to an SSA office or call for help. You will need to gather the important information listed on the form in order for the SSA to confirm your actual earnings and credit them to you. You will need to know the time-frame of the employment in question, the employer's business name, address, and phone number. The Employer Identification Number is helpful. List your correct Social Security (FICA) wages and provide evidence of them.

Remember: It is the SSA's duty to correct your records. The agency staff will check to see if any missing reports of earnings can be found in the SSA system. They will search the Earnings Suspense File both by your SSN and by your employer identification number in an attempt to locate your missing earnings. If the SSA is satisfied that the earnings in the suspense file belong to you based on the evidence that you provided, your account is credited with the earnings.

If the SSA cannot find the records in its system, the agency will write to your employer to get a statement of your earnings.

Your earnings record can be corrected if the time limit has not passed and if there is acceptable evidence of the wages paid to you.

Form Approved
OMB NO. 0960-0029

SOCIAL SECURITY ADMINISTRATION

REQUEST FOR CORRECTION OF EARNINGS RECORD

Privacy Act Notice: The information requested on this form is authorized by section 205(c)(4) and (5) of the Social Security Act. This information is collected to resolve any discrepancy on your earnings record. The information you provide will be used to correct your earnings record where any discrepancy exists. Your response to this request is voluntary; however, failure to provide all or part of the requested information may affect your future eligibility for benefits and the amounts of benefits to which you may become entitled. Information furnished on this form may be disclosed by the Social Security Administration to another person or governmental agency only with respect to Social Security programs to comply with Federal laws requiring the exchange of information between the Social Security Administration and another agency. *(Privacy Act continued on the back.)*

I have examined your statement (or record) of my Social Security earnings and it is not correct. I am providing the following information and accompanying evidence so that you can correct my record.

1. Print your name (First Name, Middle Initial, Last Name)	2. Enter your date of birth (Month, Day, Year)

3. Print your name as shown on your Social Security number card

4. Print any other name used in your work. (If you have used no other name enter "None.")

5. (a) Enter your Social Security number	5. (b) Enter any other Social Security number(s) used by you or your employer to report your wages or self-employment. If none, check "None."
− −	(1) ☐ None
	(2) − −
	(3) − −

6. IF NECESSARY, SSA MAY DISCLOSE MY NAME TO MY EMPLOYERS: ☐ YES ☐ NO
(Without permission to use your name, SSA cannot make a thorough investigation.)

If you disagree with wages reported to your earnings record, complete Item 7.
If you disagree with self-employment income recorded on your earnings record, go to Item 8.

7. **Print** below in date order your employment **only** for year(s) (or months) you believe our records are not correct. If you need more space, attach a separate sheet. Please make only one entry per calendar period employed. Show quarterly wage periods and amounts for years prior to 1978; annual amounts, 1978 on.

1 - Year(s) (or months) of employment 2 - Type of employment (e.g., agricultural)	Employer's business name, address, and phone number *(include number, city, state, and ZIP code)*	My correct Social Security (FICA) wages were:	My evidence of my correct earnings (enclosed)
(a) 1. 2.			☐ W2 or W-2C ☐ Other (specify)
(b) 1. 2.			☐ W2 or W-2C ☐ Other (specify)
(c) 1. 2.			☐ W2 or W-2C ☐ Other (specify)

▶ If you do not have evidence of these earnings, you must explain why you are unable to submit such evidence in the remarks section of Item 10.

▶ If you do not have self-employment income that is incorrect go on to item 10 for any remarks, and then complete Item 11.

8. Print below in date order your self-employment earnings **only** for years you believe our records are not correct. Please make only one entry per year.

Trade or business name and business address	Year(s) of self-employment	My correct self-employment earnings were:
(a)		$
(b)		$

9. Regarding your earnings from self-employment:
   a. Did you file an income tax return reporting your self-employment income? ⟶

   ☐ YES
   (If "YES," go on to Item 9b.)
   ☐ NO
   (If "NO," explain why in Item 10).

   b. Do you have a copy of your income tax return and evidence of filing such as a canceled check? ⟶

   ☐ YES
   (If "YES," please enclose copies.)
   ☐ NO
   (If "NO," go on to Item 9c.)

   c. Have you asked the Internal Revenue Service to furnish you copies from their records? ⟶

   ☐ YES
   (But none available)
   ☐ NO
   (If "NO," please do so if your return was filed less than 6 years ago.)

   d. If you are unable to submit a copy of your self-employment tax return, please explain in the remarks section (Item 10).

10. Remarks -- You may use this space for any explanations. (If you need more space, please attach a separate sheet).

Privacy Act *(Continued from the front)*:
COMPUTER MATCHING STATEMENT: We may also use the information you give us when we match records by computer. Matching programs compare our records with those of other Federal, State or local government agencies. Many agencies may use matching programs to find or prove that a person qualifies for benefits paid by the Federal government. The law allows us to do this even if you do not agree to it.

Explanations about these and other reasons why information you provide us may be used or given out are available in Social Security Offices. If you want to learn more about this, contact any Social Security Office.

Paperwork Reduction Act Statement - This information collection meets the requirements of 44 U.S.C. § 3507, as amended by Section 2 of the Paperwork Reduction Act of 1995. You do not need to answer these questions unless we display a valid Office of Management and Budget control number. We estimate that it will take about 10 minutes to read the instructions, gather the facts, and answer the questions. **SEND THE COMPLETED FORM TO YOUR LOCAL SOCIAL SECURITY OFFICE. The office is listed under U.S. Government agencies in your telephone directory or you may call Social Security at 1-800-772-1213.** *You may send comments on our time estimate above to: SSA, 1338 Annex Building, Baltimore, MD 21235-6401. Send only comments relating to our time estimate to this address, not the completed form.*

11. **I declare under penalty of perjury that I have examined all the information on this form, and on any accompanying statements or forms, and it is true and correct to the best of my knowledge. I understand that anyone who knowingly gives a false or misleading statement about a material fact in this information, or causes someone else to do so, commits a crime and may be sent to prison, or may face other penalties, or both.**

Signature of person making statement *(First Name, Middle Initial, Last Name)*

Mailing Address *(Number & Street, Apt. No., P.O. Box, Rural Route)*

City   State   ZIP Code   -

Date   Telephone Number (Include Area Code):
              1. Work (   )   -   2. Home (   )   -

When you have filled out this form, mail it in an envelope addressed to:

Social Security Administration
300 N. Greene Street
Baltimore, Maryland 21201

Form **SSA-7008** (2-2005) ef (2-2005)

If the correction of alien earnings occurs within the period of the employer's tax withholding liability for those wages (i.e., 3 years, 3 months, and 15 days of the earnings), then the SSA reports the correction to the Internal Revenue Service (IRS). Withholdings corrections by employers are then due.

Evidence of Wages

The best proof of your earnings must be based directly on your employer's records, if available, and may consist of Form W-2, *Wage and Tax Statement*, or any other statement signed by an employer or the employer's accountant.

What do you do if the company you worked for does not exist anymore? Then you can submit pay envelopes, pay stubs, vouchers, or union records. Your federal or state income tax returns are helpful, but they must be certified and show the actual wages paid to you. Section 7.2 explains how to get certified copies of your tax returns from the IRS. Get records of state unemployment compensation if you can.

The documents provided as evidence must clearly show the amount of your wages and when they were paid.

Important: If everything seems to be failing, don't give up. The SSA may accept well organized personal records and the statements of persons having knowledge of the facts. For more information see §1732 in the *Social Security Handbook*, which is available online at www.ssa.gov/OP_Home/handbook/handbook-toc.html. Search the handbook for "§1732."

Persons who know about your employment and wages should make their statements on the Form SSA-795, *Statement of Claimant or Other Person*, available at all Social Security offices and at www.ssa.gov/online/ssa-795.pdf. The statements must lay down the facts on which the person bases his or her conclusions about the wages paid to you and show the periods for which the wages were paid. Statements of supervisors, coworkers, and union officials are accepted, as well as statements from bank employees where you cashed paychecks, or from the staff of an employment agency that found the job for you.

Evidence of Wages for Self-Employed

If you are self-employed, you may establish your earnings by submitting certified copies of tax returns. Include the applicable schedules and evidence that your return was filed on time with the IRS. Acceptable evidence for having filed a return includes canceled checks, IRS receipts, etc.

Where to Learn More

🏛 See §1416 of the Social Security Handbook, www.ssa.gov/OP_Home/handbook/handbook-toc.html. Go to chapter 14 and then to section 1416.

📖 *Surviving in the U.S. While Waiting for Your Green Card* explains problems with Social Security numbers pertaining to undocumented immigrants. See the Appendix on page 262.

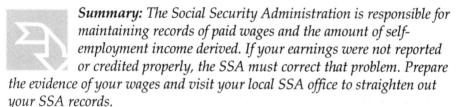

Summary: *The Social Security Administration is responsible for maintaining records of paid wages and the amount of self-employment income derived. If your earnings were not reported or credited properly, the SSA must correct that problem. Prepare the evidence of your wages and visit your local SSA office to straighten out your SSA records.*

8.6. Problems that Can Be Resolved

Scrambled Earnings

Scrambled earnings occur when a person worked under another person's SSN. Sometimes it occurs as a result of identity theft, but it most often happens when an alien worker earned a living using an SSN of a family member or a friend.

Many immigrants give their employers false Social Security numbers and work for years, dutifully paying taxes. When they start working legally, most want the Social Security Administration to credit their accounts with those earnings.

The SSA won't transfer the contents of one account into another unless the agency is presented with proof that you were the worker who used the false number. In order for the agency to unscramble your earnings, you have to show W-2 forms, paycheck stubs, or tax returns for the years in question. If this is not possible, the SSA may accept a statement from your employer or from your coworkers. You must fill out SSA Form 7008, *Request for Correction of Earnings Record,* and write the reason for the change in line 10. Take a look at the following sample explanation:

"While being an undocumented alien, I filed federal and local taxes under the name of Smith, which was my mother's maiden name. My Social Security number at this time was 987-65-4321. Now, upon legalization of my immigration status, I would like to correct my data and start using my last name and Social Security number assigned to me recently by the SSA, which is 123-45-6789."

If You Used Somebody Else's Social Security Number

Not all fake numbers are valid and in use. The real problems start for somebody who used a name of another person, whose data exists in the SSA files.

Example: Let's assume that you came to the U.S. temporarily and gave your employer the name and Social Security number of your cousin who already left the U.S. You are happy, thinking that you have circumvented regulations. Your cousin might not mind either, because you will be adding to his retirement account. But if you work for several years and then decide to stay in the U.S. permanently, you are at risk of losing those years and potential benefits.

The only solution at that point is to obtain a sworn statement from the person, whose Social Security number you used, testifying that you worked during that time. Use SSA Form 7008, *Request for Correction of Earnings Record.* The SSA might agree to transfer the earnings into your own account only if you document your case very well.

🏵 SSA Form 7008, *Request for Correction of Earnings Record* can be downloaded from www.ssa.gov/online/ssa-7008.pdf or ordered by phone from the SSA at 1-800-772-1213.

Wage Disputes

If you and your employer disagree about the amount of wages paid, when they were paid, or whether your work was covered by Social Security or not, the SSA will help you obtain evidence to settle the matter. The agency will examine wage reports sent by the employer to the SSA (W-2 and W-3) or to the IRS (Form 941, *Employer's Quarterly Federal Tax Return*).

If the employer refuses to cooperate, the SSA will attempt to contact him and may subpoena the employer's records, if necessary.

If the employer withheld FICA taxes from your earnings but never sent them to the government, the SSA will investigate this matter and try to recover your withheld taxes.

The SSA will then decide whether your earnings can be credited, their amount, and the period to which they should be credited. The SSA will notify you of their decision and if any changes were made to your record.

If Your Employer Did Not Pay Withheld Taxes to the Government

If you are concerned that your employer did not send your taxes to the government, you should report this by calling the IRS information hotline at 1-800-829-1040. Failure to remit withheld payroll taxes is a very serious offense. Employers who do not comply with employment tax laws may be subject to criminal and civil sanctions for willfully failing to pay employment taxes.

Here what you should do to resolve the situation. Ask your employer for your W-2 form from last year. If you are unable to obtain your W-2 statement from the employer, you should complete Form 4852, *Substitute for W-2*, using the best information available to calculate wages and withholdings. Attach Form 4852 to your tax return. You will pay your share of the FICA (Social Security and Medicare) and the employer will have to pay his share (see page 101).

Attention: Withheld payroll taxes are called "trust fund taxes" and they belong to the government. Companies should not use these funds to pay salaries, business expenses, or for any other purpose. Domestic employers must not keep that money for themselves. When an employer fails to pay withheld payroll taxes to the government, IRC section 6672(a) imposes a penalty equal to the entire amount of the trust fund taxes on every "responsible person" who "willfully" fails to see that the taxes are paid.

> **Employees with concerns about an employer can contact the IRS information hotline at 1-800-829-1040 or report suspected tax fraud by calling 1-800-829-0433.**

Many states help employees fight payroll tax reporting fraud. For more information contact your state department of labor.

 Summary: The SSA is obligated by law to maintain correct earning records of all workers in the U.S. and to make an effort to correct any discrepancies. Get SSA Form 7008, Request for Correction of Earnings Record, collect required documentation, and visit your local Social Security office. Correct your SSA records as soon as possible, because there is some time limitation.

8.7. Changing Your Social Security Number

You may think that the mess in your tax, Social Security, and credit records could be cleaned up more easily if you obtain a new Social Security number. Be advised, however, that changing your SSN can be done only in extreme circumstances.

Tip: If you have a valid SSN, even one that is not valid for employment, you don't have to change the number after obtaining your Green Card (see section 4.1 for details).

When a Replacement Number Can Be Assigned

If you have a Green Card or a work visa, and you never had an SSN before, obtaining your first SSN is simple. On the other hand, getting a second number is different. Generally, the Social Security Administration assigns only one Social Security number per person to use all of his or her life. The SSA can assign a replacement number only in the following circumstances:

- Sequential numbers assigned to members of a family are causing problems.
- More than one person has been assigned, or is using, the same number.
- An individual has religious or cultural objections to certain numbers or digits in the original number.

- A victim of identity theft continues to be disadvantaged by using the original number. See Publication No. 05-10064, *Identity Theft and Your Social Security Number*, www.ssa.gov/pubs/10064.html.
- Situations of harassment, abuse, or life endangerment, including domestic violence. See Publication No. 05-10093, *New Numbers for Domestic Violence Victims*, www.ssa.gov/pubs/10093.html.

How to Apply for a New Social Security Number

Before applying for a new number, you have to demonstrate that you did all you could to resolve your problem and that obtaining a second number is your last resort. The SSA explicitly states in its instructions that you cannot get a new SSN if you filed for bankruptcy or intend to avoid legal responsibility. You will not get a second number if your Social Security card is lost or stolen but there is no evidence that someone is using the number.

This means that if someone knows your number, you cannot get a new one only because you fear it may be used. The SSA will issue a second number only after you become a victim of identity theft or fraudulent SSN usage, and you do your best to solve the problem, but the trouble persists. Your original number will be retained and cross-referenced with the new one in the SSA database.

To apply for a different number, you should fill out Form SS-5, *Application for a Social Security Card*, provide proof of your identity and legal immigration status, as well as show the evidence to support your need for a new number. Read section 13.6 for more information.

If your name or Social Security number changed, your employer should notify the SSA on Form W-2c, *Statement of Corrected Income and Tax Amounts*.

Summary: *A Social Security number can be replaced only under extreme circumstances.*

9. GET TO KNOW COMPANIES WHICH GATHER INFORMATION ON PEOPLE

If you ever seem to be rejected for any credit you apply for, your insurance premiums unexplainably skyrocket, or your driver's license suddenly gets suspended, you may not simply be having a streak of bad luck. The companies you are dealing with may be finding negative information about you stored in various databases. This is why you should be aware who collects information about you in the U.S., when, and how this information is used.

9.1. What Are Consumer Reporting Agencies?

What Others Know About You

It is possible that you are suffering consequences of your own past slip-ups, mistakes made by others, or stolen identity. If you ever shared your documents with someone else (for example, a fellow immigrant), and he used your personal information as you, then his activities and obligations appear in the records as yours. The havoc can be also caused by errors in your files in various databases or by identity theft.

In the U.S., your personal details are stored in countless places, ready to be retrieved by people and companies who want to provide employment, sell something, insure you, rent out apartment, or lend you money. This information is critical to your livelihood in the United States, so knowing who has it and whether it is correct should be important to you.

Consumer Reporting Agencies

A **consumer reporting agency** (CRA) is a company which collects and sells information about consumers. The reports are used by businesses (banks, insurance companies, landlords, and others) to evaluate potential customers and risk involved in serving them. As members of the CRA, those businesses send information to the CRA about their customers. For that, they are called **information providers**.

Credit bureaus: The best known CRAs are credit bureaus (see section 10.5). They gather information about how consumers use credit. Businesses purchase credit reports from credit bureaus about prospective customers and use them to decide how much credit to extend, if any.

Specialty CRAs: Consumer reports can be issued for purposes other than issuing credit. A number of companies specialize in providing reports for specific purposes such as evaluating prospective employees or tenants. They are called "specialty" consumer reporting agencies.

Specialty CRAs operate much like credit bureaus. They collect information from various sources, including public records, court information, credit history, bankruptcy filings, medical data, driving records, information from various companies that did business with the customer. From these records specialty CRA create reports for various users such as insurance companies, landlords, and employers.

The Fair and Accurate Credit Transaction Act (FACTA) covers reports issued by specialty CRAs when reports relate to medical records or payments, residential or tenant history, check writing history, employment history, or insurance claims.

For more on specialty CRAs, read Fact Sheet 6(b), *What You Should Know About "Specialty" Reports*, www. privacyrights.org/fs/fs6b-SpecReports.htm

Where Reporting Companies Take Their Data From

Consumer reporting agencies (CRAs) obtain their information from many different sources: public records, publicly available information, and nonpublic information.

• **Public records**, a primary source of information about consumers, can be obtained from government agencies. Available to anyone, public records include, among others, birth and death records, property records, tax liens, voter registrations, licensing records, and court information (including criminal records, bankruptcy filings, civil case files, and legal judgments).

• **Publicly available information** is not found in public records but is available through other sources such as telephone directories, business directories, print publications (classified ads or magazines), Internet sites, and other sources accessible by the general public.

• **Nonpublic information** is derived from proprietary (nonpublic) sources such as credit data, product warranty registrations, lists of magazine or catalog subscribers, and application information provided to private businesses directly by consumers.

Summary: Consumer reporting agencies (CRAs) are organizations that collect information on individuals and sell reports to creditors, landlords, or employers who want to evaluate potential customers or employees. It is very important that information about you in CRAs' databases is positive and correct.

9.2. Credit, Consumer, and Investigative Reports

Credit reporting agencies (CRAs) pack consumer data in various reports, depending on the purpose.

A **credit report** is prepared by a credit bureau and contains information about where you live, how you pay your bills, and whether you've been sued, arrested, or filed for bankruptcy. (See section 10.1).

A **consumer report** contains not only credit information but also your driving, criminal, employment and academic records, as well as your public records. It also may contain your personal and credit characteristics, character, general reputation, and lifestyle. The following information might be included in a consumer report:

• personal data: current and previous addresses, marital status, Social Security number
• current and former employers
• any workers' compensation claims you have made in the past
• your medical records, military records
• owned property
• criminal history
• academic records, professional certifications and state licenses.

An **investigative consumer report** goes beyond a typical credit report. It might include very personal details such as your reputation and personal character. The investigators get this information by interviewing neighbors, friends, business associates, etc.

An investigative report may be ordered by insurance companies or very nosy employers.

9.3. Your Rights Under the FCRA

Laws that Protect You

Federal laws protect your rights with national consumer reporting agencies (CRAs) similar to how your rights are protected with the three nationwide credit bureaus – Experian, Trans Union, and Equifax.

The Fair Credit Reporting Act (FCRA) is a federal law that regulates how consumer reporting agencies use your information. Enacted in 1970, the FCRA restricts who has access to your sensitive credit information and how that information can be used. In 2003, the FCRA got amended by the Fair and Accurate Credit Transactions Act (FACTA), and since then covers also national specialty CRAs.

The full statute of the FCRA can be found on the website of the Federal Trade Commission:
www.ftc.gov/os/statutes/031224fcra.pdf.

Your state laws can give you additional rights.

How You Are Protected

Under the FCRA, you have the following rights:

You must be told when information in your file has been used against you. Anyone who uses information from a CRA to take action against you (so called "**adverse action**") – such as denying an application for credit, housing, insurance, or employment – must tell you which CRA provided the consumer report and must explain your rights. Usually, companies send you a copy of a publication called *Summary of Your Rights under the Fair Credit Reporting Act* (www. ftc.gov/bcp/conline/pubs/credit/fcrasummary.pdf). You have 60 days after receiving the adverse action notice to request your free consumer report from the CRA indicated on the adverse action letter (FCRA §612(b), 15 USC §1681j(b)).

You have the right to receive a free copy of your consumer file from nationwide CRAs once a year. In addition, you are entitled to a free copy of your file if:

- within the past 60 days you have been subject to adverse action as a result of information in your file
- you are unemployed but expect to apply for employment within 60 days
- you have been a victim of identity theft and you placed a fraud alert in your file
- your file contains inaccurate information as a result of fraud
- you are on public assistance.

Access to your file is limited. A consumer reporting agency may provide information about you only with your consent to people with a valid need – usually to consider an application with a creditor, insurer, employer, or landlord. For more information, go to www. ftc.gov/credit.

You may limit "prescreened" (preapproved) offers of credit and insurance. These offers are based on information in your credit report that indicates you meet criteria set by the company. Usually these are preapproved offers of credit cards that come via mail. You may opt-out with the nationwide credit bureaus at 1-888-5 OPTOUT (1-888-567-8688) and with ChexSystems at 1-877-OPTOUT-5 (1-877-678-6885).

You have the right to dispute information that is incomplete or inaccurate, and have your claims investigated and any errors deleted or corrected, as provided by the law (see the following section).

Information Excluded from Your Report

Matters the FCRA prohibits from being included in a report include:

- bankruptcies after 10 years
- civil suits, civil judgments, and records of arrest, from date of entry, after 7 years
- paid tax liens after 7 years
- accounts placed for collection after 7 years
- any other negative information (except criminal convictions) after 7 years

- information about arrest which did not lead to conviction, except in cases where the matter has not yet come to trial.

Important: It is important to note that the FCRA does not apply to investigations performed by companies which are not consumer reporting agencies. This means that employers, insurance agencies, landlords, or banks can investigate you themselves without limitations of the FCRA.

Problems with Specialty CRAs

While the law requires the three major credit bureaus (Experian, TransUnion, and Equifax) to create a centralized source for accepting consumer requests for free credit reports (website, a toll-free telephone number, and a single postal address, see section 10.5), specialty CRAs don't have to create one access point for consumers. They are only required to maintain a toll-free phone number, provide consumers with a copy of their report upon request, and must allow consumers to dispute inaccurate information.

This sounds good, but in practice, you may find it difficult to access and correct information held by specialty CRAs because there may be hundreds of them and no master list exists.

For example, if you are looking for a job and you want to confirm the accuracy of your background information, you would need to request your consumer report from dozens of CRAs which specialize in employee screening.

Summary: The Federal Credit Reporting Act gives you the right to know what is in your file and the right to correct erroneous or incomplete information. Access to the multitude of specialty CRAs is not centralized like access to three major credit bureaus, so you must deal with each of them individually.

9.4. Your Rights to Fix Inaccuracies

How the CRA Must Handle the Dispute

If you see errors on your consumer report, you have the right to dispute them. The FCRA specifies obligations of both CRAs and information providers (companies that send information to the CRAs) when you dispute the completeness or accuracy of your record.

The dispute process is detailed in section 611 of the FCRA (15 USC §1681i).

- The CRA must complete the investigation within 30 days after receiving the notice of dispute, unless they consider your dispute "frivolous or irrelevant."
- The CRA may extend investigation for 15 more days if you provide additional information within the first 30-day period.
- In conducting an investigation, the CRA must review and consider all relevant information you submitted.
- Within five days of receiving the dispute, the CRA must notify the company that provided the disputed information (the information provider), and send them any information you submitted to substantiate your claim.
- The CRA will follow up with the information provider after 20 days if the company does not respond and again after 28 days without a response. If the provider does not respond within 30 days, the CRA will remove the information from its database.

Responsibilities of the Information Provider to CRAs

After receiving a dispute from a CRA, the company that provided the information contained in your consumer file (the information provider, for example a bank, insurance company, landlord, etc.) must take the following steps:

- investigate the dispute and review all relevant information provided by the CRA
- report the findings to the CRA
- if the investigation finds that the information is incomplete or inaccurate, the company must provide corrections to all nationwide CRAs that received the information
- complete the investigation before the end of the 30 day period that the CRA has to finish its investigation.

You may take your dispute about information reported to CRAs directly to the information provider. Then it has the same obligation as listed above.

Information providers must inform CRAs they belong, to about your late payments, accounts placed for collection, and voluntary account closings, etc.

Conclusion of the Investigation

No later than five business days after the completion of an investigation, a CRA must send you written notice explaining the results of the investigation and your rights.

If, during the investigation, the CRA finds that a disputed item is inaccurate, incomplete, or cannot be verified, the CRA must delete or modify the item.

If the CRA or information provider will not correct the information you dispute, you are entitled to a reinvestigation. In some cases, a reinvestigation may not resolve your dispute with the CRA. Then, ask the CRA to include in your file and in future reports a short statement (also called "**100-word statement**") that explains your side of the story. Remember that companies are not allowed to add such notations to the database. There is no fee to include your 100-word statement.

At your request, the CRA will provide your statement to anyone who received a copy of the old report in the recent past. There usually is a fee for this service.

If you tell the information provider that you dispute an item, a notice of your dispute must be included anytime the information provider reports the item to a CRA.

In section 10.6, we explain the dispute process with a credit bureau.

Summary: *A consumer reporting agency (CRA) must correct or delete inaccurate or unverifiable information from your consumer file. The CRA is not required to remove accurate data from your file unless it is outdated or cannot be verified.*

9.5. How You Are Scored

Many Consumer Scores

Before a company gives your credit, sells you an insurance policy, or rents you an apartment, it wants to evaluate risk of doing that. It pulls out your record from a CRA that specializes in the given field and looks at your score that the CRA usually computes. Instead of manually evaluating your report, companies can just look at a number: your score. Consumer scores have the purpose of making a decision process easier and more objective.

There are many types of scores. The credit score (FICO, see page 138) tells lenders how likely you are to default on a loan. An insurance score (nScore at Equifax, the Experian/Fair Isaac Insurance Score at Experian, and the Fair Isaac Insurance Risk Score® at TransUnion) indicates to an insurance company how likely you are to cause an accident and file a claim. A rental score (SCOREX at Experian) tells a landlord how responsible of a tenant you are likely to be.

The consumer's score considers both positive and negative information in your consumer report.

By understanding how consumer scores work, you can figure out what lenders, insurers, employers, and landlords are looking for and how you can improve your score to meet their expectations.

How Your Consumer Scores Are Determined

Score numbers are generated by computer programs that apply certain formulas to input data. The formula is usually secret. Some scores are standard, used throughout the industry, while some are custom built for a company's particular needs. Even your FICO score (see page 138) will differ among the credit reporting companies because they all may have slightly different information on you in their databases.

Your consumer scores result from data found in:

- your credit report
- criminal record
- other reports depending on the type of the score (rental, employment, Worker's Compensation, utility, etc.)
- information the businesses (such as banks and leasing companies) already have about you, for example your income, bill-paying history, the number and type of accounts you have, collection actions, outstanding debt
- information you provided on your application.

The final number represents an estimated level of risk as compared to the performance of other consumers in a range of scores. Because your consumer score is based upon real data, it is more reliable than subjective methods of evaluating your information.

> *The formulas that generate consumer scores are complex and kept secret. However, it is known that they look for verification that you're a responsible person.*

Consumer scoring is supposed to treat all applicants consistently and impartially. Additionally, your scores never use certain characteristics – like race, color, sex, familial status, handicap, national origin, or religion – as factors. Therefore, the fact that you are a foreigner has no bearing on your chances for approval.

How Your Score Is Used

Consumer reporting agencies (CRAs) that produce consumer scores don't decide on approving your application. They provide businesses with the consumer report and the score which businesses may consider in their decision. Businesses are free to take any additional information or circumstances under consideration. For example, a bank can approve your loan application despite your mediocre FICO score, if you are a long-term, loyal customer timely paying his obligations at that bank.

Business decisions are based upon how much risk the company is prepared to accept. A minimum score is required for approval of an application. Once you reach that minimum, the price of credit, insurance, or leasing can depend on the quality of your score: the higher the score, the lower the price and the faster your approval. The reason is that businesses need good customers and they try to attract them with competitive prices.

> *It pays to be a responsible person with a solid financial background; you will pay less for credit and insurance, as well as you will find a better job and apartment. Your life in America will be significantly easier.*

How to Improve Your Score and Chances for Approval

While seeking fresh start in life, your priority should be to improve your consumer scores. Consumer scores are generated with a secret formula, so you can't know for sure how they are created. Some scores you cannot even see. However, you can make educated guesses.

Keep your credit score in top shape. Things that improve your credit score are likely the same things that improve your score calculated for insurance, rental, or employment. Paying bills on time, avoiding excessive debts and bankruptcy, in addition to having well-established accounts will keep you looking good.

Consider other factors, besides credit history, might affect your rates, depending on the industry. For example, traffic tickets will not affect your credit score, but may ruin your insurance score.

Make sure that you are scored on good information. In the following chapter you will see how to check various types of reports and how to correct them, if needed. The law allows you free access to information that various consumer reporting agencies keep on you.

Bear in mind that **your scores can be different** depending on where you apply. Since information is taken from a variety of sources and run through different scoring formulas, some businesses may treat you better than others.

Summary: A consumer score is a number that helps lenders, insurers, or landlords to predict how likely you are to be a good customer. The higher the score, the more likely you are to be approved and the lower rates you will pay. There are many consumer scores calculated for various purposes. You have the right to see your score, although for a fee. It pays to improve your consumer scores and keep them high.

10. STRAIGHTEN OUT YOUR CREDIT HISTORY

As we discussed in section 5.6, it is important for people starting a new life in the U.S. to establish a credit history. Even those with an excellent credit rating back home must start from scratch in America, because foreign credit history does not apply in the U.S. Those who already have some American credit record may need to clean it up if they had financial problems before. This chapter explains how to proceed.

10.1. Credit, Credit History, and Credit Score

What Is Credit?

The term credit has two meanings. It can mean money available for you to borrow, or it can describe your financial reputation. Having "good credit" (a good credit report) indicates that you are a reliable person who repaid obligations in the past.

Using credit (loaned money) is commonplace in America. Essentially, you get credit by promising to pay in the future for something you receive now. However, obtaining credit does not necessarily mean indebtedness.

Credit is a convenience, which relieves you from carrying large amounts of cash by allowing you to charge expenses on credit cards. It gives you financial flexibility by letting you handle emergencies and borrow, if necessary. Very few people would be able to buy a house without assuming a mortgage. Furthermore, credit cards are also popular additional proofs of identification required by stores before they accept checks. So even if you are not eager to borrow money, it is important to establish your credit history.

Credit History and Credit Report

Credit history is a record of your current and past debt payments kept by credit bureaus (consumer reporting agencies, see section

10.5). A credit history helps lenders, insurance companies, and landlords to determine whether you are a good potential borrower or customer.

A **credit report** is a statement taken from your credit record created by a credit bureau and updated using information from banks, merchants, and other creditors. (A creditor is a person or company to whom the debtor owes money). Your credit record is a snapshot of your credit history – a sequence of information depicting your financial situation and your ability to handle debt.

You have the right to see your credit report (see section 10.5).

Credit Score

A **credit score** is a number assigned by credit reporting agencies based on information available on your credit report.

The best known credit score is the Fair Isaac or FICO score (see www.myfico.com). FICO scores range between 500 and 990. A rating over 901 is considered "excellent," between 801-900 is "very good," from 701 to 800 is "good," between 701 and 600 is "acceptable," and a score below 600 is "risky."

> *A credit score is a measure of your financial health. Having a good credit score is very important in the United States.*

How the quality of your credit score affects various aspects of your life was explained in section 5.6.

Summary: Establishing credit history is very important in the United States. Your ability to pay bills is measured with a FICO score. The higher your FICO score, the easier it is to obtain credit, rent an apartment, or get a good job.

10.2. Consequences of Unpaid Bills

Some aliens go back to their native countries leaving unpaid bills behind. If they choose to return to the U.S. later, even with a Green Card, they will soon realize that their financial irresponsibility is catching up to them.

What Happens with Unpaid Bills

Example: During Pedro's "extended vacation" in the U.S., he got into an accident and was taken to a hospital with a broken rib. The hospital bill came up to $5,000. Pedro had no health insurance and did not pay the bill, knowing that he would be going back to his country right after he recovered. Three years later, Pedro had received a Green Card and was back in the U.S. trying to restart his life with a clean slate. Now he faces serious problems because of his unpaid debts.

What should Pedro have done to avoid troubles? After he was discharged from the hospital, the hospital kept sending him bills. At that time he could have negotiated a payment plan or a lower cost that he could have afforded. If he had no money, he should have admitted it and worked with the billing department. They could have arranged government insurance (Medicaid) or a charity care program to cover the cost of the treatment.

Consequences of Nonpayment

If you refuse to pay, the hospital hires a collection agency (a company specializing in collecting debts) and eventually will notify a credit bureau about your unpaid bills. The collection agency will press you for payment. Any unpaid debts will ruin your credit history and may cause many problems in the future.

The hospital may take legal action against you. If the due amount is low and you are not able to pay, the hospital may accept the loss. If the amount is high, the hospital will go to court to get a judgment against you. All hospitals will pursue this action because a court judgment is often a condition for receiving government refunds for such financial losses.

Warning: A court judgment stays legally binding for a long period of time – in some states up to 20 years. Most visitors staying temporarily in the U.S. with expired visas do not worry about court judgments, but some of them will eventually become rightful residents or citizens of the U.S. and will have to face the consequences.

If a debtor opens a bank account in the future, the money may be garnished by a court order. If he buys a house, a lien will be imposed that will prevent the sale of the property as long as the debt remains unpaid.

It is very important to pay your debts. The consequences of not doing so can ruin your credit history and even jeopardize your chances for naturalization, as you will not be a person of "good moral character" (see page 24).

Other Debts

Other financial responsibilities sometimes "forgotten" by aliens who temporarily stayed in the U.S., include rents, phone and other utility bills, credit card payments (if a person managed to obtain a credit card), and personal loans.

Your unpaid financial obligations will be reflected in your credit history. The creditor may hire a collection agency (see below) or sue you in court.

Attention: You may be held responsible for another person's debts! This happens when you take out a loan or a credit card with another person, when you co-sign a loan, or make someone an authorized user of your credit card. If that person runs up debt and disappears or refuses to pay for it, the collection agency will be after you.

If You Cannot Afford to Repay Your Debt

Contact your creditors immediately if you're having trouble making ends meet. Don't wait until your accounts have been turned over to a debt collector. Try to work out a modified payment plan that reduces your payments to a manageable amount.

Propose to the creditor that you could pay off the debt in regular, specific payments. Write a letter explaining your current difficult financial situation and propose paying monthly. Make sure that the payments are in an amount you can afford. Include your first payment with that letter. The payments should be in an amount that would pay off the debt in a reasonable amount of time. If the creditor approves the new plan, it is extremely important that you do not miss any payments. If you do, your account goes into default and creditors can demand immediate full payment of the debt plus interest.

Summary: Paying debts on time is important. Being irresponsible reflects poorly on your credit history. If you cannot afford to pay your obligations, ask your family or friends for help. As a last resort, ask the creditor to reschedule your payments.

10.3. How to Deal with Collection Agencies

About Collection Agencies

Definition: A collection agency is a business that pursues payments on debts owed by individuals or businesses. Creditors typically hire a collection agency only after they have made efforts to collect the debt themselves through letters and telephone calls to the person who owes them. Some collection agencies operate as agents and collect debts for a fee or percentage of the due amount. Others purchase debts from a creditor for less than the dollar amount of the debt, but all aggressively try to persuade the debtor to make his payments.

In the U.S., debt collection is heavily regulated by the Fair Debt Collection Practices Act (FDCPA). Under the FDCPA, a collection agency cannot harass, intimidate, threaten, or embarrass you. It cannot threaten violence, criminal prosecution, or use offensive language. You also cannot be called between 9 p.m. and 8 a.m. If you send a written statement requesting a collection agency to stop pursuing you, it cannot continue to call or write to you.

When a Debt Collector Calls

The first time a collection agency contacts you, it must give its name, address, and the name of the original creditor (the business or person whom you owe money). It must tell you the amount of the debt and any fees. You must also be informed of your right to dispute the information.

Within five days after contacting you about paying a debt, the collector must validate the debt, which means that he must send you a written notice that includes:

- the name of the creditor and the amount of debt
- any fees which have been added, such as interest or collection fees
- the statement that the debt will be assumed to be valid unless disputed within 30 days. If disputed, the collector will verify it and send a copy of the verification or of a judgment against the consumer.

During the period when a debt is being verified, the collector may not attempt to obtain payment from you.

How to Stop Debt Collection

You can stop a debt collection agency from contacting you by writing a letter telling them to do so ("cease and desist letter," see the sample below). Send the letter by certified mail with a return receipt requested, and keep a copy for your records. Once the collector receives your letter, he may not contact you again except to notify you that the agency or the creditor intends to take some specific action.

Keep in mind that sending such a letter to a collector does not make the debt disappear. The creditor can still sue you for nonpayment and, with a court judgment (order), he can garnish your wages (take from your paycheck directly) or levy your bank account (seize your account and collect the money from it). Court judgment against you will remain in force for many years and will stay in your credit report for 7 years. It can ruin your reputation and will make building your life in the U.S. even more difficult. For this reason, it is imperative that you pay up or resolve the issue with the creditor.

Sample Letter Stopping Debt Collectors

Collection Agency

Ref: Account #123456

Under provisions of the Fair Debt Collection Practices Act, I request that you cease all communication with me in regard to the debt referenced in your letter of January 5, 20XX (account #123456). I will contact the original creditor to resolve this matter directly, as circumstances warrant.

Please also be advised that I will take the appropriate legal actions should any adverse information be placed against my credit reports.

If you fail to heed this notice, I will file a formal complaint against you with the Federal Trade Commission, the State Attorney General office and the American Collectors Association.

Sincerely,

Your name

Ask for Debt Verification

There are con artists who perpetrate scams on honest people by impersonating debt collectors. There are also collection agencies that violate the law by going after people who have names similar to those of debtors. Others try to force family members, who are not responsible for debts, to pay. For those reasons, do not make any payments until you have verified that the collection agency has basis for collection.

Important: If a debt collector failed to send you a written notice, but keeps demanding payment verbally, ask him to send you validation of the debt. You may use the sample letter shown below. If the debt cannot be verified, the collection agency must cease activity on your account.

If You Do Not Owe the Money

Your outstanding debt can be a result of a mistake. You may have already paid the bill or it is for something you never ordered or never received. The item may have been defective when you received it.

The way to dispute the bill depends on whom you are dealing with. If the agency collects on behalf of the creditor, you should settle the conflict with that creditor. If the collection agency purchased your debt from the creditor, talk directly with the agency. Sometimes lawyers are hired to send you letters, which seem to look more serious, but do not panic.

Here are some of the ways you can present your position:

> **Request for Debt Verification**
>
> Collection Agency,
>
> Ref: Account #123456
>
> I am being contacted by your employee [*name*] trying to collect a debt. Pursuant to the Fair Debt Collection Act, please send me the following:
>
> 1. Proof that I am liable for the original debt and its amount (copy of the original loan agreement or credit card application signed by me).
>
> 2. Proof that your collection company owns the debt or has been assigned the debt (your contract with the original creditor establishing the contract between you).
>
> 3. Payment history: what fees and interest were added to the debt and how the fees were determined (according to Fields v. Wilber Law Firm, Donald L. Wilber and Kenneth Wilber, USCA-02-C-0072, 7th Circuit Court, Sept 2004).
>
> Sincerely,
>
> Your name

- Send a copy of a receipt proving you've already paid the debt, along with a letter of explanation.
- In the event you never owed the debt, explain this in detail. Maybe you were mistaken with someone else, so providing the collector with your detailed personal information may be helpful.
- If you have a defense to their claim, present explanations.

You should dispute the debt within 30 days of receiving the initial notice. During the dispute, the collector may not disclose any information about the debt without also stating that it is being disputed.

If You Owe the Money

If you are responsible for the bill, you may try to negotiate a settlement. Not being able to afford repayment may work to your advantage, because the agency may not attempt to collect further.

Try to bargain for forgiveness of interest, finance charges, and collection charges if you pay in full by a certain date. Try paying in installments, but remember that if you don't send payments on time, the extra charges will not be forgiven.

The collection agency may agree to a settlement because they are in business of collecting debts in a profitable manner, and this is done only if they work quickly and efficiently. They don't make money harassing people or filing lawsuits. If you pay voluntarily, the collection agency gets the money; if you don't, their only option may be to file a lawsuit against you, which is slow and very expensive for them as well as for you.

Where to Learn More

🏛 The Fair Debt Collection Practices Act can be found here: www.ftc.gov/bcp/edu/pubs/consumer/credit/cre27.pdf

🏛 The Federal Trade Commission has useful commentary on the Fair Debt Collection Practices Act at its website: www.ftc.gov/os/statutes/fdcpa/commentary.htm#809

🏛 *Debt Collection Practices: When Hardball Tactics Go Too Far*, a fact sheet from www.PrivacyRights.org.

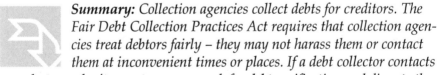

Summary: Collection agencies collect debts for creditors. The Fair Debt Collection Practices Act requires that collection agencies treat debtors fairly – they may not harass them or contact them at inconvenient times or places. If a debt collector contacts you, but you don't owe any money, ask for debt verification and dispute the bill. If the bill is your responsibility, try to negotiate a settlement.

10.4. Financial Obligations of an Immigrant Sponsor

Be aware that sometimes you may be responsible for somebody else's obligations if you choose to become the sponsor of a person immigrating to the U.S.

Affidavit of Support

Before an immigrant can come to the U.S., the government needs to be sure that somebody will be financially responsible for the newcomer. For that purpose, the sponsor – a person who brings the foreigner to the U.S. – has to sign an Affidavit of Support.

Definition: An Affidavit of Support is the document in which a sponsor pledges to financially support the visitor or immigrating relative, so he will not become a public burden. There are two types of affidavits:

- **USCIS Form I-134,** *Affidavit of Support,* is used for temporary visitors (i.e. tourists, students), public interest parolees, and diversity visa immigrants (visa lottery winners). This document is not legally binding on the sponsor.
- **USCIS Form I-864,** *Affidavit of Support Under Section 213A of the Act,* is required in all family visa petitions and some employment visa petitions (when a business owner hires a relative).

After you sign Form I-864, the government (or the sponsored immigrant) can sue you to recover the cost of public benefits paid to the immigrant. The affidavit is binding until the immigrant is credited with at least 40 quarters of work (10 years), obtains citizenship, or leaves the country.

What Is Required of You as a Sponsor

In an Affidavit of Support the sponsor must prove that the immigrant whom he brings to the U.S. will have enough financial backing to live without becoming reliant on U.S. government welfare.

If the sponsored immigrant uses federal means-tested public benefits, the sponsor is responsible for repaying the cost of the benefits. Means-tested benefits are those meant for people with low incomes and sometimes low assets. Federal means-tested public benefits are the following:

- food stamps
- Supplemental Security Income (SSI)
- Medicaid (medical insurance for low-income people, see page 49)
- Temporary Assistance for Needy Families (TANF)
- State Child Health Insurance Program (SCHIP, page 49).

Some Things That a Sponsor Is Not Responsible For

The following types of assistance are not considered means-tested public benefits and do not have to be repaid to the government:

- emergency Medicaid (page 49)
- immunizations and treatment for communicable diseases
- student assistance to attend colleges
- some kinds of foster care or adoption assistance
- job training programs
- Head Start (an education program for small children from low-income families)
- school lunches
- short-term non-cash emergency relief.

The sponsor is not liable for private debts that the immigrant may incur: credit card bills, loans, and unpaid utility bills.

Remember: If a sponsor changes his address, he is required by law to notify the USCIS within 30 days by filing USCIS Form I-865, *Sponsor's Notice of Change of Address* (see section 3.5). Failure of doing so may result in a fine.

Where to Learn More

Read instructions to USCIS Form I-864, *Affidavit of Support Under Section 213A of the Act*; www.uscis.gov/files/form/I-864.pdf (see section 3.7).

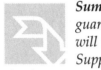

Summary: By signing the I-864, Affidavit of Support, you guarantee the U.S. government that your immigrant relative will not use government help such as welfare, Social Security Supplemental Income (SSI), or food stamps. You are not liable for the immigrant's private debts or unpaid bills.

10.5. Find out what Credit Bureaus Know About You

Credit Bureaus

Definition: Credit bureaus are credit reporting agencies (CRAs) – companies that gather information about credit users and sell it to credit providers such as banks, finance companies, stores, and others. Credit bureaus have records of almost all the people in the United

States who have ever borrowed money, had line of credit, or bought something on credit. It is likely that they know about you too. The three major credit bureaus are:

☎ Experian, P.O. Box 8030, Layton, UT 84041-8030, tel. 1-800-682-7654 or 1-800-392-1122, www.experian.com

☎ Equifax, P. O. Box 740241, Atlanta, GA 30374-0241, tel. 1-800-685-1111, www.equifax.com

☎ Trans-Union, 760 West Sproul Rd., P.O. Box 390, Springfield, PA 19064, tel. 1-800-916-8800, www.transunion.com.

Credit bureaus collect and manage information about people obtained from financial institutions. Each time you buy something on credit, you add overdraft protection to your checking account, take out a loan, or are late with a payment, a credit bureau is informed. Each inquiry about you is also recorded.

How to Get Your Credit Report for Free

Under the Fair Credit Reporting Act, you can request your credit report for free from each of the three major consumer reporting agencies (see section 9.3) in the following ways:

- over the Internet at www.annualcreditreport.com
- by phone calling 1-877-322-8228, a toll-free number where you will reach the Annual Credit Report Service
- by mail; complete the Annual Credit Report Request Form and mail it to: Annual Credit Report Request Service, P.O. Box 105281, Atlanta, GA 30348-5281. The form is at the back of the brochure you will receive by mail or you can download it from www. ftc.gov/credit.

A sample credit report is shown on the following page.

You are allowed to order one free copy of your credit report from each of the nationwide consumer reporting companies every 12 months.

Sample Credit Report

Please address all future
correspondence to the address
shown on the right.

Credit Reporting Office
Business Address
City, State 00000

John Doe
123 Home Address
City, State 00000

Date 03/04/20XX
Social Security Number 123-45-6789
Date of Birth 04/19/57
Spouse Jane

CREDIT HISTORY

Company Name	Account Number	Whose Acct.	Date Opened	Months Re-viewed	Date of Last Activity	High Credit	Terms	Items as of Date Reported			Date Reported
								Balance	Past Due	Status	
Sears	1125151	J	05/01	66	12/08	3500	0	0			02/09
Citibank	2953900 0001004	I	11/01	48	11/07	9388	48M	0			12/08
AMEX	3554112 51511	A	06/97	24	10/09	500		0 Closed Account		O1	12/09
Chase	5422977	I	05/95	48	01/08	5000	340	3000	680	R3	

*Amount in H / C Column is Credit Limit

\>>>Prior Paying History   30 (03)   60 (04)   90+ (01)   08/08 - R2,   02/08 - R3,   10/07 - R4   <<<

\>>>Collection Reported 06/09; Assigned 09/09 TO PRO COLL (800) 555-1234
 Client - ABC Hospital; Amount - $978; Stat Unpaid 06/90; Balance - $978 06/05
 Date of Last Activity 09/09; Individual; Account Number 787652JC

\>>>>>>>>>>>>>>>>>>>> COLLECTION AGENCY TELEPHONE NUMBER (S) <<<<<<<<<<<<<<<<<<<<<<<<<<<<<<<<
PRO COLL (800) 555-1234

*****************************COURTHOUSE RECORDS***
\>>> Lien Filed 03 /92; Fulton Cty; CASE NUMBER - 32114; AMOUNT - $26,667; Class - City/County;
Released 07/03; Verified 09/03

\>>>Bankruptcy Filed 12/09; Northern Dist Ct; Case Number - 673HC12; Liabilities - $15,787; Personal
 Individual; Discharged; Assets $780

\>>>Judgment Filed 12/09; Fulton Cty; Case Number 898872; Defendant - John Doe; Amount - $8,984
 Plaintiff - ABC Real Estate; Satisfied 03/02; Verified 05/03

******************************ADDITIONAL INFORMATION***
Former Address 456 Jupiter Rd, Atlanta, GA 30245

Former Address P.O. Box 2138, Savannah, GA 31406

Last Reported Employment   Engineer, Space Patrol

Checking Account Opened 09/07
Closed 05/09 Reason: Nonsufficient funds
In the amount of $400

*********************COMPANIES THAT REQUESTED YOUR CREDIT HISTORY***************************
03/04/04 EQUIFAX
12/16/03 PRM VISA
06/11/03 NATIONS BANK

02/12/04 MACYS
08/01/03 AM CITIBANK
04/29/03 GE CAPITAL

To get your free report, you need to provide your name, address, Social Security number, and date of birth. If you have moved in the last two years, provide your previous address too. To maintain the security of your file, you may be asked for some information that only you would know such as the amount of your monthly mortgage payment. Each credit bureau may ask you a different security question.

Under federal law, you are entitled to another free report in several situations described in section 9.3. Otherwise, any of the three consumer reporting companies may charge you a fee for another copy of your report issued within a 12-month period.

Summary: Credit bureaus collect information on the borrowing activities of people in the U.S. Once a year you may get a copy of your credit report from each of the three biggest credit bureaus: Experian, Equifax, and TransUnion. You can also obtain a free credit report if you were denied credit, an apartment, or employment due to bad credit history.

10.6. Clean up Your Credit Report

Under the Fair Credit Reporting Act, credit bureaus and information providers are responsible for correcting any inaccurate or incomplete information in your report.

Correct Errors in Your Credit Report

Mistakes do happen. Another person's data can appear on your record, or debts that have already been paid off may show up as delinquent. If you believe that information in your report is incorrect, the Federal Credit Reporting Act (FCRA) allows you to dispute inaccuracies (see section 9.4).

With every copy of your credit report, you get a dispute form, where you should list mistakes found in your report. If you need more space for explanations, write a separate letter. The form and the letter should provide your complete name, address, and telephone number (see the sample on the following page). Enclose a copy of your report with the items in question circled. Clearly identify each item in your report that is inaccurate, state the facts, explain why you dispute the information, and request that the information be deleted or corrected.

Include copies, not the originals, of all documents that support your position.

Send your letter by certified mail with a return receipt requested so you have proof of what the credit bureau received. Keep copies of your dispute letter and enclosures.

Consumer reporting agencies (credit bureaus) must investigate the items in question, usually within 30 days, unless they consider your dispute "frivolous or irrelevant." They also must forward all the relevant data you supplied about the inaccuracy to the organization that provided the information (information provider).

After the information provider (for example, a bank) receives notice of a dispute from the credit bureau, it must check the relevant information and report the results back to the credit bureau. If the information provider finds the disputed information inaccurate, it must notify all three nationwide credit bureaus so they can correct the information in your file.

When the investigation is complete, the consumer reporting company must give you the written results and a free copy of your report if the dispute results in a change (this free report does not count as your annual free report under the FCRA). If an item is changed or deleted, the consumer reporting company cannot put the disputed information back in your file unless the information provider verifies that the information is accurate and complete. The credit bureau also must send you a written notice that includes the name, address, and phone number of the information provider.

Letter Requesting Error Correction

Manager, Credit Bureau
Ref.: Letter of 11/05/20XX

Dear Credit Bureau,

I am writing to inform you that there is an error in my credit report that I received on 12/30/XX. Your report states that I owe $1,500 on a car loan that I took out from ABC Bank two years ago. I repaid that loan in full on 02/03/XX. I have enclosed a copy of a check with my final payment and a copy of the letter I received from my bank on 03/10/20XX acknowledging that I had paid off the loan in full.

I would like you to rectify this error as soon as possible. If you need verification of my payment, please call Ms. Jones at ABC Bank at 1-213-123-3211. Thank you for your cooperation in this matter.

Sincerely,

Your name

At your request, the consumer reporting company must send notices of any correction to everyone who received your report in the past 6 months. A corrected copy of your report can be sent to anyone who received your report during the past two years for employment purposes.

100-Word Statement

If an investigation doesn't resolve your dispute with the consumer reporting company, you can ask that a statement of the dispute be included in your file and in future reports. You can also ask the consumer reporting company to provide your 100-word statement to anyone who received a copy of your report in the recent past. Expect to pay a fee for this service.

For more information see section 13.5.

What You Cannot Do About Accurate Negative Information

Some negative information in your credit report may be accurate. Maybe in the past you left an apartment without paying the last rent. Maybe you owe money to a hospital or overdue taxes to the Internal Revenue Service. If you disregarded any unpaid bills or if you received a default judgment from the IRS or civil court, be aware that this information will show on your credit report and will ruin your credit score.

Some problems may not be of your own doing. If you ever gave your Social Security number away to someone who used it and got into financial troubles under your name, his actions may be now reflected on your credit report. Your credit report would also suffer if you ever co-signed a loan or guaranteed an apartment to another person who failed to pay on time.

Only Time Will Cure Bad Credit

When negative information in your report is accurate, only the passage of time can assure its removal. Most information stays in your file for 7 years, and personal bankruptcy is reported for 10 years. In certain situations, those time limits do not apply. Negative credit history information may be reported indefinitely when you apply for:

- a loan of $150,000 or more

- employment at an annual salary over $75,000
- a life insurance policy with a face value of $150,000 or more.

There is a standard method for calculating the 7-year reporting period. Generally, the period runs from the date when the delinquency occurred, immediately before collection activity starts.

Stay Away from "Credit Doctors"

Don't believe in the assurances of "credit doctors" or "credit clinics," who for high fees say they can clean up your bad credit record. They are a new breed of computerized con artists. At best they would do what you could do for yourself. At worst, they would steal computerized files of someone with good credit and a name similar to yours and seriously commingle the credit data. It is possible that your charges may later appear on that person's credit report or his on yours. Unscrambling such a mess takes a lot of effort and time.

You can remedy credit problems by yourself without paying someone else to do it. Just apply the knowledge you gain by reading this book.

Summary: Contact a credit bureau if you believe there is incorrect information in your report. The credit bureau has the obligation to check the accuracy of the disputed item. You cannot remove truthful negative information from your credit file. It will be removed from your file only after 7 or 10 years. Be wary of con artists who claim they can fix your credit record for you.

10.7. How to Improve Your Credit

Credit impacts your life. Whether you're trying to obtain a credit card from a bank, buy a house, or even get a job, people look at your credit report or score to determine your financial trustworthiness. Improving your credit report (which is reflected in your credit score) makes your life in the U.S. easier.

If you had financial problems before, don't give up. Opening new accounts responsibly and paying them off on time will raise your credit score in the long term and help reestablish your good name.

Factors that Affect Your FICO Score

FICO scores are calculated from a lot of different credit data in your credit report. This data can be grouped into five categories as outlined below. The percentages reflect how important each of the categories is in determining your FICO score.

Your payment history (affects about 35 percent of a FICO score). Late payments, bankruptcies, and other negative items hurt your credit score. The longer your delinquencies, the lower the score.

Amount of debts compared to your credit limit (30 percent of a FICO score). The more you owe compared to your credit limit, the lower your score will be.

Length of your credit history (15 percent) is time since accounts opened and time since account activity. A longer credit history increases your score.

New credit (10 percent). Number of recently opened accounts and recent credit inquiries is taken under consideration, as well as time since account opening.

Types of credit used (10 percent). Number of various types of accounts (credit cards, retail accounts, installment loans, mortgage, consumer finance accounts, etc.) is calculated. One big debt on a credit card is no good, but several various credit accounts with small balances work to your advantage.

Tips on Improving Your Credit Score

Start by **getting a copy of your credit report** from each of the three major credit bureaus to examine your situation. If your credit report contains incorrect information, you have the right to have it removed (see section 10.6).

Pay your bills on time – this is the most important point. Get up to date on delinquent accounts. Even making only the minimum payments for a while will improve your credit because it proves that you are responsible. If you have missed payments, get current and stay current.

Don't take on any more debt you cannot afford to pay off. Shred those tempting offers to open a new credit card or apply for a loan. Only take out a loan you know you can pay off.

Keep balances low on credit cards and other "revolving credit" accounts. The higher amount of your credit limit you use, the riskier customer you are.

Ask the bank to increase your credit limit. The bank may agree to this if you are in good standing and have your card for a year or longer. A smaller ratio of your debt to your credit limit is an advantage.

Keep your old credit accounts. The length of your credit history provides insight on how you manage your credit, so it is a positive factor. However, you can get a high score with a short credit history if the rest of your credit report shows responsible credit management.

Actions that Don't Help Your Score

Closing unused credit cards can in the short run lower your score. The reason is that the ratio of your debts to your available credit will go up. However, getting rid of unnecessary cards is a good thing. Keep the old ones, if possible.

Although the total available credit works to your advantage, **opening many new accounts** just to increase your available credit has the opposite effect. Rate shopping for the best mortgage rate or car loan will not hurt your credit rating. But applying for too many credit cards or opening multiple accounts has a negative impact, because it makes you look desperate for credit.

Paying off a collection account will not remove it from your credit report. It will stay on your report for 7 years. Avoid collection action at all cost; talk to the creditor if you have problems making ends meet.

Note that **closing a delinquent account** doesn't make it go away. A closed account will still show up on your credit report, and may be considered by the score. If you choose to close an account, pay all balances and fees and ask the bank to report that your account was "closed at the customer request."

It is OK to check your own credit report. This won't affect your score, as long as you order your credit report directly from the credit reporting agency or through an organization authorized to provide credit reports to consumers.

Where to Learn More

The following organizations may be helpful:

- National Foundation for Consumer Credit, 1-800-388-2227, www.nfcc.org

- National Association of Consumer Advocates, 1-202-452-1989, www.naca.net

- National Consumer Law Center, 1-917-542-8010, www.consumerlaw.com

- Public Interest Research Group, 1-202-546-9707, www.pirg.com

- Privacy Rights Clearinghouse, www.privacyrights.com; be sure to read *Your Credit Score: How It All Adds Up*, and other brochures.

Summary: *Improving your FICO score can be compared to losing weight: it takes time as well as effort and there is no quick fix. The best advice is to manage credit responsibly over time.*

11. CHECK THE "OTHER" CONSUMER REPORTS

You may be familiar with large consumer reporting agencies (CRAs), such as Equifax, TransUnion, and Experian, but may not be aware that there are other CRAs that have your information, unless you have been denied a particular service.

For example, the Medical Information Bureau collects information on a consumer's individual life, health, disability, and long-term care insurances. ChoicePoint deals with information regarding insurance claims, employment, and tenant history. Many banks and credit institutions rely on reporting agencies, such as ChexSystems, which provide consumers' bank account and check-writing history. Many companies provide pre-employment background checks to employers willing to screen their job candidates. Other CRAs help landlords to obtain information on their potential tenants.

Chances are that information about you is hidden in databases of many specialty CRAs. If this information is negative or erroneous, it may constitute a serious problem.

Information in your specialty report may overlap information in your credit report. It is important to correct inaccuracies no matter where they appear. If someone else has been using your identity (a thief or your fellow immigrants), then order all available reports.

11.1. How Negative Banking History Can Hurt You

Before a bank or a credit union opens an account for you, it will search your prior banking history, probably through a company called ChexSystems. If your name is listed in the ChexSystems database, the bank may turn you down.

Example: Richard's friend came to the U.S. for a year. He had no Social Security number and no proof of address, so he could not open a bank account to keep his money safe. To help him out, Richard opened an account on his name, and added the friend as a co-owner, so he could conduct transactions. Deposited money belonged to the friend, so Richard thought there was no risk for him. It turned out that he was wrong. The friend overdrew the account and bounced checks numerous times. When one year later Richard moved to another town and wanted to open an account for himself in a local bank, he was declined because his friend's financial irresponsibility made him listed in ChexSystems.

About ChexSystems

ChexSystems is a consumer reporting agency (CRA) which collects information that helps banks to identify customers who mishandled their accounts. People who bounce excessive number of checks, who had their accounts closed because of insufficient funds, or who have closed accounts but left an overdrawn balance, are listed in the Chex-Systems' database. Over 80 percent of U.S. banks and credit unions belong to the ChexSystems network. ChexSystems also serves retailers as a check verification agency (see section 11.2).

Member banks contribute information to ChexSystems which is shared among other members. Banks report only negative events such as:

- excessive overdrafting your account while using your ATM, debit card, or automatic debit
- bouncing too many checks resulting in non-sufficient funds
- nonpayment of overdraft fees
- having your account closed "for cause" – due to insufficient funds, unpaid fees, etc.
- fraudulent handling of checking account
- lying on your account application.

☎ Another company which collects negative banking history is Tele Check, www.Telecheck.com; PMB 4513, Houston, TX, 77210-4513; tel. 1-800-366-2425.

As nationwide specialty consumer reporting agencies (CRAs), ChexSystems and TeleCheck are governed by the Fair Credit Reporting Act (FCRA) and other laws (see page 129).

Consequences of Being Blacklisted

When you go to a bank to open an account, the bank service representative will run your name and Social Security number through ChexSystems on his computer to verify the validity of your Social Security number and your good standing. If your name is found, you are in trouble.

Being blacklisted by ChexSystems is not a small matter. You will likely be denied opening a checking, savings, or CD account anywhere in the country, for at least the next five years. You should know that in the U.S. a person without a bank account is treated with suspicion, just like someone without a phone number.

Without banking services, you will be limited to using cash only. Some companies pay salaries only through direct deposit to a bank account. If you manage to get a paycheck, you will have to use check cashing places, which charge notoriously high fees. Without a bank account, you will not be able to keep your money safe. You will have no ATM, debit, or credit card, so you will have to carry lots of cash.

What Is in Your Record

You will not know that you are listed in ChexSystems until you find that you are having trouble opening a bank account. But don't worry – most people don't have a ChexSystems file.

If you handle your bank accounts properly and responsibly, by not overdrawing your accounts, always covering bank fees, and ensuring proper closing of accounts, you will not have a file in ChexSystems.

In case you are blacklisted in ChexSystems, your record contains the following:

- reports of accounts that have been mishandled or with outstanding debts
- inquiries initiated by your action such as applying for a credit card or completing an application at a financial institution
- inquiries not initiated by your action – this means inquiries by current creditors, pre-approval creditors, and potential investors
- retail information about returned checks written on an account and certain collection accounts (see section 11.2)
- history of checks ordered within the past three years

- Social Security number validation which indicates whether the SSN has appropriate format. The name is not matched with the Social Security Administration database
- drivers license validation.

Each report submitted to ChexSystems remains on the files for five years, unless the bank that filed the report requests its removal.

You can see a sample ChexSystems Report at www.consumer-debit.com.

How to See and Correct Your Record

You are allowed to see and correct your ChexSystems report according to the FCRA (see page 129). With your free report you will get information how to dispute its content. Contact ChexSystems:

- online: www.consumerdebit.com
- by phone: 1-800-428-9623
- by mail: 7805 Hudson Road, Suite 100, Woodbury, MN 55125.

Note: Paying back money you owe will not remove your record from the ChexSystems file. However, banks are supposed to report the payment or settlement to ChexSystems.

> **Dispute Letter**
>
> ChexSystems
>
> Ref: Dispute of report
>
> I would like to notify you that the following information in my consumer report is incorrect:
>
> **ABC Bank:** I have never had an account with this institution. Please remove this entry from my record.
>
> **First National Bank:** The non-sufficient funds amount of $100 has been paid in full on 09/17/20XX.
>
> The above errors are in a violation of the FCRA, and therefore need to be investigated. I respectfully request that, within 30 days of the receipt date of this letter, I be provided proof of these alleged items. If this is not provided to me within 30 days I am formally requesting that these item must be removed from my report.
>
> Thank you.
>
> Your name and signature

How to Prevent Problems

To avoid being blacklisted by ChexSystems, keep an eye on your bank accounts to be sure that you always have sufficient funds. Sign up for Internet banking, for easy access to your account, so you could know what's going on with your money. Here are some tips:

- Don't write checks without being sure that there is money in the account to cover them. Be aware that some checks take longer than others to clear. It is also possible that checks are converted into electronic form and clear immediately.
- Make sure you are aware of not just your "total balance" but your "available balance" – the amount that is currently available for withdrawal.
- Close your account properly. Bringing the balance of the account to zero does not mean closing it. Before you close a checking account, make sure all the checks have cleared, fees got paid, and all automatic debits have been stopped.
- Provide a forwarding address to all institutions when you move.
- Obtain written confirmation that an account has been properly closed at your request.
- Don't open several accounts in a short period of time. Having numerous open accounts does not affect you in any way as far as ChexSystems is concerned, only opening many of them within a short period.
- If your checks got stolen or an account was set up fraudulently in your name, notify the bank immediately and put stop payments on missing checks. Cancel your existing account and obtain a new one. See section 13.1 for more information.

> *Even responsible people may be listed in ChexSystems*
> *if they are not careful.*

If you got reported to ChexSystems anyway, don't close any bank accounts, and keep the balances positive. Pay all overdraft fees as soon as you can, make good on the checks. Once you have paid the overdraft fees and you have satisfied everyone who received a bounced check, get a short explanation inserted into your ChexSystems file (see "100-word statement" on page 133).

What to Do if You Were Turned Down by a Bank

If a bank or a credit union refused to open an account for you because of your ChexSystems report, here is what you need to do.

Check your ChexSystems file. At least one report a year is free (see page 130).

Remove any errors from your record (see section 9.4). If the report is correct, do the following.

Pay off what you owe to the bank. If you don't have money, work out a payment plan. Remember, though, that even if you pay, the debt will remain on your report. The bank has no obligation to remove accurate information about account mishandling. However, if a collection amount is reported, the bank is obligated to mark the account as paid.

Apply for an account without overdraft protection. You may be denied an account only because you had indicated on your application that you would like the overdraft protection option (it works as a line of instant credit). When your application includes this request, the bank will verify your credit in addition to verifying your ChexSystems record. If you have both bad credit and a negative ChexSystems record, then the bank is more likely to reject your application. In this case, leave off the overdraft protection request and re-apply.

Go elsewhere. There are financial institutions that are more flexible or that don't subscribe to the ChexSystems services.

- **Try another bank** and ask for savings account first. Some banks don't check with ChexSystems when you are only opening a savings account. Later, as an established customer, you may ask for a checking account and a debit card. Avoid big banks. Smaller, local banks may be willing to open a savings account even if you are in ChexSystems.
- **Look for a non-ChexSystems bank**, but don't get scammed. Make sure that the bank is insured by the Federal Deposit Insurance Corporation (FDIC) and has physical branches. Search the web for "non-ChexSystems bank."
- **Go to a credit union.** They are more understanding, as their goal is to serve the "underserved" – less affluent people, immigrants, or ethnic minorities. To find a credit union near you, go to www. creditunion.coop and click on "Locate a Credit Union."
- **Bank online.** Many online banks will open a checking account for you without verifying your ChexSystems or TeleCheck report. They will allow you deposit your paychecks directly, pay bills online, and add cash in some ATMs.
- **Try non-banks**. There are places you can get a debit card without using a bank such as financial institutions (Western Union, NetS-

pend) and big department stores (such as Wal-Mart). The cards have a Visa or MasterCard logo; you can use them anywhere in the world in places that accept credit cards.

So don't give up!

Where to Learn More

StopChex at www.stopchex.com has sample letters, useful information about fighting ChexSystems, and tips on banks that don't check ChexSystems files.

Summary: You need a bank account to live a normal life in America. You earn the privilege of having a bank account by being financially responsible. If you mishandle your accounts, the bank will report you to ChexSystems and can even close your account. Once that happens, you will have serious problems opening a bank account.

11.2. Check Writing History: Consequences of Bouncing Checks

Let's say you went to a store to buy groceries and you wanted to pay with a check. When you presented your check to a sales clerk, she passed it through a special reader. She told you that your check got rejected because you were in the TeleCheck system. You never heard of TeleCheck, you have never written a fraudulent check. You left the store shocked and embarrassed. What happened?

What Is Check Verification Company?

Merchants (retailers) subscribe to the services of check verification companies (also called check acceptance companies or check services) which protect them from fraudulent or bounced checks. Check verification companies maintain a database of returned checks and instances of fraud.

The three major companies that report on check writing history are SCAN, TeleCheck and ChexSystems.

- **SCAN** (Shared Check Authorization Network): 7805 Hudson Road, Suite 100 Woodbury, MN 55125; tel. 1-800-262-7771; www.consumerdebit.com/consumer-info/us/en/scan/index.htm

- **TeleCheck:** 5251 Westheimer, Houston, TX 77056; tel. 1-800-TELECHECK; tel. 1-800-366-2425; www.telecheck.com
- **ChexSystems,** 7805 Hudson Road, Suite 100, Woodbury, MN 55125; tel. 1-800-428-9623; www.consumerdebit.com.

Before accepting checks, the retailer runs customers' checks through a check reader, which verifies them in seconds. Customers are identified by their checking account number or driver's license. Every bad transaction is added to the database. It is estimated that over 25 million Americans are currently blacklisted by check verification companies all over the country.

If a check bounced after a merchant verified it through a check service company, that company is responsible for the loss. You can be sure that it will start writing to you in attempt to collect the money.

Why Would a Retailer Decline My Check?

Retailers decline to accept checks when the TeleCheck or SCAN marks the customer or his account as risky. This happens when:

- checks were bounced in the past at the account from which your checks are paid
- checks were bounced by a person who identified himself with your identification document, usually a driver's license (this could be you or an identity thief)
- the bank account number has been reported to the database as closed
- there are other reasons not involving the SCAN or TeleCheck database (see below).

The merchant who rejects your check will give you a card with the check verification company contact information and with the "code" or "record number" which identifies the problem. You are supposed to call the company to discuss the declined check and see if you can correct the problem.

In the past, check verification was straightforward and strictly negative. If you wrote a check without sufficient funds, your name would appear in the database, and your checks would be declined in the future. But today also positive information is gathered and decisions may be based on a statistical scoring formula that compares you to other customers. This means that you may be rejected despite the fact that you never bounced a check in your life. The factor raising a red flag could be, for example, a high dollar amount of the check, writing too many checks over certain limits, not having written checks for a long time, or because of other check acceptance policies of the retailer.

> *Approval of a check is not based on the actual amount of money you have in your account or on your credit history, but sometimes depends on company's mysterious risk guidelines.*

Since the formulas used to calculate scores are not public information, SCAN or TeleCheck representatives may not be able to explain exactly why your check was declined. If you did nothing wrong, send in your correct personal information and hope for the better.

How to See what Is in Your File

Check verification agencies are consumer reporting agencies (CRAs) governed by the Fair Credit Reporting Act (FCRA) and other laws (see page 129). You have a right to obtain any reports that these companies compile about you. Contact the check verification company to order a copy of your consumer report. Have your driver's license and a check from your account handy.

How to Remove Negative Information

If your own checks are rejected at stores where you shop, contact the check verification company that the merchant uses.

The majority of returned checks are written by honest people who did not realize they had insufficient funds. Luckily, after covering the check, you have the right to have the negative information removed from the database of the check verification company once the merchant informs the company that the issue is resolved.

How to Correct Inaccurate Information

Check verification companies are obligated by the Fair Credit Reporting Act to help people who believe their file contains inaccurate or incomplete information.

With your report, you will get instructions on how to dispute erroneous information.

Your personal information in the TeleCheck database may not be correct. If, for example, your driver's license number was mistyped by a clerk, your record gets associated with someone else's. Mismatch of data can make your account "negative." Provide TeleCheck with the information listed below, so it can update your file and improve the likelihood your checks will be approved in the future. Send to TeleCheck (or another check verification agency) copies of documents showing:

- rejection code number (record number) provided on a card or printed on your check that got rejected
- your driver's license number and the state where it was issued
- numbers printed along the bottom of your check
- your Social Security number, if you were referred by a financial institution.

Even if you are not listed in the TeleCheck file, sending them copies of your identification information will establish a positive file which will improve your chances for approval in the future.

It is possible you were a victim of fraud. If your checks got forged, counterfeited, lost, or stolen, fax or mail one of these documents below to the forgery department of the check verification company:

- a notarized Affidavit of Forgery (see page 129)
- a notarized Identity Theft Affidavit (page 209)
- a filed police report with the assigned case/incident number (section 12.8).

The document should include all information needed for identifying you as well as checks in question.

More information about dealing with check verification companies can be found at www.consumerdebit.com.

How to Prevent Problems with Checks

Try to limit the use of checks. They are old fashioned and are being replaced with more modern alternatives. In stores, pay with debit or credit cards for your purchases. They are more convenient and provide consumer protection. Also pay your bills through online banking. Almost all banks allow their customers to pay bills electronically.

Utility companies also encourage their customers to pay bills over the Internet or to have them charged automatically to credit cards.

If you prefer or must use checks, follow these tips:

- Always have sufficient funds in your bank account to cover the checks you write or ATM withdrawals you make.
- Establish overdraft protection in your checking account. It is a service that allows a checking account to be linked to another savings account or a line of credit (instant loan) to provide protection against insufficient funds.
- Order checks only from a reputable check printer. Do not order checks from unknown websites.
- Write checks in permanent blue ink that cannot be easily erased.
- When writing the amount of the check, do not leave spaces or gaps that can be used to alter the amount of your check.
- Do not try to cash checks at a store; go to a bank instead. Stores have very strict restrictions for first-time check cashers, even those that have shopped for years and have perfect credit.
- Prevent your checks from showing through envelopes by using security envelopes or folding a piece of paper around the check.
- Reconcile your checking account statement promptly after you receive it. Report any discrepancies to the bank immediately.
- Keep your checks in a safe place at home. Do not carry them with you if not needed.
- Shred bank statements and deposit tickets you want to dispose of.

Summary: Check verification companies collect information about returned checks or fraud. If you paid with a check and your check returned, the merchant will report you to a verification network. When you offer the same checking account to purchase something from another merchant, your check may be rejected. You have the right to see your recorded checking history and to correct it, if necessary.

11.3. Insurance Claims Report: How Insurers Size You Up

You look at your bills and you see that your car insurance premiums are going sky-high, much higher than those of other drivers. Your friend, who is in a situation similar to yours and has the same car, pays much less for the same coverage. Maybe your home insurance suddenly got cancelled, and when you call other insurance companies, you are quoted unaffordable rates or are told they will not cover the property.

If this scenario sounds familiar, then you may have joined millions of Americans who have a negative CLUE report.

About CLUE

CLUE, which stands for Comprehensive Loss Underwriting Exchange, is a database developed by ChoicePoint Asset Company, used by insurance companies to exchange information about customers' claim history and history of homes including claims, injuries, losses, and other pertinent information.

When you apply for home or car insurance, the insurance company looks at your claims information and your insurance score and then decides whether to sell you the policy or not.

Explanation: A claim is your demand for payment made under an insurance contract. If you damage your insured car in an accident, you file a claim so the insurance company pays for losses and repair. You may think you are entitled to receive claim payments, because you pay insurance premiums. However, the higher claims you file, the lower your insurance score becomes. If your insurance score drops, the insurance company may raise your premiums or not renew the policy at all.

Three Types of CLUE Reports

Your CLUE personal property report provides 7 year history of property claims you have filed. You are identified by your name and your Social Security number.

Your CLUE auto report includes a 7 year history of claims made by you (the owner) for this vehicle. It is separate from the claims report for your homeowner's insurance.

Your home's CLUE report includes information about all claims of damage filed for the property itself. This could include claims filed by you and previous owners of the property. The property is identified by its address and other identifiers.

Your CLUE Report

The CLUE report is a loss (claim) history report extracted from the CLUE database. This report shows all claims made by you (by Social Security number), made on a specific vehicle (by Vehicle Identification Number), or made on a specific property (by address).

CLUE report includes policy information such as customer's name, date of birth, and policy number; claim information such as date of loss; type of loss and amounts paid; and a description of the property covered. For homeowner's coverage, the report includes the property address and for auto coverage, it includes specific vehicle information. No other sources of data, credit reports, criminal records, civil lawsuits, or legal judgments are incorporated into CLUE reports.

Another common loss history database used by companies is known as A-Plus and is managed by Insurance Services Office (ISO). You can get your A-PLUS report free by calling the A-PLUS Consumer Report Request Line at 1-800-627-3487.

Information in the CLUE and A-Plus databases is provided by member insurance companies.

What Claims Are Entered into the CLUE Database

Not only all paid claims are recorded in the CLUE database, but also unpaid ones. If you filed an actual claim, but the insurer denied the payment, this information would be recorded by the company and may appear in a CLUE report.

Some companies count a payment due to an accident for which you were not even responsible ("no fault" claim payment) as a loss on your account if it reaches a certain dollar threshold.

Note: You should be aware that contacting your insurance company or an agent to discuss an actual loss might be considered reporting a claim, even if you don't file a claim and the company does not end up making a payment.

Tip: If you are interested in purchasing a home, you may want to get a CLUE report for the physical address because sometimes insurance rates will be high based on the residence's past. Not being an owner yet, you cannot get the report yourself, so ask the owner or the real estate agent to get it for you.

Your Insurance Score

When you fill out a new auto insurance application, the potential insurer queries ChoicePoint (ISO, Equifax, Experian, TransUnion, or another consumer reporting company) for your insurance score. Some big insurers, such as State Farm, use their own scoring system.

Your insurance score is a number derived from your credit history, driver's record (for auto insurance only), your personal claims (CLUE) history, where you live, and other factors according to a certain formula. Based on your score, the insurance company places you in a rate class (for example, preferred, standard, or high-risk) and sets a price for you within that class.

The higher your insurance score, the more reliable you seem to be, and the lower premiums you will pay.

Learning what factors are used in calculating your rates can help you reduce your insurance premiums over time.

ChoicePoint can sell you your Home Insurance Score or your Auto Insurance Score for a moderate fee. You will get your credit report as a bonus.

How to See and Correct Your CLUE Report

If you are shopping for new homeowner's or automobile insurance, order a copy of your CLUE claims report. Also, if you have filed claims on existing policies, check the report to make sure the information is accurate. You can obtain a copy of your CLUE report as directed by the FCRA (see page 130).

- For your CLUE report contact: ChoicePoint Consumer Disclosure, P.O. Box 105108, Atlanta, Georgia 30348-5108; 1-866-312-8076. Online go to www.ChoiceTrust.com.

- For your A-Plus report contact ISO: Consumer Inquiry Center, 545 Washington Boulevard, Jersey City, NJ 07310; 1-800-627-3487; www.iso.com.

With your report, you will get instructions how to correct it, if necessary.

How to Improve Your Score and Lower Your Car Insurance Premiums

The tips below may help you obtain affordable car insurance.

Shop around and get insurance quotes from a variety of sources, as some may treat you better than others. Many companies will give you quotes online. Visit www.esurence.com, www.insure.com and others.

Develop and maintain a good credit history. This factor greatly influences the insurance score. For that, follow tips in section 5.6.

> *If you have good credit, you'll pay less for insurance. Almost all insurers look at your credit report. Studies have shown a direct correlation between your credit score and the likelihood that you will file a claim.*

Don't file claims for small damages, especially if they are smaller then your deductible (the amount paid by you – the policyholder).

Drive safely. Bad driving is costly. Your premiums can increase by as much as 40 percent after your first at-fault accident. Some insurance companies have a "forgive the first accident" policy. The qualifying variables are wide-ranging, so ask your company if it has a forgiveness policy and how to qualify.

Obey traffic rules. Even relatively minor ticket for failure to use seatbelts can have as severe an impact on auto premiums as speeding. Other minor convictions that may disqualify you from getting the lowest car insurance rates are: obstructing traffic, carrying too many passengers, having a broken headlight, etc. Major traffic convictions, on the other hand, can result in the highest insurance rates, even if they did not end up in an accident. Read chapter 14 for more information.

> *Traffic tickets affect car insurance rates for three years. Some auto insurance companies altogether cancel policies for drivers who have a combination of two tickets and one accident.*

Don't lie on your insurance application. Be truthful about your address (which greatly influences the premiums), prior citations, or convictions. If you are caught lying, the insurance company can cancel your policy and refuse paying for accident damages.

Don't lend out your car. If your friend borrows your car and crashes it, you'll have to file a claim with your insurance company. As the result, your rates will probably go up. Tip: If your friend didn't have your permission to take your car, in most cases you won't be held liable for the damage. But if your friend is uninsured and causes damage that exceeds your policy limits, the injured party can come after you for medical and property-damage expenses.

Don't buy fancy vehicles. The car model affects the price of insurance. You will pay more for expensive cars, sport models, or cars popular with thieves.

Be careful while switching carriers. You may think that dropping the old insurer is as simple as stopping payments. Not so. If you don't pay a bill for the next term, your carrier will not only cancel the policy but also may report your nonpayment to the credit bureaus. This could mean you'll pay higher rates or be declined by the new carrier. To avoid the issue, ask your current carrier for a policy cancellation form.

Where to Learn More

- ☙ *CLUE and You: How Insurers Size You Up*, a fact sheet published by Privacy Rights, www.privacyrights.org/fs/fs26-CLUE.htm

- 📖 *A U.S. Driver's License* explains how to fight traffic tickets and keep your driving history clean (see the Appendix on page 262).

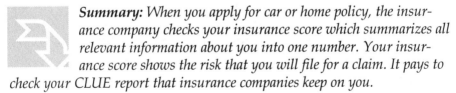 *Summary: When you apply for car or home policy, the insurance company checks your insurance score which summarizes all relevant information about you into one number. Your insurance score shows the risk that you will file for a claim. It pays to check your CLUE report that insurance companies keep on you.*

11.4. Employment Background Check: How Employers Look into Your Past

Employers can request credit, consumer or investigative reports on their employees before hiring or promoting them. If you're not landing jobs despite your good education and experience, you might consider looking at your own report.

What May Be Included in Your Background Check

Pre-employment background checks can be as simple as a verification of your Social Security number or as complex as investigative consumer report (see section 9.2). Most potential employers request standard consumer credit and criminal checks (see 15.1).

Background checks conducted for employment purposes can access a full range of data including the following:

- credit history, bankruptcies (see section 10.1)
- national and state criminal records, DWI, as well as sex offender lists (see section 15.1)
- driving history and violations (see chapter 14)
- financial information: vehicle or boats registered, real estate ownership,
- court records, judgments, tax liens, evictions
- medical records, drug test records, Worker's Compensation claims (see section 11.6)
- identity verification – this check may discover other Social Security numbers used in the past or other names associated with your SSN; address verification, periods of occupancy
- employment history, references, gaps in employment
- "employee misconduct investigation" – if the employer suspects you of violation of laws, regulations, or previous employer's policies
- education verification – school grades, degrees, and any professional qualifications obtained
- professional licenses, credentials, and certifications
- military records.

How Your Rights Are Protected

The Fair Credit Reporting Act (FCRA) provides employees with important protection. For example, the employer must get your permission in writing to obtain your credit or consumer report. Some states, including California, give workers additional rights.

Employer must get your permission before obtaining school, military, and medical records. Schools do not need your consent to release your name, address, dates of attendance, and degrees earned. Only name, rank, salary, duty assignments and status, and awards may be released by military officials, unless you give permission for the release of other information.

No medical records are freely available except for a physical examination that might be required by the employer once a job is offered. An employer may check your medical history only after offering you a job and after obtaining your explicit affirmative consent.

If You Are Rejected Because of Your Background

Under the Fair Credit Reporting Act, you have certain rights in case you get rejected for employment because of the content of your consumer report (read about "adverse action" on page 129). At the workplace, adverse action means eliminating you as a job candidate, firing you, or bypassing you for promotion based on your consumer report.

The employer must keep the information about your consumer report confidential and cannot store it in your personnel file where others might have access to it.

The FCRA Does Not Always Protect You

If the employer suspects you of job-related misconduct or violations of laws, regulations, or employer policies, then he may order a so called "misconduct investigation." He may order this investigation at a specialty credit reporting agency (CRA) and not inform you about it. The reason is that a misconduct investigation is not considered to be a consumer report by the Fair Credit Reporting Act.

What does it mean for you? You would not even know about the investigation because the employer does not have to get your permission. Furthermore, you cannot dispute the findings. If you find yourself in this position, you will probably want to seek the advice of an employment law attorney. You will receive only a summary of the investigation report, but not the more detailed report that may include sources.

Where to Complain if You Are Mistreated

If you experience treatment by an employer that you feel has violated the Fair Credit Reporting Act, you can file a complaint with the Federal Trade Commission online at www.ftc.gov or call 1-877-FTC-

HELP (1-877-382-4357). If you can prove damages caused by an inaccurate consumer report, you might have grounds for a lawsuit against the agency and possibly even the employer who used the report against you. Be sure to check with a lawyer before taking any legal action.

How to Prepare for a Background Check

There are some things you can do to increase your chances for employment and assure a fresh start in life.

- Check all your consumer files: order a free copy of your credit report (section 10.5), criminal report (section 15.2), driver's report at your state DMV (section 14.5), and medical report (section 11.6). Correct mistakes if found.
- Do your own background check through a company that specializes in pre-employment screening. Verify your own information before your employer sees it.
- Request to see a copy of your personnel file from your old or current job. Some state laws allow access to your files, while others don't.
- Ask for your previous background report, if you have been subject to the check covered by the FCRA. State and federal law entitle you to a free copy of your report if any employer requests your permission for a background check. If you do not know the name of the screening company, ask the employer who requested the check.
- When you apply for a job, you may be given notice that a background check will be conducted. At this point ask for the name of the screening company. Then, make your request for a free disclosure to the screening.
- Check information about yourself on the Internet. Search yourself on Google. If you have a private web page or a profile on MySpace or other networking websites, remove inappropriate entries.

How to Check Your Own Background

Consider ordering an employment history report if you've been frequently turned down when applying for jobs.

⚜ The National Association of Professional Background Screeners lists over 300 screening companies online at www.napbs.com.

⚜ ChoicePoint does pre-employment screening. If you know you were the subject of an employment background check conducted by ChoicePoint, you can get your free file disclosure by contacting the company at 1-866-312-8075 or www.choicetrust.com. Click on "Employment History Report."

Where to Learn More

📖 *Employment Background Checks: A Jobseeker's Guide*, Privacy Rights at www.privacyrights.org/fs/fs16-bck.htm

📖 *Your Rights in the Workplace*, by Barbara Kate Repa, Nolo Press, www.Nolo.com, 950 Parker Street, Berkeley, CA 94710-2524, tel. 1-800-728-3555.

📖 More information about job hunting can be found in chapter 6.

Summary: *Employers usually check your consumer record and employment history when considering you for employment or for promotion. Bad credit history or inaccuracy on your job application can ruin your career.*

11.5. Improve Your Tenant History Report to Qualify for a Good Apartment

In the U.S., landlords and management companies screen their potential tenants to find out if they can afford the rent, will pay it regularly, and not cause any disturbances. To evaluate the risk of renting the apartment to a given person, landlords order tenant history report. Whether or not the applicant will get the apartment depends not only on his income, but also on the content of that report.

Why Finding Good Housing Is not Easy for Newcomers

Attention new Americans: Renting a first apartment may not be easy for newcomers, because they have no credit history, no rental history, and probably not much past employment. People with present or past financial problems and victims of identity theft may also face rejection. Even if landlords rent to those higher risk tenants, they will charge higher rent plus a double or triple security deposit. Therefore, it pays to learn how landlords screen potential tenants, what they expect, and how to improve your chances.

Even people with good background and sufficient income can have housing problems if negative information or errors creep into their credit or tenant history.

Consider the following example. John immigrated to the U.S. with his wife. As a newcomer, he couldn't get an apartment, so his brother agreed to co-sign the lease. Due to financial problems, John was late with his rent payments. Delinquencies got reported on John's credit report as well as his brother's. When the brother wanted to buy a house and applied for mortgage, his credit score was too low to qualify.

Ana rented an apartment with her friend and they both signed the lease. Ana moved out 6 months later after her company transferred her to another state. The friend stayed in the apartment, but stopped paying the rent. The landlord started the eviction process naming both Ana and her friend as defendants. Ana's credit and tenant's report is permanently scarred, and she may not even know about the case.

What Landlords Want to Know

Landlords take information about prospective tenants from the rental application and from consumer reporting agencies (CRAs).

Every apartment complex or housing agency has its own set of forms, but the information you fill out on these are mostly the same. It includes personal information, rental history (most landlords will check your previous rental references), employment information and history, financial information (banks where you have accounts, credit cards, major loans, obligations etc.) This lets the landlord gain an overview of your financial situation.

Note: Banks are obligated to secrecy and they would never reveal the balance of your accounts to a landlord or anyone else. Banks may only confirm that a customer is in "good standing." Usually landlords don't call banks for verification.

Small landlords can rent you an apartment without any formalities if they consider you a reliable person. Managers of large apartment buildings, on the other hand, will check your background to make sure that you have adequate income and are likely to pay your rent on time. Public housing agencies are even more demanding; they thoroughly check all kinds of eligibility requirements set up by regulations.

What Landlords Check

A typical tenant report ordered by a landlord from a CRA consists of the following:

- Credit report from one of the major credit bureaus (Experian, Equifax, or TransUnion, see section 10.5). It shows your credit history and judgments for money against you. Landlords want to see credit reports to evaluate your ability and willingness to pay rent.
- Check writing report from ChexSystems or TeleCheck (see section 11.2) which shows how good your checks are.
- Criminal report (see section 15.1) including Sex Offenders List. Landlords don't want tenants with past criminal activity who are likely to threaten the safety of others. Criminal convictions and open cases are shown in the report. Favorable dispositions (dismissed cases or those in which you were found not guilty) should not be taken under consideration.
- Eviction, employment, and residence report from First Advantage or another CRA.
- Reference check. CRAs can contact previous landlords or other parties listed on the rental application on behalf of the landlord.

Whether verifying such references is covered by the Federal Credit Reporting Act (FCRA) or not depends on who does the verification. A reference checked by the landlord personally or by his employee is not covered by the Act; a reference verified by a CRA hired by the landlord is covered.

How to Find out What Is in Your Tenant Report

A number of consumer reporting agencies (CRAs) prepare reports for landlords concerning individuals who have applied to rent housing.

If you want to check your file, you may have trouble, because there are many tenant screening companies and no master list exists. Start with First Advantage or ChoicePoint, because they are the major ones. You may save yourself a lot of time and trouble by simply asking the landlord which screening company he uses.

To obtain a free copy of your consumer report, get a disclosure request form from the CRA, which you may obtain online, by calling, or by writing the reporting agency (see the box on the following page). The rules set up by the FCRA apply (see page 130).

How CRAs Collect Information

Credit, criminal, and check writing reports were discussed in other chapters. Let's talk about evictions.

Landlords do not tell CRAs about evictions. Instead, Experian, Equifax, TransUnion, First Advantage, and others look up cases in courts, place the information into their computer database, and then sell reports to landlords.

First Advantage, the largest screening agency, writes down the names of every defendant in an eviction case after the eviction action was filed, and keeps the names on their records for up to 7 years. First Advantage is not supposed to report eviction cases where the defendant was the prevailing party or where the action was resolved by settlement agreement, but various mistakes may happen.

Major Consumer Reporting Agencies Providing Tenant Reports

ChoicePoint, 1-877-448-5732, 1-800-487-3246, www.choice-trust.com, www.residentdata.com

First Advantage SafeRent, 7300 Westmore Rd, Suite 3, Rockville, MD 20850; 1-800-811-3495; www.fadvsaferent.com

Tenant Net, Inc., P.O. Box 420, 37 Beach Street, Saco, Maine, 04072, 1-800-883-2074 or 1-207-282-2074, www.goodtenants.net

Kroll Factual Data, Residential Qualifier/Tenant Screening, 5200 Hahns Peak Drive, Loveland, CO 80538; 1-800-929-3400, www.krollfactualdata.com/services

MrLandlord.com, Box 64442, Virginia Beach, VA 23467; 1-800-950-2250, 1-757-436-2606, www.mrlandlord.com

Tenant Tracker, P.O. Drawer 1990, McKinney, TX, 75070, 1-800-658-9369, ext. 507, www.tenanttracker.com

TheCreditBureau.com, P.O. Box 4898, Clifton Park, NY 12065, 1-800-374-6055 or 1-800-897-8054, www.thecreditbureau.com (see sample consumer report)

Rent Port, service of TransUnion, 1-888-387-1750, www.rentport.com

RentGrow, Inc., 307 Waverley Oaks Road, Suite 301, Waltham, MA 02452; 1-800-RENT-GROW, 1-888-401-7999, www.rentgrow.com

In contrast, credit bureaus collect money judgments if a ruling was filed against you, but not otherwise.

Your Rental Score

Many landlords rely upon rental scores to estimate the relative financial risk of renting an apartment to you. For example, Equifax has a rental score system called SCOREX.

Your rental score is determined by a certain formula which assigns points to certain factors based on information in your credit report, your application, and previous rental history. Such information includes your bill-paying history, debt load, collection actions, outstanding debt, civil judgments, evictions, household income, rent level, etc. The final number, or rental score, represents an estimated level of risk as compared to other consumers.

Attention new Americans: CRAs never discriminate by using characteristics such as race, color, sex, familial status, handicap, national origin, or religion to affect your rental score. Also, landlords and real estate agencies are not allowed to use those factors in selecting tenants, because that would constitute illegal discrimination.

Factors Affecting Your Score

The following factors could negatively impact your rental score:

- Insufficient income. Most landlords expect total monthly household gross income not lower than three times the monthly rent.
- High debt load. Your personal debts are considered excessive if they exceed your family gross monthly income.
- Credit type, credit history length, credit strength.
- Payment behavior: late payments and not paying down outstanding balances, especially rents or mortgages. Some landlords let you make no more than three late payments or insufficient funds in the past two years.
- Collection accounts: utility, apartment, and other housing related bills that are in collection.
- Landlord/tenant court filings and eviction. They are the most heavily weighted factors within the scoring model.
- Bankruptcies, civil judgments.

Should your application be denied based upon your rental score, you can learn which factors most negatively influenced your score by contacting the CRA which issued the report. Under the FCRA, you can obtain a free copy of your consumer report (see page 130).

Disputing the Errors

Tenant screening services are classified as consumer reporting agencies (CRAs), and as such they must work with you to correct inaccurate information in your report in accordance with the FCRA (see section 9.4). Generally you will be required to fill out a form provided by the CRA and supply them with documentation that refutes the inaccurate information. Go online or call for instructions.

Correcting an Eviction Report

Tenants who don't pay rent on time, cause damage, or who break the terms of the rental agreement, can be evicted. Landlords do not want to rent to people who were evicted before; for that they check eviction report.

Note: Eviction is the court-ordered removal of a tenant from a rental property. The tenant is entitled to a hearing if he believes that the landlord has no right to evict him. Only the court and the sheriff's office may evict a tenant. If a landlord tries to evict you illegally, without court order, you have the right to sue him for damages.

Pay special attention to your eviction report, if you have one, since it may disqualify you from obtaining an apartment. The report may show that there was an eviction case filed against you, but it may not show that the case was dismissed, you won the case, or that the landlord allowed you to stay in your apartment under an agreement.

If your consumer report does not show the complete picture, go to the appropriate courts to get copies of all documents that show a good outcome or inaccuracies. Keep copies for yourself (which you can show to potential landlords) and mail a copy to First Advantage Safe-Rent with a request for correction.

If an eviction case is reported correctly, you have the right to place a statement in your file explaining your side of the case. For example, the eviction was "no-fault," which meant that a landlord evicted a tenant who had done nothing wrong. In addition, if the case is more than 7 years old, it should not be listed at all (see section 9.4).

If the judge ruled for the landlord and had you evicted, get a letter from the landlord proving you have completely paid off all debts and compensated him for any damaged property. Signed documentation from the landlord in question goes a long way and it shows you made it right.

How to Improve Your Chances of Getting Housing

Before you start looking for an apartment, take certain steps to improve your chances.

Obtain a copy of your own consumer report from First Advantage SafeRent to make sure there is no inaccurate or incomplete information.

Establish credit history (see section 5.6). If you have never borrowed money from any institution that reports to credit reporting agencies, you will have no credit history. Landlords may be reluctant to rent to a person who was not trusted before. You would have to convince a landlord that you can afford to pay the rent. However, you should not be denied public or subsidized housing for lack of any credit history.

Improve your credit rating by paying your bills on time, paying down outstanding balances, and not taking on new debt. For more, see section 10.6.

Gather documents showing that the circumstances have changed. If you had troubles in the past that are reflected in your consumer report, show that the hard times are behind you. For example, you could have been sick, or you did not pay the rent because of poor conditions in the apartment.

Always pay your rent on time. Having a poor rental payment history will make it difficult for you to obtain housing in the future. Rent is due on the first of the month and it is late on the second. You can be evicted for failure to pay rent. Not paying your rent on time constitutes a breach of lease. In a tight rental market, an untimely rental payment history can be the basis for not renewing your lease.

When You Apply for Apartment

Provide accurate information on your rental application. If a background check shows that you gave false or incomplete information, a landlord may deny you admission.

Explain damaging information. If your credit record is tarnished, include a letter explaining your negative credit history. Include documentation, if possible. For example, you can show that a period in which you fell behind on bills was due to illness, unemployment, or divorce. This is very helpful if your recent credit history is positive.

Apply for other apartments. Don't get discouraged. Your rental score might mean a denial at one property, while the same score might be approved at another. It all depends upon the risk a landlord is prepared to accept.

Apply to different types of housing programs. Owners of small apartment buildings may be the least demanding, especially if you are recommended by a common friend or another tenant. Larger city landlords are most likely to check your credit report. Public housing authorities conduct the most extensive review of prior housing history and your ability to pay.

Find a lease guarantor (co-signer). If your income or your credit score is too low, a landlord may require a lease co-signer or guarantor. Landlords prefer a family member who lives and owns property in the state and has ample income. The guarantor must have verifiable income as well as an excellent SCOREX score. Extensive financial documentation and cumbersome paperwork may be required.

Summary: Landlords hire specialty consumer reporting agencies (called reference-checking services or screening services) to verify information included on a rental application. An applicant with an unfavorable credit history is likely to be denied an apartment.

11.6. Medical History: What Others Know About Your Health

Consequences of Medical Identity Theft or Mistakes in Your File

About 200,000 cases of medical identity theft happen each year, and newcomers contribute to this number considerably. New arrivals almost never have medical insurance when they come to the U.S., so some of them try to obtain health care by posing as someone else, usually a relative or fellow countryman.

If you ever gave your medical insurance card to someone, you may be surprised by the consequences. That person's chronic illness or condition (AIDS, cancer, or Alzheimer's disease) may appear on your medical record. Because of that

- you may not be hired for a job, since some companies check medical records before hiring
- you may be refused a life or health insurance policy
- you may not get treatment appropriate for your health.

Luckily, there are ways to make sure that this will not happen. First, learn where your medical information is stored and then check whether it is correct.

What Is the Medical Information Bureau?

The Medical Information Bureau (MIB) is a data bank of medical information used by insurance companies. Through the MIB, more than 750 insurance companies, which issue individual life, disability income, health, long-term care or critical illness insurance, obtain information about the applicants.

When an individual applies for health, disability, or life insurance, the insurance company checks his health status to assess the risk involved with issuing the policy. With the medical records of about 15 million people on file, the MIB protects insurance companies from insurance fraud.

The MIB collects information to help its member companies avoid fraud as well as to estimate which customers are likely to live a long and healthy life, thus allowing the company to make profits.

Here how it works. When you apply for an individually underwritten (issued) insurance policy, you are asked a number of questions on the application. If you omit a question or don't provide an accurate answer, the MIB alerts the insurance company. The insurance company compares the information provided by you to what is in your MIB file. The information in your MIB file is used only as an alert, and you should not be refused coverage solely on the basis of the MIB report.

How Information Gets into Your MIB File

The MIB obtains information only from member insurance companies. The MIB does not receive information from doctors, hospitals, or clinics.

When you apply for life or health insurance as an individual, you disclose information about your health on the application. Sometimes you are examined by a doctor or have your blood and urine tested before the policy is issued. Then results may be forwarded to the MIB.

Insurance companies may report information to MIB only with your written consent and only if you have a condition significant to health or longevity. The insurance company must provide you with the MIB Pre-Notice and obtain your signature.

After you get coverage, the insurance company will report to the MIB your medical conditions considered significant, for which you file claims. For example, if you file a claim for an emergency-room visit, chances are your insurance company will send that information to the MIB.

Do You Have an MIB File?

According to the MIB, about one or two in 10 people in the U.S. have a record with MIB. You may have an MIB record if you have ever applied for individual life, health, or disability income insurance in the last 7 years with an insurance company who is a member of MIB, and if you have a condition that is considered significant to your health or longevity.

The easiest way for you to check if the MIB has a file on you and to see whether that file is accurate, is to request a copy of your record.

How to See Your MIB File

The federal laws (Fair Credit Reporting Act and the Fair and Accurate Credit Transactions Act) allow you free access to your MIB records once year and in some circumstances (see page 130). The MIB website at www.mib.com explains how to request your file. To get a copy of your MIB:

- call MIB's toll-free telephone number: 1-866-692-6901
- email your request at infoline@mib.com to request the form or
- send a letter to: MIB, Inc., 50 Braintree Hill Park Suite 400, Braintree, MA 02184-8734.

Only you can request an MIB file on yourself. You will be asked for some personal identifying information so that your record can be located. If a record exists, a copy of it will be mailed to you within 15 days.

Note: Unless otherwise required by law, only member companies have access to information in the MIB database and only when you are applying for individually underwritten insurance. When you get coverage through a group policy (such as at work), your MIB file is not checked.

What Is in Your File?

The MIB collects information about medical conditions, medical tests and results, hazardous jobs and hobbies, as well as motor vehicle reports (poor driving history and accidents). The MIB has no actual "reports" or "medical records" on file, only the coded data provided by the member insurance company which pertains to your health or factors that may affect your health and longevity. Those codes identify:

- medical conditions or medical tests that are reported to the MIB under broad categories
- potentially hazardous sport activities (such as skydiving) or hobbies
- habits that may impact your health (for example smoking, overeating, gambling, drugs)
- results of a motor vehicle report showing a poor driving history.

Information stays in the MIB database for 7 years. Under the Fair Credit Reporting Act, you have a right to see and correct any information about you the MIB has (see section 9.3 and 9.4).

How to Correct Medical Records

Because the Medical Information Bureau maintains data on millions of Americans, mistakes and input errors can and do happen. Errors can occur because of simple coding errors, transcription errors, or even inaccurate diagnosis entered to justify insurance payments. Some unscrupulous managed care companies can assign a fraudulent diagnosis to you that will allow the treatment or the test to be covered (paid) by the insurance company.

You may fix inaccurate information in your MIB record in accordance with the Fair Credit Reporting Act procedures (see section 9.4). With your medical report you will receive information how to proceed. In essence, on a Request for Reinvestigation Form, you should indicate the specific information with which you disagree.

Summary: If you are applying for private health, life, long-term care, or disability insurance, order your MIB report from the Medical Information Bureau. If your MIB report contains erroneous or outdated information, make sure it is corrected before you apply for insurance.

12. FIGHT AND PREVENT IDENTITY THEFT

Undocumented aliens, desperately trying to get work documents, may unknowingly become identity thieves when they borrow Social Security cards from their relatives or friends. Those relatives often become identity theft victims when they are faced with the mess created by multiple users of their Social Security numbers.

Newcomers without papers often become thieves and victims at the same time. Some criminal rings specialize in creating identities for undocumented aliens by stealing information about people, forging documents, and selling them to unsuspecting immigrants. The immigrant uses the false name and SSN to obtain employment, a driver's license, professional licenses, and then to establish credit. He is not aware that the whole time he is impersonating someone else and thus engaging in "total identity steal," which is a criminal activity. He is often caught when the victim discovers his impersonator's employment or credit and contacts the authorities.

Undoubtedly, illegal immigration vastly contributes to the growing problem of identity theft. As you legalized your status, chances are that you may be affected by the consequences of the identity fraud.

12.1. How an Identity Thief Can Harm You

What Identity Theft Is

Definition: Identity theft (fraud) occurs when your name and other personal information is stolen for fraudulent purposes.

Identity fraud occurs not only for illegal immigration, but also for purposes of espionage, evading criminal prosecution, or obtaining medical treatment by people lacking health insurance. Most commonly, identity fraud is done by criminals for their financial gain.

> *In the U.S., identity theft is estimated to cost about $60 billion annually, approximately $6,500 per victim.*

In today's computerized world, a thief does not need to break into your home or steal cash from your pocket. Your personal information is the key to your money. Your Social Security number, place and date of birth, bank account or credit card number, and other identifying data can be used by thieves to take funds out of your bank account or credit card. In the worst cases, thieves take over their victims' identities altogether and run up vast debts or commit crimes in their victims' name.

Real-life example: In a widely publicized case, Michelle Brown, a victim of identity fraud, testified before a U.S. Senate Committee Hearing on Identity Theft. Ms. Brown stated that over a year and a half, one individual impersonated her to procure over $50,000 in goods and services. Not only did the crook damage her credit, but she also engaged in drug trafficking. The crime resulted in Ms. Brown's false arrest record and eventually a prison record when the criminal was booked under her name as an inmate in the Chicago Federal Prison.

In many cases, a victim's damages include not only out-of-pocket financial losses, but substantial additional financial costs associated with trying to restore his reputation in the community and correcting erroneous information for which the criminal is responsible. Cleaning up your consumer report, explained in section 10.6, may take a lot of time and effort.

Identity thieves don't steal only your money; they steal your name and reputation. Cleaning up your credit history and rebuilding that reputation can take a long time.

How Identity Thieves Get Your Personal Information

You may not realize that criminals can easily obtain your personal data without breaking into your home. Techniques for obtaining information include:

- Stealing mail or rummaging through trash, where thieves can find bank and credit card statements, credit card offers, new checks, and tax information.
- Eavesdropping on public transactions to obtain personal data (called shoulder surfing). Thieves may watch you as you punch in your telephone calling card number or credit card number or

they may listen in if you give your credit-card number over the telephone to a hotel or rental car company.

- Stealing personal customer records from companies. This is done by cracking into a company computer system or by bribing employees.
- Impersonating a trusted organization in an electronic communication (phishing) or by phone (pretexting). By claiming that you have a problem with your bank or credit card account, criminals may obtain from you important financial information, which would give them access to your money.
- Electronic spam – unsolicited e-mails that promise some benefit but request identifying data. For example, you may get a message that you won a lottery and you must enter personal information to claim the prize.
- Stealing your wallet or purse.
- Stealing your credit or debit card numbers by capturing the information in a data storage device – a practice known as "skimming." The information can be stolen at the time of purchase, or the skimming device can be attached to an ATM machine, where you enter or swipe your card.
- Unauthorized use of your personal information by your immigrant friends or relatives.

What Thieves Can Do with Your Information

After stealing enough of your information, criminals can pose as you to conduct various illegal transactions.

- Thieves may file applications for loans and credit cards in your name. When they use credit cards and don't pay the bills, the delinquent accounts are reported on your credit report.
- They can make fraudulent withdrawals from your bank accounts by means of electronic transfers, counterfeit checks, as well as credit and debit cards.
- Some crooks may call your credit card issuer, pretend to be you, and ask to change the mailing address. When they run up a bill, you will not realize for a long time that there's a problem, because the bills are sent to a different address.

- They may open a bank account in your name and write bad checks on that account. A bad check is written against a bank account with insufficient funds.
- They may establish phone or wireless service in your name and run up bills.
- They may take out loans in your name (car loans, for example) and make you legally liable for the payments.
- Criminals may even file for bankruptcy under your name to avoid paying debts they've incurred using your information, or to avoid eviction from an apartment they rented impersonating you.
- They may get identification such as a driver's license issued with their picture but with your name.
- They may get a job or file fraudulent tax returns in your name (the most frequent problem in ethnic communities).
- They may give your name to the police or the Immigration Service during an arrest. After they don't show up for their court date, a warrant for arrest is issued with your name. If you are not a U.S. citizen, this can get you deported.

You may not be aware of the activities of identity thieves if bank and credit card statements showing the unauthorized withdrawals are sent to another address. Meanwhile, the criminal is inflicting substantial damage on your assets, credit, and reputation.

 Summary: *Sharing documents and personal information with anyone can lead to identity fraud. This will cause disarray in your tax, Social Security, and credit files as well as will put your money and reputation at stake. Criminals who gain access to your data can purchase goods and obtain loans or money in your name. They will disappear and you will get stuck with a bill.*

12.2. How to Protect Yourself

Guard Your Information

Never give your identification documents to anyone, even your countrymen. Irresponsible people can ruin your reputation and bring havoc in your tax, Social Security, driving and criminal records.

To effectively guard your personal information from thieves, you should understand the reason why someone may ask you for your data. If you call your bank to ask for your account balance, the bank employee has the duty to ask for your mother's maiden name or your birthday so that he can verify your identity. The bank already has this information on file and asks you only for confirmation. A person who calls you and says he's from your bank, however, doesn't need to know your personal information (Social Security number, date of birth, etc.) because the bank already has it. The only purpose of such a call (or e-mail) would be to acquire your sensitive information for that person's personal benefit.

Take the following precautions to guard your information from identity thieves:

- Don't carry unnecessary documents in your wallet. Leave your Social Security card, birth certificate, and unused credit cards in a secure place at home. Carry your cards separately from your wallet, in a zippered pocket or compartment.
- Do not carry checks – they should be left at home. If you must carry a check, don't keep it in your purse or wallet. Losing checks can create serious problems, as explained in section 13.1.
- Do not give out your credit card number, account number, or password to people who contact you, especially if they offer a prize or a business opportunity. Only reveal your number if you call a store or service provider to make a purchase.
- Never disclose your Social Security number by phone. Do not use it as identification number, and don't print it on your checks. Do not carry your Social Security card in your wallet.
- Shred important documents before throwing them out: cancelled checks, credit card or bank statements, and other records that typically bear your name, address, telephone number, etc. Never leave transaction receipts at ATM machines, on counters at financial institutions, or at gasoline pumps. Collecting these types of records make it easier for criminals to take over accounts in your name and assume your identity.

Don't Become a Victim

The practice of getting your personal information under false pretenses is called pretexting. For example, a pretexter may call claiming that he works for a survey firm, and ask you a few questions. Others may call to inform you that you won a prize and some information is needed for your identification and processing of payment. Do not believe them!

Beware of emails that warn you about problems with your bank account and ask you to confirm your account number and password. This is a trap called "phishing." To check such a request, don't click on the link but go to your bank's website directly. Contact customer service to confirm the request.

Be Cautious

Check your financial information frequently. Examine your bank and credit card statements for anything unusual. If you don't get your statements when expected, contact the sender. If you spot any unauthorized charges, contact the card issuer (bank, store, airline, gas station chain, or other company that issued the card) to dispute them. If you do this promptly, you will not be financially responsible (see your rights in section 12.4).

Check your credit report periodically. You may obtain one free credit report from each of the three major credit bureaus annually, which means that you are entitled to three free credit reports per year. Order them every four months and check their accuracy (see section 10.5). Remember that your report may also be free if you were denied credit within the recent past or if you are the victim of a suspected fraud.

Consider using monitoring services at any of the three credit bureaus. This gives you regular access to your credit file for a moderate fee. As a subscriber to a monitoring service, you will receive unlimited copies of your report and immediate notifications when significant changes happen in your credit file at one or all of the credit bureaus. This way you may learn immediately when somebody requested your credit report or when a new credit account has been opened.

Bear in mind that credit monitoring, just like fraud alerts (described in section 12.6), is not a bullet-proof solution. For example, it will not detect when an identity thief has taken a job using your name and Social Security number. In some states, this type of employment fraud constitutes one-third of all identity theft cases, especially in immigrant communities.

If Your Wallet Was Stolen

After your credit cards and important documents got stolen, you can minimize the risk for identity theft by taking the following measures:

- Immediately report lost or stolen credit cards to the banks that issued those cards. You will find the phone number on your monthly statements. The banks will cancel the cards and issue replacements free of charge. If you have cards issued by a department store, airline, gas station chain etc., contact that company. After reporting the incident promptly, you will not be liable for any financial losses (see section 12.4).
- Close your bank account and open a new one, but don't use for password typical identifiers such as your mother's maiden name, your birthday, or four last digits of your Social Security number.
- Set up fraud alert on your credit reports (see page 204). An alert will warn you about someone opening a new credit account in your name.
- Place a security freeze on your credit report (see the section below). This is a stronger measure than fraud alert because it prevents creditors from seeing your credit file.
- File a report about the theft with the police.

Hopefully, these precautions will prevent any further damage.

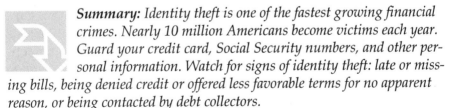

Summary: Identity theft is one of the fastest growing financial crimes. Nearly 10 million Americans become victims each year. Guard your credit card, Social Security numbers, and other personal information. Watch for signs of identity theft: late or missing bills, being denied credit or offered less favorable terms for no apparent reason, or being contacted by debt collectors.

12.3. How a Credit Freeze Protects You

What Is a Credit Freeze?

American consumers who are serious about preventing identity theft can activate a credit security freeze, if their state's law allows it.

Definition: A credit freeze is a "lock" on your credit file. If your file is "frozen," nobody can access it, so no new credit can be issued.

A credit freeze locks your credit file so potential lenders, insurers, landlords and even potential employers cannot see your credit information. When you apply for a credit card, a loan, car lease or cell phone, the company issuing credit can see your credit file only with your permission. This means that a crook who has stolen your personal information cannot apply for credit in your name. The criminal may have all your personal information – Social Security number, date of birth, your mother's maiden name – but still will not gain access to your credit.

When you want to get new credit while you have a credit freeze, you must plan ahead. You will need to contact the credit bureau to request that they temporarily lift your freeze and report your credit file to the credit grantor you identify. You use a predetermined personal identification number (PIN) to unlock access to the credit file.

A credit freeze gives you an extra layer of security. It makes your credit file completely inaccessible, unless you unlock it using a PIN number.

Freezing your credit is a stronger measure than fraud alert (see section 12.6).

How to Freeze Your Credit

More than half of the states have enacted legislation granting consumers the right to prevent identity theft by placing a security freeze on their credit reports. Some of them only provide this option to identity theft victims. For a complete list of states and information on state credit freeze laws search the web for "state security freeze laws" or visit www.consumersunion.org.

To place a credit freeze on your credit file, contact each of the three credit reporting bureaus:

- Equifax, 1-800-685-1111, Equifax Security Freeze, P.O. Box 105788, Atlanta, GA 30348
- Experian, 1-888-397-3742, Experian Security Freeze, P.O. Box 9554, Allen, TX 75013

- TransUnion, 1-800-909-8872, TransUnion Security Freeze, P.O. Box 6790, Fullerton, CA 92834-6790.

In most states, victims of identity theft who have a police report (see section 12.7) can freeze their credit at no cost. Non-victims, who wish to activate the freeze for prevention, usually have to pay a fee. Each bureau has a different procedure for freezing files. However, in each of them you are required to make your request in writing providing your full name, current and past addresses, Social Security number, and birth date. Include any necessary payment. Identity fraud victims must send in a valid copy of a police report, investigative report or complaint filed with a law enforcement agency.

Summary: A security freeze lets you stop thieves from getting credit in your name. It locks, or freezes, access to your credit report and credit score. Without this information, a business will not issue new credit to a thief. When you want to get new credit, you use a PIN to unlock access to the credit file.

12.4. How Laws Protect Your Rights as a Consumer

Lost Credit Cards

Your rights as a credit card user are stated in the Truth in Lending Act, which was established to protect consumers in credit transactions. The statute is contained in Title I of the Consumer Credit Protection Act (15 USC 1601 et seq.). The regulation implementing the statute known as "Regulation Z" is codified at 12 CFR Part 226.

Here are your basic rights:

- If you report the loss before the card is used, you can't be held responsible for any unauthorized charges.
- If a thief uses your card before you report it missing, the most you'll owe for unauthorized charges is $50. The credit card issuer is responsible for the rest.

To minimize your liability, report the loss as soon as possible. Most credit card issuers have 24-hour toll-free telephone numbers to receive emergency information. It's a good idea to follow up with a letter to the issuer. Include your account number, the date you noticed your card was missing, and the date you reported the loss.

🔖 For the full text of the law, go to www.fdic.gov or search the web for "Regulation Z."

Unauthorized Charges

Your rights listed above also pertain to unauthorized charges. If you discovered charges not made by you on your statement, you cannot be liable for more than $50.

It is good to know that major American credit cards (MasterCard, Visa, and Discover) will not hold you responsible for any unauthorized purchases made on a U.S. issued card. This coverage extends to purchases made in a store, over the telephone, or online. For example, "zero liability" is provided by MasterCard under the following conditions:

- your account is in good standing
- you have exercised reasonable care in safeguarding your card
- you have not reported two or more unauthorized events in the past 12 months.

Under a Visa plan, you will not be liable for any charges unless the card issuer determines that the fraud is related to gross negligence on your part, or if the transaction wasn't processed by the Visa network.

If you gave your card to someone who made charges you did not approve of, you demonstrated negligence in safeguarding your card. Your credit card is for your use only.

Unsatisfactory Goods or Services

The Fair Credit Billing Act (FCBA, codified at 15 U.S.C. § 1601 et seq.) is federal legislation requiring credit card issuers to proceed in a certain manner when resolving credit card billing disputes raised by customers.

The Fair Credit Billing Act allows you to dispute charges for unsatisfactory goods or services. To do so, you must first make a "good faith effort" to resolve the dispute with the seller. No special procedures are required. If the matter is not resolved to your satisfaction, you may dispute the charges, providing that:

- you have made the purchase in your home state or within 100 miles of your current billing address

- the charge is more than $50.

Note that the dollar and distance limitations do not apply if the seller is the card issuer or if a special business relationship exists between the seller and the card issuer (for example, the card was issued by a finance company that is a subsidiary of the seller).

Few issuers actually enforce the $50 or 100-mile rule on purchases, but all are allowed to do so. There is a good chance that you'll be able to dispute credit card charges on defective merchandise purchased outside your home state, over the Internet, or by mail or phone order.

When you prove your point, the bank initiates a **chargeback** on your behalf, which means that the credit card transaction is billed back to the merchant. In the end you get your money back.

If you want to learn more, search the web for "The Fair Credit Billing Act."

Billing Errors

Under the Fair Credit Billing Act (15 USC §1666, Correction of Billing Errors), if you find an error on your credit or charge card statement, you may dispute the charge and withhold payment on the challenged amount while the charge is contested. The error might be a charge for the wrong amount, for merchandise you did not accept, or for an item that was not delivered as agreed. Of course, you still must pay any part of the bill that is not in dispute, including finance charges on the undisputed amount.

In order to dispute a charge, do the following.

- Write to the creditor at the address indicated on the monthly statement for billing inquiries. Include your name, address, credit card number, and a description of the billing error.
- Send your letter so that it reaches the creditor within 60 days after the first bill containing the error was mailed to you.

The creditor must acknowledge your complaint in writing within 30 days of receiving it, unless the problem is resolved. The creditor must resolve the dispute within two billing cycles (but not more than 90 days) after receiving the letter.

🕸 For the full text of the Fair Credit Billing Act visit the website of the Federal Trade Commission at www.ftc.gov/os/statutes/fcb/fcb.pdf.

Lost or Stolen ATM or Debit Cards

The Electronic Funds Transfer Act (15 USC §1693, 12 CRF 205), also called Regulation E, covers electronic financial transactions involving ATM, debit cards, or any electronic ways to debit or credit an account. It also limits your liability for unauthorized electronic fund transfers. ("To debit" means to subtract from the balance of an account; "to credit" means to add funds.)

Remember: Debit cards are payment devices, not credit instruments. They allow you to access your funds from your bank account by making a withdrawal at an ATM or by making a payment at a store. Many debit cards bear the Visa or MasterCard logo and are used as easily as credit cards. But debit card purchases have much weaker consumer safeguards than do credit card purchases.

If your credit card is lost or stolen, you can't lose more than $50. However, if you lose your ATM or debit card, you can lose much more. The amount you can be held responsible for depends on how quickly you report the loss.

- If you report the loss or theft of your ATM or debit card to the card issuer before it's used without your permission, you can't be held responsible for any unauthorized withdrawals.
- If you report the loss or theft within two business days of discovery, you won't be responsible for more than $50 for unauthorized use.
- If you report the loss or theft after two business days, but within 60 days after the unauthorized electronic fund transfer appears on your statement, you could lose up to $500 of what the thief withdraws.
- If you wait more than 60 days to report the loss or theft, you could lose all the money that was taken from your account. This may include the balance of your account plus the line of credit established for overdrafts.

> *Once you report the loss or theft of your ATM or debit card, you are not responsible for additional unauthorized transfers occurring after that time.*

Note: VISA and MasterCard have voluntarily agreed to limit consumers' liability for unauthorized use of their debit cards in most instances to $50 per card, no matter how much time has elapsed since the discovery of the loss or theft of the card. However, no debit cards allow chargebacks (see page 197).

🏛 The Cornell University website provides access to all U.S. legal code. The Electronic Funds Transfer Act can be found at www4.law.cornell.edu/uscode/15. Go to Title 15, Chapter 41 and Subchapter VI. Also, the FDIC posts that Act here: www.fdic.gov/regulations/laws/rules/6500-3100.html.

Unauthorized or Erroneous Electronic Transactions

According to the Electronic Funds Transfer Act, you have 60 days from the date your bank account statement is sent to you to report in writing any money withdrawn from your account without your permission. This includes instances when your ATM or debit card is "skimmed."

Skimming is when a thief captures your name, account number, and PIN without stealing your card. Usually the information is collected from the customers' ATM or debit cards using a device called a skimmer. It records the names, account numbers and other identifying information from the magnetic strips to be downloaded onto a personal computer later. That data can then be used to make fake cards.

If you fail to notify the bank (or other financial institution) of the problem within 60 days, you may have little recourse. Under federal law, the bank has no obligation to conduct an investigation if you've missed the 60-day deadline.

Once you've notified the bank about a problem on your statement, it has 10 business days to investigate. The bank must tell you the results of its investigation within three business days after completing the inquiry and must correct any errors within one business day after finding a mistake. In case the bank needs more time, it may take up to 45 days to complete the investigation, but it must return the money in dispute to your account and notify you of the credit. If the investigation finds no error, the bank may take the money back and send you a written explanation.

Stolen Checks

Although no federal law limits your losses if someone uses your checks and forges your signature, you have some protection under state law.

Most states hold the bank responsible for losses from forged checks. However, most states also require the customer to take reasonable care of his or her account. You may be held liable for the forgery if you don't notify the bank in a timely manner that a check was lost or stolen, or if you don't monitor your account statements and promptly report an unauthorized transaction. Pay attention to your accounts. Usually, if you can show that you took reasonable precautions, you will not lose any money.

☀ Contact your state consumer protection office to learn more about your rights. Consumer Action Website will help you locate the office in your state at
www.consumeraction.gov/caw_state_resources.shtml.

Many banks purchase a form of insurance called a "banker's blanket bond" that protects the bank from robbery, burglary, embezzlement and other causes of disappearing funds. The banker's blanket bond would cover the bank and, most likely, ensure that funds taken from your account would be covered.

If your checks got stolen, call the bank to stop their payment. Stopped checks will not clear and therefore the thief will not gain access to your money. However, if you are unaware of theft (which happens when checks are stolen in the mail), but later you discover on your bank statement that forged checks cleared, your bank will handle the matter. Banks are likely to be easier to work with than check verification agencies, and they are prepared to absorb the cost of the forgery. For more information see section 13.1.

Stolen Stored Value Cards

Stored value cards (also called prepaid or cash cards) are a popular payment instrument. These cards are issued by many banks and major stores, have a pre-determined limit of cash stored on them, which is drawn down with every purchase. Some cards are Visa- or Master-Card-branded, allowing them to be used wherever major credit cards are accepted.

If a stored value card is lost or stolen, it's like losing cash, and no federal law protects you. Only stored value cards connected to the bank account are covered by the Regulation E of Electronic Fund Transfer Act, which covers debit cards linked to traditional checking accounts.

Where to Learn More

🏛 Read more in the *Consumer Handbook Credit Protection Laws*, a booklet provided by the Federal Reserve Board, http://federal-reserve.gov/pubs/consumerhdbk/default.htm.

Copies of this handbook and other consumer pamphlets are available upon request from Publications Services, Division of Support Services, Board of Governors of the Federal Reserve System, Washington, D.C. 20551, tel. 1-202-452-3245.

🏛 A full list of publications provided by the Federal Reserve Board is available online at www.federalreserve.gov/publications.htm.

Summary: Many federal regulations protect you in case of credit or debit card loss, stolen checks, unauthorized use of your cards, erroneous transactions, etc. MasterCard and Visa give you total protection. If you monitor your monthly credit card or bank account statements and report incidents promptly, you will not be liable for any financial losses.

12.5. What to Do First if You Are a Victim of Identity Theft

You may become a victim of identity theft and not even know about it until long after the crime has been committed. Be watchful of the following signs: you are suddenly denied credit, your credit card interest is unexpectedly increased, or you started getting phone calls from debt collectors. You may start seeing unauthorized transactions on your credit cards.

If someone else has been using your identity, report this fact to the following institutions immediately:

202 Starting Over in the U.S. After Getting Your Green Card

- financial institutions where you have accounts
- credit bureaus (consumer reporting companies)
- your local police, and
- the Federal Trade Commission.

Contact Your Bank

Contacting the financial institution where you keep your money or have credit is the most important thing to do first.

Checks: If your checks have been stolen, or if you believe they have been used, contact your financial institution (bank, credit union, or breakage house) and stop payment right away. Most states hold the financial institution responsible for losses related to a forged check. However, it is your responsibility to notify the financial institution of the possible forgery in a timely manner.

Next, report theft or fraudulent use of your checks to major check verification companies (also called check service companies, see page 213). These companies will alert the retailers who use their databases to not accept your checks.

You can also find out whether the thief has been passing bad checks in your name by calling Shared Check Authorization Network (SCAN) at 1-800-262-7771.

If you suspect your accounts have been compromised, cancel your checking and savings accounts and obtain new account numbers. Your bank will assist you.

ATM Cards: Report the incident to all institutions with which you hold ATM cards, and close those accounts. If fraudulent withdrawals were made, ask the financial institution to send you a fraud dispute form to complete. When reopening new accounts, be sure to use new PINs to reduce the risk of future identity theft.

Investment accounts: If you suspect that your investment (brokerage) account has been altered without your permission, report the incident to your broker and the Securities and Exchange Commission (SEC). You can file a report using the SEC's online Complaint Center at www.sec.gov/complaint.shtml. Address: SEC Complaint Center, 100 F Street NE, Washington, D.C. 20549-0213. You can also send a fax to 1-202-772-9295.

If your financial institution is not assisting you with the issues related to your identity theft, you may contact the agency with jurisdiction over your financial institution. You can locate the agency at the website of the Federal Financial Institutions Examination Council (FFIEC) www.ffiec.gov/enforcement.htm.

Every institution has its own procedures for handling cases of identity theft, so ask what is expected of you and what you can expect of them. Request instructions by mail, fax, or e-mail.

Contact Your Creditors

Contact the fraud department of each of your creditors: credit cards issuers, banks where you have loans, utilities, telephone, and cable companies. Report your identity theft to each creditor, even if you don't believe that your account at that institution has not been tampered with. Close the accounts that you think have been affected. Write down the names of representatives you spoke with on the phone, as well as day and time of the conversation.

Confirm all conversations in writing. Follow your each phone call with a letter and any necessary documentation to support your claim (for example, a police report). Send your letters by certified mail, return receipt requested, so you can document what the company received and when. Send copies, not originals of your documents. Keep a file of your correspondence and enclosures. You should follow these suggestions in your dealings will all institutions.

The Federal Trade Commission provides an Identity (ID) Theft Affidavit (www.consumer.gov/idtheft/pdf/affidavit.pdf), a standardized form used to report new accounts fraudulently opened in your name (see page 209). Check with the creditor to see if they accept this form. If not, request that they send you their fraud dispute form.

> *Summary: If you notice that an imposter has used your personal information to obtain credit, cancel all accounts and credit cards that got compromised. Send all correspondence by registered mail and keep copies for your records.*

12.6. Report Fraud to Credit Bureaus

Initial Fraud Alert

Place a fraud alert on your credit file by calling the fraud department of any of the three credit bureaus. The numbers are listed in the box on the next page.

Your telephone call will be handled by an automated telephone system. You will not be able to talk to a live person at this point. The system will ask you to enter information needed for your identification: your name, Social Security number, date of birth, etc. The credit bureau will flag your file and will contact the other two bureaus, which will place a fraud alert on their versions of your report. This initial alert remains for 90 days, but may be extended.

The fraud alert tells creditors to contact you before extending any new credit and helps stop a thief from opening new accounts in your name.

Once you place the fraud alert in your file, you're entitled to order free copies of your credit reports from each of the three credit bureau. Each bureau will send you a letter confirming your fraud alert with instructions on how to get a free copy of your credit report. Each report you receive will contain a telephone number that you can call to speak to someone in the credit bureau's fraud department in case you have further questions.

Extended Fraud Alert

Anyone can place the initial fraud alert as a precaution. A victim of identity theft, however, can have an extended alert placed on his credit report. For that, you need to provide the credit bureau with a copy of a police

---

> **Where to Report Fraud**
>
> Call the fraud units of the one of three principal credit reporting companies:
>
> **Equifax:** Consumer Fraud Division, tel. 1-800-525-6285 or write to P.O. Box 740250, Atlanta, GA 30374-0250. To order a copy of your credit report, write to P.O. Box 740241, Atlanta, GA 30374-0241, or call 1-800-685-1111.
>
> **Experian:** Experian's National Consumer Assistance, tel. 1-888-EXPE-RIAN or 1-888-397-3742, fax to 1-800-301-7196, or write to P.O. Box 1017, Allen, TX 75013. To order a copy of your credit report: P.O. Box 2104, Allen TX 75013, or call 1-888-EXPERIAN.
>
> **TransUnion:** Fraud Victim Assistance Department, tel. 1-800-680-7289 or write to P.O. Box 6790, Fullerton, CA 92634. To order a copy of your credit report, write to P.O. Box 390, Springfield, PA 19064 or call 1-800-888-4213.

report (identity theft report, section 12.7). When you place an extended alert on your credit report, you're entitled to two free credit reports within 12 months from each of the three nationwide consumer reporting companies. In addition, the credit bureau will remove your name from marketing lists for pre-screened credit offers for five years unless you request that your name is put back on the list sooner.

How Fraud Alert Works

When a business sees the alert on your credit report, they must contact you before issuing you credit. In your alert, include a cell phone number where you can be reached easily. Remember to keep all contact information up to date.

> *Bear in mind that fraud alerts are sometimes ignored by creditors, but an alert can stop many instant credit applications (approved instantly, usually online, based solely on your credit score).*

A credit fraud alert will only warn you of the fact that someone is applying for credit in your name and will signal creditors to contact you for permission to issue credit in your name. Creditors, however, aren't required to check the alert or abide it. If they see that you have a good credit history, they may issue credit regardless of the alert (after all, they are in the business of lending money). A credit freeze is a stronger measure (see section 12.3).

To remove a fraud alert, you will be required to provide appropriate proof of your identity – your name, Social Security number, address, and other personal information. Unlike a credit freeze, which can be lifted for one creditor, fraud alert only offers a global lift (removing the restriction for all creditors).

Where to Learn More

🏵 Visit www.ftc.gov and read *Identity Crime: When Bad Things Happen to Your Good Name*. This brochure contains sample dispute letters and tips on resolving credit problems.

> *Summary: A credit fraud alert tells creditors to contact you before issuing new credit. Initial fraud alert can be used preventively. To set extended fraud alert, you must be a victim of a crime.*

12.7. Report the Incident to Law Enforcement Agencies

After contacting financial institutions, victims of identity fraud should file a police report.

File a Police Report

Go to your local police precinct to report the identity theft. You might also report the crime to the police department in the area where the crime occurred.

You need to report the crime for two reasons: First, to help police investigate the crime and catch the crooks. Second, you need to obtain a copy of an "identity fraud report." This will help establish that you are a victim of a crime and not a credit abuser. You need to send copies of this report to creditors and the credit bureaus as proof of crime. Also, obtain the police report number, and the name of the investigator.

Since identity theft is not a violent crime like a burglary or assault, some understaffed police agencies may be reluctant to take your report. The following tips may help you get a report if you are having difficulties:

- **Provide as much documentation** as you can to demonstrate the seriousness of your case: copies of your credit report, debt collection letters, your notarized ID Theft Affidavit (more about this on page 209), and other evidence.
- **Be persistent**. Stress the importance of a police report. Explain that many creditors require one to resolve your dispute. Remind the police that credit bureaus will block bad debts and fraudulently open accounts from your credit report, but only if you can give them a copy of the police report.
- If you are told that identity theft is not a crime under your state's laws, **ask to file a "Miscellaneous Incident Report"** instead.

Also, request **information on fraudulent accounts**. When you file your police report of identity theft, the officer may give you forms to use to request account information from credit grantors, utilities, or cell phone service companies. If the police do not have these forms, you can use the form available from the California Office of Privacy

Protection, 1325 J Street, Suite 1650, Sacramento, CA 95814, or call at 1-916-323-7300, www.privacy.ca.gov/cover/identitytheft.htm. The form is called *Identity Theft Victim's Request for Fraudulent Transaction/Account Information*. It can be found in Consumer Information Sheet 3A, *Requesting Information on Fraudulent Accounts*. Download this sheet from www.oispp.ca.gov/consumer_privacy/identitytheft.asp. Residents of all states can use this form for guidance.

When you write to creditors where the thief opened accounts, send copies of those forms, along with copies of the police report. Give the information you receive from creditors to the officer investigating your case.

If the Police Refuse to Accept Your Report of Identity Theft

If the local police station refuses to accept your report, **go elsewhere**. FTC regulations define an "identity theft report" as a "report made to local, state, or federal law-enforcement agencies." Therefore, if your local police department refuses to file a report, try your county police or your state police.

If your case involves fraudulent use of the U.S. mail (the thief sent letters by mail), you may use your identity theft report from the **U.S. Postal Inspector**. Notify the Postal Inspector if you think an identity thief has stolen your mail, used mail to defraud you, sent a forged check through the mail, or filed a change of address request in your name. To find the nearest Postal Inspector, call the U.S. Postal Service at 1-800-275-8777 or visit www.usps.com/ncsc/locators/find-is.html. Obtain a Mail Fraud Report here: www.usps.gov/websites/depart/inspect/ps8165.pdf. Mail the completed report to the address provided on the form.

If your case involves fraudulent use of a driver's license in your name, you may be able to obtain a report from your state **Department of Motor Vehicle**.

You will find your state DMV at www.dmv.org.

Federal Trade Commission

File a complaint with the Federal Trade Commission (FTC):

- online at www.ftc.gov/bcp/edu/microsites/idtheft
- by telephone toll-free at 1-877-ID THEFT (1-877-438-4338)

- by mail to Identity Theft Clearinghouse, FTC, 600 Pennsylvania Avenue, N.W., Washington, DC 20580.

Do not expect any intervention from the FTC in your particular case. The FTC just collects information and maintains a database of identity theft cases that is then used by law-enforcement agencies for investigations. Filing a complaint helps them track down identity thieves across the country and put stop to their illegal activities.

The FTC prepared a form, ID Theft Affidavit, which gives you a single, standard document to report your ID theft to multiple institutions. See page 209.

Where to Learn More

📖 The FTC provides a lot of useful information for identity theft victims. Read *Take Charge: Fighting Back Against Identity Theft*, published by the U.S. Federal Trade Commission. It is a guide that describes what to do to clear your name, and which legal rights protect you. Order the guide by calling 1-877-FTC-HELP (1-877-382-4357) or download it from www.ftc.gov/bcp/edu/pubs/consumer/idtheft/idt04.shtm.

📖 *Organizing Your Identity Theft Case,* a fact sheet by the Identity Theft Resource Center, is available at www.idtheftcenter.org or by calling 1-858-693-7935.

Summary: *You need evidence of your identity theft. Go to the local police precinct to file a police report. Also inform the Federal Trade Commission.*

12.8. Proving That You Have Been Victimized

The police would believe a report of robbery at gunpoint without any evidence. However, when reporting identity theft to your creditors, you will have to prove that you are a victim, not a crook or a deadbeat trying to get out of paying debts. In order to do that, you need the right documents.

Police Report

As explained in the previous section, a police report is an important document for providing proof of the crime. Many creditors want to see a copy before they absolve you of the fraudulent debts. Also, you must send a copy of the police report to each of the three major credit bureaus if you want them to block or remove the disputed information from your credit file.

ID Theft Affidavit

When you report identity theft, creditors may ask you to provide all required information in writing. The Federal Trade Commission, together with banks and consumer advocates, developed a document called the ID Theft Affidavit to make it easier for fraud victims to report information.

The FTC's affidavit is accepted by the credit bureaus and by most major creditors. The form is available on the FTC website at www. ftc.gov/bcp/edu/resources/forms/affidavit.pdf. Fill out this form and send copies to creditors where fraudulent charges were made, to the credit bureaus, and to the police. File a complaint of identity theft with the FTC. See their website at www.consumer.gov/idtheft.

Documentation from Creditors

If you need proof that you did not make certain transactions, you need some documents from the creditor. For example, a copy of the credit application may reveal that the signature is not yours. Federal law (see FCRA § 609(e)), in addition to state laws, gives identity theft victims the right to receive copies of documents related to fraudulent transactions made on accounts opened using victims' personal information. Be sure to ask the company representative where you should mail your request. Companies must provide these records at no charge to you within 30 days of receipt of your request and supporting documents.

Bank Discharge Statement

Most victims can get their accounts closed and debts dismissed by presenting the police report and completing the creditor's fraud paperwork (or the ID Theft Affidavit). Insist on getting a letter from your creditor stating that they have closed the disputed accounts and have discharged the fraudulent debts.

Before the creditor releases a discharge statement or any documentation, the company can ask you for proof of your identity, a police report and a completed affidavit, which may be the ID Theft Affidavit.

Where to Learn More

⊕ The Federal Trade Commission offers many useful brochures in the electronic form on its website at <u>www.ftc.gov/bcp/consumer. shtm</u>.

Summary: In case you become a victim of identity fraud, you need to collect appropriate documents that will be necessary for removing the charges and straightening your records.

13. RECOVER FROM UNAUTHORIZED FINANCIAL TRANSACTIONS

For users of financial services in the U.S., transaction errors, fraud, or identity theft can create serious problems. But generally honest people are protected in the U.S. It pays to know how to avoid troubles and financial losses.

13.1. What to Do About Stolen Checks

What Happens When a Check Is Forged

It may be a surprise to you, but stolen checks can cause even more damage than unauthorized charges on your credit card.

Let's say that your wallet with a checkbook was stolen. Immediately, you stop payment on those checks or close the account altogether. However, this will not stop the thief from using the checks. He does not even have to convincingly forge your signature.

The criminal may use your checks to pay for purchases, at a department store, for example. Before accepting a check, the cashier scans it together with your driver's license (let's assume that the criminal has it). The information is run through the database of a check verification company to which the store subscribes (see page 213). When the verification system indicates that your record is clean, the cashier accepts the check. Later your check bounces, because you stopped the payment, and the retailer reports this fact to a check verification company. The company enters information about you and your bad check into the nationwide database, so other merchants are warned. You will start getting intimidating letters from the check verification company or directly from larger stores which have their own collection programs.

Closing your checking account after you discovered that your checks were stolen is not any better, especially if you have many outstanding checks. When the good and the bad checks get bounced, your account is marked as "bad" by the check service company. People who bounce many checks may find it difficult to open new checking accounts. Therefore, work closely with your bank, so it understands that you are a victim of fraud and not an irresponsible person.

What to Do Immediately After a Check Is Stolen

If a checkbook was stolen from you or lost, do the following.

- Call the bank and ask them to stop the payment on all stolen and misused checks. Ask your bank to notify the check verification service with which it does business.
- Report stolen checks to major check verification companies (see page 213). Follow your phone call or personal conversation with a letter.
- Open a new bank account.
- Close the old account as soon as all outstanding checks clear.
- Prepare an Affidavit of Forgery for every forged check (see below).
- Report the crime to the police and keep the police report, which you will need as proof of the forgery (see section 12.7).

Affidavit of Forgery

Definition: An Affidavit of Forgery is a notarized sworn statement attesting that the signature which appears on the questioned check has been forged and is not authorized by you. You must prepare an Affidavit of Forgery before reporting the crime to the police. This document provides basis for criminal charges against any suspected criminal. You should take the Affidavit of Forgery to your bank (if it is financially responsible for the forged check) or to a check verification company, if the merchant (a store or a service) accepted the bad check and sustained losses. You need one affidavit for each forged check – if you have five forged checks, you must prepare five affidavits.

Some police departments provide blank affidavits. You may also obtain a form from your bank or from a check verification company.

🏛 An organization Bankers on Line provides a sample Affidavit of Forgery at www. bankersonline.com/forms/forgery.html. You can also search the web for "Affidavit of Forgery."

Important: Ask your bank to contact the check service company it uses to report your stolen checks as soon as possible. This way no one will be able to use your checks for payments.

How to Deal with the Bank

If a bank honored a forged check, it will be responsible for the loss and will handle the matter. In such a situation, the bank is relatively easy to work with. If the signature on the check differs from yours, the case is straightforward. Even in the case of skillful forgery, the bank may absorb the full cost.

Most states hold the bank responsible for losses from a forged check. At the same time, however, most states require you to take reasonable care of your account. You may be held responsible for the forgery if you fail to notify the bank in a timely manner that a check was lost or stolen.

Provide your bank with the following documents, so you are not held responsible for the fraud:

- a letter explaining the check forgery; include your personal information, account number and check numbers
- a notarized Affidavit of Forgery (as was explained above)
- a copy of the police report
- a copy of your ID document such as driver's license.

How to Deal with Check Verification Companies

Check verification companies are consumer reporting agencies, and therefore they are regulated by the Fair Credit Reporting Act just like the credit bureaus (see section 9.1). However, some of them may be more difficult to deal with. Each one has its own procedure for resolving problems.

If your identity has been assumed by someone else, you must convince the check verification company that you are a victim of forgery or identity theft, and not a crook. Contact the company to check for requirements and forms the company uses. Most of them have the information posted on the web. To prove your innocence, you will need to send them the same documents as listed above in subsection *How to Deal with the Bank.*

If your checks were lost or stolen, you should inform the bank, and then the bank should alert the check verification company. You may contact the company yourself by sending/faxing an Affidavit of Forgery (see page 212). Your account number will be flagged and nobody will be able to use your checks.

If your check was fraudulently used, you want to clear it from your record. However, the check verification company will not, even upon your request, remove a bad check reported by a merchant. You need to deal directly with the merchant to resolve the issue and then get the action removed. You may not know which merchant accepted your check from a thief. You can find that merchant by the reference number that is printed on the back of your denied check. Contact the check verification company and, by using the reference number, get the name and address of a merchant that submitted the bad check report. After you resolve the issue with the merchant and he reports about it to the check verification company, the record will be removed from the database within a few days.

How to Dispute Inaccurate Information

Each record submitted to a check verification company by a merchant remains in the database until the merchant indicates that the check is paid or otherwise resolved.

When a checking account is reported as closed by a bank, it will remain flagged until the bank notifies the company of a change in the account status. Information reported to check verification companies may remain on their databases for up to 7 years.

Check verification companies are obligated by the Fair Credit Reporting Act to help people who believe their file contains inaccurate or incomplete information. Contact the check verification company to order a copy of your consumer report. You are entitled to one free report annually. Have your driver's license and a check from your account handy. If you have been denied an account at a bank or credit union within the past 60 days, you are also eligible to receive your report for free. With your report, you will get instructions on how to dispute erroneous information. Basically, the procedure is similar to cleaning up your credit report (see section 10.6).

⚜ More information about dealing with check verification companies can be found at www.consumerdebit.com.

Stolen Driver's License

If the crook used your driver's license to cash counterfeit or stolen checks, the check verification company marks this driver's license as "bad" in the nationwide check verification system database. As the result, you will not be able to use your driver's license to cash checks again and you may have problems opening a new bank account. In this situation, you must change your driver's license.

Summary: Crooks may cause more damage by stealing your checks than by using your credit card. When stolen checks bounce, your checking account is marked as "bad" by the check service company. Because of this, stores may not accept your checks in the future, and you may have problems opening a new checking account. You must inform check verification companies of the incident and clear your name.

13.2. Fraudulent Credit Accounts Opened in Your Name

Finding out About Fake Accounts

How would you know that an imposter opened new credit accounts in your name? You can learn about this either from your credit report or from a collection agency.

The company where the fraudulent account was opened will be listed in your credit report. It can be a credit card company, bank, phone or utility company, gas station chain, or department store. You can obtain the phone number from the credit bureau, the toll-free telephone directory (1-800-555-1212), or Yellow Pages on the Internet: www.yellow-pages.com, www.superpages.com, or www.yellow.com.

A phone call or letter from a collection agency is bad news. This means that someone took out a loan or made purchases using your name, did not pay, and creditors are now after you to get their money back. It is very important to resolve the issue.

More about collection agencies can be found in section 10.3.

Contact the Creditor

As described before, contact the fraud department of each creditor first by phone and then in writing. Tell the creditor that you are an identity theft victim and ask not to be held responsible for accounts opened by the thief.

To dispute charges and to obtain fraud documentation, you need to establish your identity and the fact that you are a victim of identity fraud.

Creditors will ask you to fill out the appropriate fraud dispute forms and provide a police report (Identity Theft Report). To save yourself time, ask if the company accepts the FTC affidavit (ID Theft Affidavit, see page 209). If not, ask the representative to send you the company's fraud dispute forms. Find out what other documentation may be needed.

See the sample dispute letter to your creditor on this page about a new fraudulently opened account.

Recent amendments to the Fair Credit Reporting Act (FCRA §623(6) (B)) prevent businesses from reporting fraudulent accounts to the credit bureaus. This means that fraudulent activity will not be shown on your credit report.

Obtain Documentation of Fraud

Creditors' policies on confidentiality may make it difficult to get the paperwork you need. However, if you are an identity fraud victim and you submit your request in writing, the law (FCRA § 609(e)) says that companies must give you a copy of business

---

Dispute Letter to a Creditor

Name of the Creditor
Ref: Acct. # 123456

Dear Sir or Madam:

I am writing to dispute account number 123456 opened fraudulently in my name. I became victim of identity theft and I did not open account number 123 456. Therefore, I am not responsible for any charges made to this account.

Enclosed are copies of [police report, ID Theft Affidavit, Request for Fraudulent Account Information, etc.] supporting my position.

Send me any dispute forms your policies may require. Pursuant to FCRA § 609(e), I am also requesting copies of any documentation such as applications and transaction records showing the transactions on this account.

After you resolve the problem, please issue me a discharge letter, stating the disputed account was established as a result of identity fraud against me and the issue has been closed.

Sincerely,

Your name

transaction records relating to your case.

Ask your creditors in writing to provide you with copies of documents such as the fraudulent application and transaction records (see the sample letter). The creditors must provide copies of these records to you, the fraud victim, within 30 days of your request, at no charge. The law also allows you to authorize a law-enforcement investigator to get access to these records, which can help investigate the crime and prevent repeated violations.

Discharge Letter

Important: After resolving the controversy with the creditor, ask for a letter stating that the company closed the disputed account and discharged the debts. Keep this letter in your files. You may need it if the account reappears on your credit report.

You must also notify the credit bureaus about the fraudulent accounts.

 Summary: If someone opened a credit account in your name, you may learn about it from your credit report or from a collection agency. Contact the creditor immediately and explain that you are a victim of identity fraud. Close the account and dispute all unauthorized charges. Follow with a letter and enclose all necessary documentation.

13.3. Unauthorized Charges on Your Credit Card

When you notice any unauthorized purchases or withdrawals on your monthly credit card statement, notify the bank immediately and close the account. You won't be liable if you report suspicious activity promptly (see section 12.4).

Remember: If you have automatic bill payments set up with that credit card, inform all merchants about the incident, so they stop automatic charges to your card. Once you have a new card, you'll need to reestablish automatic bill payments with your new card at the participating merchants.

How to Dispute the Charges

You should dispute any unauthorized charges. The Fair Credit Billing Act (FCBA) limits your liability to $50. To take advantage of the law's consumer protections, you must do the following.

- Write to the creditor at the address given for "billing inquiries," not the address for sending your payments. Provide an ID Theft Affidavit (page 209) or a dispute form (most creditors have their own). Include your name, address, account number and a description of the problem.
- Send your letter so that it reaches the creditor within 60 days after the first bill showing the problem was mailed to you.

> **Letter Disputing Unauthorized Charges**
>
> Name of the Creditor
> Ref: Acct. # 1234-2345
>
> Dear Sir or Madam:
>
> I am writing to disputed an unauthorized charge in the amount of $1,231 on my MasterCard, account number 1234-2345. I noticed the charge on my April 20XX billing statement and called you immediately on May 10, 20XX. I requested that the card be canceled and a new one be issued to prevent unauthorized charges from reoccurring.
>
> I am not responsible for the charge of $1,231 made on April 14, 20XX, because I have never been in [name of the town] or shopped at [merchant's name]. Please correct the error and do not apply any charges that could be related to the disputed amount. Also, please send me an accurate statement.
>
> Enclosed are copies of [police report, sales slips, payment records] supporting my position. Please investigate this matter and correct the billing error as soon as possible.
>
> Sincerely,
>
> Your name

If the address on your account was changed by an identity thief and you never received the bill, your dispute letter still must reach the creditor within 60 days of when the creditor would have mailed the bill. This is why it is very important to keep track of your billing statements and immediately follow up when your bills don't arrive on time.

You should know that MasterCard and Visa offer zero liability if your card is lost or stolen. You will not be responsible for any unauthorized card transactions. However, you must dispute the charges.

Send a Dispute Letter to Your Creditor

To dispute the charges, send your letter by certified mail and request a return receipt. This will be your proof of the date the creditor received the letter.

Include copies (not originals) of sales slips or other documents that support your position. Keep a copy of your dispute letter.

Many organizations provide sample letters, for example:

* Credit InfoCenter, www.creditinfocenter.com/forms

* Privacy Rights Clearinghouse, www.privacyrights.org/Letters/letters.htm.

Unauthorized charges and other errors tend to be fixed quickly, because card issuers want to maintain your faith in the security of their cards. Many clerical errors are easily handled with a single call to customer service. However, you pay for fraud in your annual fees and finance charges, which are very high for credit cards in comparison to other forms of credit.

Note: Unfamiliar charges may not be fraudulent. Many consumers question their bills because the merchant identifier on the monthly statement shows a merchant's corporate name rather than the store name. Banks clear up to 80 percent of these cases on the first call without a formal dispute being filed.

A Creditor's Obligations

Although most financial institutions will cooperate with you, you should know about their legal obligations specified by the federal Fair Credit Billing Act and Federal Reserve System Regulation Z. These safeguards establish deadlines for investigating, responding to, and resolving complaints about billing errors (which include unauthorized charges).

The creditor must acknowledge your complaint letter in writing within 30 days of receiving it, unless the problem has been resolved. The creditor must resolve the dispute within two billing cycles (but not more than 90 days) after receiving your letter.

You may withhold payment on the disputed amount and related charges during the investigation. You must pay any part of the bill not in question, including finance charges on the undisputed amount.

The creditor may not take any legal or other action to collect the disputed amount and related charges during the investigation. While your account cannot be closed or restricted, the disputed amount may be applied against your credit limit.

The creditor may not threaten your credit rating or report you as delinquent while your bill is in dispute. However, the creditor may report that you are challenging your bill. According to the Equal Credit Opportunity Act, you cannot be denied credit simply because you have disputed a bill.

If a Debt Collector Contacts You

If a thief used your identity to purchase goods or services, you might be contacted by the creditor when the bill isn't paid. Explain that the bill he is trying to collect was not incurred by you. Ask the creditor whether or not you need to complete a particular form. If you do, ask for it to be sent to you.

Using certified mail, send a follow-up letter to the creditor restating the important points of the telephone conversation. Include required forms, copies of a police report, as well as any other documentation showing that you have been a victim of identity theft. Finally, ask the creditor to confirm to you in writing that you are not responsible for the debt and that the account has been closed. For more information see section 10.3.

Where to Learn More

✦ The Federal Trade Commission offers many useful brochures in electronic form on its website: www.ftc.gov/bcp/consumer. shtm.

Summary: Under federal law, if your credit card is used without your authorization, you can be held liable for only a maximum of $50 per card. If you report fraudulent transactions promptly, the credit card issuer will not hold you responsible for any unauthorized charges. MasterCard and Visa offer unlimited protection. It is your duty, however, to contact the creditor and dispute the charges.

13.4. How to Recover Stolen Money from Your Debit Account

Debit card problems can be resolved similarly to how you deal with credit card issues. Remember, however, that different regulations apply.

How the Electronic Fund Transfer Act Protects You

If the theft of your money involved an ATM, debit card, or other electronic means of accessing debit or credit account, you are protected by the Electronic Fund Transfer Act. Your liability in this case depends on how quickly you report unauthorized transactions or the loss of your ATM or debit card (see section 12.4).

If you report an ATM or debit card missing before it is used without your permission, the card issuer cannot hold you responsible for any unauthorized transfers. If you report the loss within two business days, your liability is limited to $50. If you inform the bank after two days but within 60 days, you may be liable for up to $500. After that period of time, you may lose everything the thief withdrew.

In instances of unauthorized electronic transactions, the Electronic Funds Transfer Act gives you 60 days, from the date your bank account statement is sent to you, to report in writing any money withdrawn from your account. If you miss this deadline, you may not be able to recover any of your money.

How to Proceed

To protect yourself, call the financial institution immediately after you discovered suspicious activity, and follow up in writing. It is important to send the letter by certified mail with a return receipt requested in order to have proof of when the bank received your letter. Keep everything for your records. Victims of a crime (those whose wallet or personal information was stolen) should include the police report and the ID Theft Affidavit described on page 209.

Ask credit issuers to close compromised accounts and to report them to credit bureaus as "closed at consumer's request."

The Electronic Fund Transfer Act requires a bank to investigate your problem within 10 business days of receiving your letter, and must report the results within three business days of completing the investigation. The bank must correct an error within one business day after determining that the error has occurred. If the bank needs more time, it may take up to 45 days to complete the investigation, but only if it provisionally returns you the money in dispute and notifies you of the credit. If no error has been found, the institution may take the money back with a written explanation. You may ask for copies of the documents that were used in the investigation.

Summary: *Report the theft of your ATM or debit card or an unauthorized transaction as soon as you discover the problem so you will not be held responsible for losses. Close the account and establish a new one. The bank has the obligation to investigate the matter.*

13.5. How to Correct Fraudulent Information in Your Credit Report

What Is in Your Credit File?

Credit bureaus (also called consumer reporting agencies) compile information about the credit activities of millions of American consumers and sell this information to businesses. If someone stole your personal information and fraudulently assumed credit in your name, information about this action will be reflected in your credit record. It is up to you to remove fraudulent charges from your credit file.

The Fair Credit Reporting Act (FCRA) makes both the credit bureau and the company that provided the information to the bureau (such as a bank or credit card company) responsible for correcting inaccurate or incomplete information in your report (see section 9.4).

Contact the Credit Bureau

Get a copy of your credit report (see section 10.5). If you believe that some information is inaccurate, contact both the credit bureau and the information provider. Send them a dispute letter, a police report, and full documentation of your case (see section 12.5).

It is possible that some fraudulently opened accounts will not be listed in your credit file, because not all creditors supply information to credit bureaus. Some travel, entertainment, and gasoline card companies, local retailers, as well as small credit unions are among the creditors who don't.

There are two ways to correct fraudulent information.

- You may complete and return the dispute form that is part of each credit bureau report. Attach a copy of any documentation you have pertaining to the disputed account.
- You may file the dispute electronically. Go to the website of the credit bureau for instructions on filing an online dispute (Equifax: www.equifax.com, Experian: www.experian.com, TransUnion: www.transunion.com). You will still have to send supporting documents by mail.

Write a Dispute Letter

Whether you attempt to correct false information in your credit file by mail or electronically, you will need to write a letter explaining what information you think is inaccurate. You can use the sample dispute letter shown below.

Include documents that support your position. Never send originals because they may get lost. Clearly identify each item you dispute in your report. Explain why you dispute the information and request that it be removed or corrected. Enclose a copy of your report with the items in question circled. Send your letter by certified mail and request return receipt so you can document what and when you sent. Keep copies of your dispute letter and enclosures. If you filed the dis-

---

Dispute Letter to a Creditor

Complaint Department
Name of Credit Bureau

Ref: [Reference number, file or report number, your full name and address]

Dear Sir or Madam:

As per our conversation on [date], I am a victim of identity fraud and I am writing to you to dispute the following information in my file.

Item #1. I have never opened a credit card account number 12345678 at XYZ Bank. The MasterCard at that bank was obtained fraudulently by an imposter and I am not responsible for the outstanding balance of $ _____.

Item #2. I did not sign up for a cellular phone service at AT&T, therefore I am not responsible for the account number 987654 and the outstanding balance of $ _____.

I have marked the fraudulent accounts on the attached copy of my credit report. I am requesting that the items be corrected.

Please investigate these matters and block the disputed items as soon as possible. Enclosed are copies of [list enclosed documentation] supporting my position.

Sincerely,

Your name

pute electronically, keep printouts showing the date.

Important: If you are a victim of identity fraud and provide a copy of your police report confirming the crime, the credit bureaus will automatically block the inaccurate information from appearing on your credit reports sent to companies that request your report. The investigation may take up to 30 or 45 days. The credit bureaus have the right to remove the block if they believe it was wrongly placed; however, information blocking is not required by the FCRA. Except for a few states which have made it a law, blocking the inaccurate information based on a police report is a voluntary initiative by the credit bureaus.

Investigation by Credit Bureaus

Credit bureaus must investigate the items in question unless they consider your dispute frivolous. Once you have notified the credit bureau of any mistakes in your report, the bureau will have 45 days to investigate the disputed items if you obtained a free annual copy of your report from www.annualcreditreport.com. It will have 30 days to investigate in all other cases, but may extend this time period to 45 days if it later receives additional information from you that is relevant to the investigation.

They also must forward all the relevant data you supplied to the information provider (the bank or credit card company). After the information provider receives notice of a dispute from the credit bureau, it must investigate, review the relevant information, and report the results back to the credit bureau.

- If the information provider finds the disputed **information inaccurate**, it must notify all three nationwide credit bureaus so they can correct the information in your file.
- Disputed **information that cannot be verified** must be deleted from your file.
- Information that does not belong to you must be deleted from your file.
- If an item is **incomplete**, the credit bureau must complete it. For example, if your file shows that you have been late making payments, but it fails to show that you are no longer delinquent, the credit bureau must show that your loan payments are current.

When the investigation is complete, the credit bureau must give you the results in writing and provide you with a free copy of your updated report. If an item is changed or deleted, the credit bureau cannot put the disputed information back in your file unless the information provider verifies that it is accurate and complete. The credit bureau must also send you a written notice that includes the name, address, and phone number of the information provider.

At your request, the credit bureau must send **notices of correction** to anyone who received your report in the past 6 months. You can have a corrected copy of your report sent to anyone who received a copy during the past two years for employment purposes.

Statement of Dispute

In case an investigation doesn't resolve your dispute with the credit bureau or your financial problems were caused by certain mitigating factors, you can ask that a statement of the dispute (up to 100 words) be included in your file and in future reports. In that statement you have the right to explain your side of the story.

The credit bureau must provide your statement to anyone who received a copy of your report in the recent past. You can expect to pay a fee for this service.

Accurate Negative Information

> ### Letter Requesting the Addition of 100-Word Statement
>
> Name of Credit Bureau,
> Ref: Acct. # 123456
>
> To Whom It May Concern
>
> I am writing to request that this short statement be added as part of my credit file in accordance with the Fair Credit Reporting Act (FCRA). As your reinvestigation failed to resolve my problem to my satisfaction, I wish to include the following information as "Section 611b Statement of Dispute" so that any credit inquiries will include this statement automatically.
>
> "As a result of [illness, death in the family, layoff, divorce, extended military service], I was unable to pay my debts in a timely fashion during the period [state the dates]. Since that time, I have [returned to work, improved my financial situation, gotten another job] and brought the payments up to date. Before that difficult period of my life I had an impeccable credit history and I still intend to pay my obligations on time."
>
> Please send me a copy of my updated credit report with my Section 611b Statement as soon as possible. Thank you for your prompt attention to this matter.
>
> Sincerely,
>
> Your name

When negative information in your report is accurate, only the passage of time can ensure its removal. Accurate negative information can generally stay on your report for 7 years. There are certain exceptions:

- bankruptcy information may be reported for 10 years
- credit information reported in response to an application for a job with a salary of more than $75,000 has no time limit
- credit information reported because of an application for more than $150,000 worth of credit or life insurance has no time limit
- information about a lawsuit or an unpaid judgment against you can be reported for 7 years or until the statute of limitations runs out, whichever is longer.

 Summary: *In order to correct an error on your credit report, contact the credit bureau immediately. Write a letter and include all supporting documents. The company is then responsible for researching and changing or removing incorrect data. This process may take as long as 45 days. At your request, a corrected report will be sent to the parties that you specify, who have received your report within the past 6 months, or employers who have received it within the last two years.*

13.6. When Someone Uses Your Social Security Number

Can You Get a New Social Security Number?

Under certain circumstances, the Social Security Administration may issue a new Social Security number for a victim of identity fraud. As explained in section 8.7, the SSA rarely replaces an SSN. However, since November 4, 1998, the SSA has made it easier to assign new Social Security numbers to victims of identity fraud (reason called "SSN misuse and disadvantage") as well as to victims of domestic abuse ("harassment, abuse, or life endangerment").

The SSA may consider changing your SSN at your request only if you prove that you tried to resolve problems brought about by identity theft, but your SSN is still being misused by the thief. For example, you get arrested each time you are stopped for a traffic violation (because there is a warrant on your name) or new accounts are still being opened using your name and Social Security number. The SSA may facilitate the change of the SSN to some domestic violence victims or people under witness protection program, whose prospective testimony puts them in immediate danger.

You cannot get a new Social Security number if:

- you have filed for bankruptcy
- you intend to avoid the law or your legal responsibility (for example, to change your identity or avoid paying child support), or
- your Social Security card is lost or stolen, but there is no evidence that someone is using your number.

Warning: People or companies offering to get you a Social Security number for a fee are usually swindlers. If they supply you with a fraudulent number, using it is a crime.

Disadvantages of a New SSN

It is natural that as a victim of identity theft, you would try to distance yourself from the thief and quickly close compromised accounts. However, changing your Social Security number (SSN) may do more harm than good.

Your original Social Security number will not be voided or canceled when the new one is assigned. It will be retained by the Social Security Administration (SSA). The original SSN will be cross-referenced to the new one to make sure that you get credit for your earnings and to ensure the integrity of the SSA's data.

Although the SSA may issue a new SSN for you, it does not have the authority to control its use by other institutions. The Internal Revenue Service, banks, schools, the military, credit bureaus, departments of motor vehicles, insurance companies, Medicare, Medicaid, etc., use your SSN as an identifier. They will be using your original SSN until you notify them of your new number, and it may take a long time for them to enter the change into their system.

By changing your Social Security number, you are not guaranteed a fresh start, because a new number does not ensure a new credit record.

Credit bureaus use more pieces of information than only your SSN for creating database identifiers such as your name, birth date, address, mother's maiden name, and spouse's name. If these identifiers remain the same, a credit bureau may combine your credit records, so the old bad credit moves to the new number.

If your old credit does not get associated with the new SSN, you will become totally creditless, which can cause even more trouble. You will not be able to obtain new credit, rent an apartment, get utilities (for example, cell phone service), or even get a job (because you have no employment history in your credit file).

Should You Get a New SSN or Not?

Generally, obtaining a new SSN is not advisable. Only the following situations may justify this decision:

- you are a newcomer to the U.S. or a young person who has not yet established a credit history
- your problems are so extreme that a competent attorney advises you to change your SSN
- you are a victim of serious domestic abuse, or you are under a witness protection plan. In this case, the Social Security Administration must ensure additional safeguards on your Social Security records to protect your safety.

How to Change Your SSN

To change your Social Security number, you must apply in person at a Social Security Administration office. Make an appointment at a local office by calling the SSA at 1-800-772-1213.

Prepare evidence documenting your identity theft such as a police report and the ID Theft Affidavit (see page 209). When going to the SSA office, bring evidence of your identity, age, and U.S. immigration status, using documents such as a birth certificate, driver's license, or passport. Have the originals with you, as photocopies are not acceptable.

Some SSA representatives may not be familiar with the policy for assigning new SSNs for victims of identity fraud, because SSNs are rarely changed. You can inform them that your situation is called "SSN misuse and disadvantage," and the appropriate policies can be found in Program Operations Manual System (POMS), chapter RM 00205.054.

If you are a victim of "harassment, abuse, or life endangerment," refer the SSA representative to Program Operations Manual System (POMS) chapter RM 00205.058. If there are problems, ask to speak with a supervisor or the field office manager.

Help available: The National Coalition Against Domestic Violence (www.ncadv.org), a nonprofit organization working since 1978, suggests that if, after going through all of these steps, you are still experiencing difficulty with your local SSA office, you should contact NCADV's Public Policy Office at 1-202-745-1211.

To get a new Social Security number, you will fill out a Form SS-5, *Application for a Social Security Card*. Be prepared to complete a statement explaining the need for a new number. You may download this form from the Internet (www.ssa.gov/online/ss-5.html) and fill it out ahead of time at home.

After a new SSN is assigned to you, request a letter from the Social Security Administration indicating that your number was changed due to fraud. Such letter, showing your old and new number, will be very useful to explain the change of the SSN to an employer and other institutions.

After Getting a New SSN

A new Social Security number is only the beginning of restoring your credit. Now you must ensure that all credit reporting is done under your new number.

Make a list of all the financial institutions listed on your credit report. Write a letter (see the sample below) to each of them stating that you have changed your SSN and they should update the number in their files. With your letter, enclose a copy of your police report and either the letter from the Social Security Administration granting your new number or copies of both your old and new Social Security cards.

Send similar letters and attachments to all other institutions that have your data: your employer, the college you graduated from, your insurance company, and all banks, even if you have no credit there.

Send a similar package to all three credit bureaus. Demand that they remove all credit entries containing your old Social Security number. For a while, credit bureaus will post the entries reported to them under the old number, but once all creditors report under your new number and references to the old numbers are erased from you credit file, your old number becomes "credit-less." Therefore, any request for credit made by the thief under the old number will be rejected.

Finally, change your driver's license (see page 247) and monitor your credit report frequently in all three credit bureaus to keep it clean.

Remember that once you receive a new SSN, you must not use the old one under any circumstances. Be advised that restoring your good credit may take a lot of work and years of time.

A sample letter at the right could be used to inform your bank, employer, or credit bureaus about the SSN change. Remember to provide your full name, address, and account number when writing to a financial institution.

Letter About the SSN Change

Name of the Bank
Ref: Acct. #123456

Dear Bank XYZ,

The Social Administration changed my Social Security number from _____ to _____ because I have become a victim of identity theft. Please change my Social Security number in your records. Make sure that all future tax and credit reporting be done under that new number.

Enclosed you will find a copy of my new Social Security card, the letter from the SSA, as well as my identity theft documentation.

Sincerely,

Your name

If Someone Uses Your Number for Work

Sometimes an identity thief will use someone else's Social Security number for work. Most often these are illegal immigrants who use other person's SSN to be eligible for employment.

If you suspect that someone else is using your number for work, you should report it to Social Security. As we explained in chapter 8.2, you can check your earnings record by calling 1-800-772-1213 and asking for your *Personal Earnings and Benefit Estimate Statement*. You may also download the application form from www.ssa.gov. Your statement will show the earnings reported to your Social Security number each year since 1951. If you find that too much or too little is reported for your number, notify the Social Security Administration. The agency will help you make corrections.

If your Social Security number has been used to run up bills or obtain credit, Social Security cannot straighten out your credit record. You must contact each creditor or credit agency yourself. If your employer made incorrect reports to state unemployment or welfare offices, the SSA cannot help you either. You need to contact the state or local agency to correct your record. If you suspect that someone else has claimed unemployment benefits using your Social Security number, call your state unemployment office.

Summary: *Generally, a new Social Security number will not solve your problems related to identity theft. In most cases, changing your SSN is not recommended. The SSA will issue a new number only if you can prove that someone has stolen your number and is using it illegally. If your card has been lost or your number has fallen into the wrong hands, that's not enough. The Social Security Administration will not give you a new SSN to aid in avoiding legal responsibility, or in hiding bad credit or a criminal record. To get a new SSN, you must visit a local Social Security office. There is no fee.*

13.7. When Someone Obtains Phone Service in Your Name

It may happen that a thief established telephone or cable service in your name, is using your calling card, or is making unauthorized calls that seem to come from your cellular phone. In this case, contact your telephone company immediately and cancel the account or calling card. Open a new account and choose a new Personal Identification Number (PIN). If you are being billed for calls you did not make, request that the charges be removed from your account.

If you are having trouble getting fraudulent phone charges removed from your telephone account or getting an unauthorized account closed, you will need to take further action.

For local service contact the Public Utility Commission in your state. If a service provider in another state is billing you for local service your imposter received, contact the Public Utility Commission in that state. To find your state Public Utility Commission, refer to your local telephone directory or visit the website of the National Association of Regulatory Utility Commissioners at www.naruc.org. Click on "State Commissions."

For long distance and cell phone billing disputes, file a complaint with the Federal Communications Commission (FCC). The FCC regulates interstate and international communications by radio, television, wire, satellite, and cable. The FCC complaint form (FCC Form 475) can be found at http://esupport.fcc.gov/complaints.htm. Completed forms can be submitted to the FCC by:

- sending to Federal Communications Commission, Consumer and Governmental Affairs Bureau, Consumer Complaints, 445 12th Street, SW, Washington, D.C. 20554
- faxing your complaint to 1-866-418-0232
- emailing your complaint to fccinfo@fcc.gov.

For questions or assistance in filing a complaint, call 1-888-225-5322 (1-888-CALL-FCC) or visit the FCC website at www.fcc.gov/cgb/complaints.html.

Summary: Identity thieves frequently establish phone or other utility services in their victims' names. If this happens to you, contact the utility or phone company. Explain that you are a victim of identity theft and that the bill they are trying to collect was not incurred by you. Send them a letter with all supporting documents. If your cell phone was stolen, report the theft to your cell phone service provider.

14. Fix Your Driving Record

Although in most of the country a driver's license is a necessity for daily life, immigrants cannot obtain one without legal status. For this reason, many newcomers try to get around the fact they are not legally allowed to drive. In the process, they may get in trouble.

Traffic violations can result in you losing your driver's license. Every year, thousands of motorists throughout the country are stopped for routine traffic violations, and many are surprised to find out that they had unknowingly been driving on a suspended license. License suspension can happen for a variety of reasons, including unpaid traffic citations, lost parking tickets, and offenses committed by identity thieves. Getting back a license is not an easy task. Fines, surcharges, and other costs may run into hundreds of dollars.

To avoid surprises and higher insurance rates, learn your obligations as a driver.

14.1. Types of Traffic Violations

Definition: Traffic violations are any acts that breach state or municipal traffic laws. As traffic laws vary by state and city, motorists are faced with dozens of regulations depending on where they are driving.

What happens after an infraction is committed depends on the type of violation. Managing the consequences is especially important for noncitizens for whom an encounter with the police may have serious immigration implications.

Types of Traffic Offenses

Traffic offenses basically fall into two categories: moving violations (that arise from the operation of a motor vehicle) and non-moving violations (parking, equipment, and regulatory violations).

Non-moving violations are small civil infractions, which are not counted against a driving record (section 14.4). However, a person can be arrested for unpaid violations. Here are examples of non-moving violations:

- parking violations such as double parking, blocking a driveway, parking in a no-parking zone, etc.
- equipment violations: broken lights, a cracked windshield, missing side or rear-view mirror, not wearing seat belts, faulty exhaust, and many others
- miscellaneous (or regulatory) violations: obtaining a driver's license through deception, lack of insurance.

Traffic offenses are either civil infractions or crimes. In most states there are three levels of criminal traffic offenses: petty or summary offenses, misdemeanors, and felonies (the most serious crimes).

Civil or Criminal Violations

Moving violations can be civil or criminal in nature.

Most traffic violations (parking and petty offenses) are **civil infractions**. Civil traffic infractions are not punishable by imprisonment. Examples include driving without a seat belt, speeding, running a stop sign, having an expired safety check sticker, and parking where prohibited. Penalties for civil infractions include fines, community service, and mandatory attendance at a driving school. Most civil traffic infractions are handled outside of court, by a branch of the DMV.

A **traffic crime** is a violation of law relating to traffic movement and control, for which you can be sentenced to a possible prison term. Examples include operating a vehicle without a license, drunk driving, and reckless driving.

The distinction between civil and criminal violations is very important, because criminal judgments are reported on your criminal record and may have immigration consequences. Repeat drunk-driving offenses and hit-and-run accidents causing injury or death are treated as felonies. If you are charged with a felony, get an attorney's help fast, especially if you are a noncitizen. A felony conviction can get you deported or make you inadmissible (ineligible for a Green Card, a temporary visa or for crossing the border into the United States).

Civil cases are handled by the town administration (Department of Motor Vehicles), while criminal cases by courts.

Summary: *Various traffic violations have different consequences. The majority of traffic infractions are civil in nature, punishable by fines. The most serious traffic violations, categorized as crimes, are punishable by prison. A conviction of a crime can make a noncitizen deportable.*

14.2. Traffic Tickets

Motorists stopped for a moving violation receive traffic tickets. A traffic ticket is a citation commonly issued by police officers to motorists who fail to obey traffic laws. A citation is a direction to appear in court to answer the charges.

Parking tickets, on the other hand, are given to car owners who commit parking violations, and direct them to pay a fine.

The owner of a car gets a parking ticket (even if someone else parked his car improperly), while a driver gets a traffic ticket, regardless of whose vehicle he drove.

Your rights to fight a ticket and procedures involved depend on local regulations and the category of the offense.

Infraction Traffic Tickets

For driving too fast, running a red light, or driving without proof of insurance, the police can charge you with an infraction and give you a "Notice to Appear" ticket. The police officer will ask you to sign the ticket. Signing doesn't mean you are guilty, it just means that you acknowledge the receipt. For getting a photo of running a red light or crossing railroad tracks when you were not supposed to, you'll get a ticket in the mail. Those tickets are handled by the Department of Motor Vehicles, not by courts.

Traffic tickets issued for infractions usually state the offense and the amount of the fine. You have a choice about how to respond.

- You can plead **guilty** by checking the "guilty" box on the ticket, pay the fine by mail or by the Internet and have it over with.

However, you will get points on your driving record and your insurance rates may go up.

- You can plead **not guilty** by checking the "not guilty" box and challenge the ticket. Do this either by going to traffic court (usually civil court or a unit of the DMV) or through trial by mail (also called a "trial by written declaration").

Read the instructions on the ticket and on your state DMV's website. Call the DMV if you have further questions.

Failure to go to court or pay the fine will cause suspension of your license. The court can charge you with a misdemeanor and issue a warrant for your arrest.

Misdemeanor Traffic Tickets

The police can give you a ticket for a more serious crime such as drunk driving, driving without a license, or driving with a suspended license. If the charges don't involve alcohol or drugs, the police officer can ask you to sign the ticket (called a "Notice to Appear") and will let you go. By signing the ticket you don't admit guilt; you only promise to come to court.

If the police officer thinks that you are driving under the influence of alcohol and/or drugs, you'll be taken into custody.

The main difference between infraction tickets and misdemeanor tickets is that misdemeanor tickets don't list the amount of the fine, so you cannot easily close the case by paying them. They only summon you to criminal court. If you are ticketed while traveling in a state far away from home, this may pose a problem. You will have to return to the local court in the place where you got the ticket to answer criminal charges. If you are found guilty, you will have to pay steep fines, and the sentence may go on your criminal record. Depending on the offense, you could also go to a city or county jail for up to one year. As a noncitizen, this is something you want to avoid at all cost.

If you fail to appear in court as ordered, the judge will suspend your license, charge you with another misdemeanor, and issue a warrant for your arrest.

Consequences of Traffic Violations

The effect of a traffic violation depends on the nature of the offense and on your driving record. The possible consequences include fines and/or jail, driving school, higher insurance premiums, and the suspension of driving privileges. A traffic violation is noted on your driving record, and it may appear on your criminal record as well, if it rises to the level of criminal offense.

Attention immigrants: As was already explained, criminal record may have immigration consequences for noncitizens, as the U.S. Citizenship and Immigration Service (USCIS) checks the criminal record of each applicant before granting him a Green Card, citizenship, or other benefits. Also, candidates for naturalization are expected to show "good moral character" – a standard of behavior expected by the Immigration Service (see page 24).

📖 More about the impact of criminal convictions on your eligibility for naturalization can be found in *Citizenship: Overcoming Obstacles to Naturalization* (see the Appendix on page 262).

📖 *A U.S. Driver's License* explains how to fight traffic tickets in administrative and criminal courts (see the Appendix on page 262).

> **Summary:** *You can pay some tickets by mail, while others may be addressed only in court. You may plead guilty or attempt to contest the ticket. Consequences of irresponsible driving can be severe.*

14.3. How You Can Lose Your License and How to Prevent It

You may lose your driver's license if the court or the DMV determines that you pose a threat to public safety or that you operate a motor vehicle improperly. License suspension also serves as a leverage to motivate individuals to obey the law.

Too Many Penalty Points

The most common way to lose a driver's license is by accumulating traffic tickets for moving violations. The effect of this accumulation can result in a license suspension of 30, 60, or 90 days. Any additional moving violations may result in a suspension of the privilege to drive for one year.

New York: If your driving record accumulates 11 or more penalty points within 18 months, your license will be suspended or revoked. You will be given the option of attending a hearing before an Administrative Law Judge (ALJ) or accepting a period of suspension, usually 31 days long.

Solution: Go to the hearing and ask for permission to attend driving school.

Drunk Driving

When you are stopped by police for drunk driving (with 0.08 blood alcohol content or more) or you refuse to submit to alcohol testing, your license gets automatically suspended by the DMV, regardless of the criminal procedure in court. All states impose mandatory license revocation for convicted drunk drivers. In many states, under the Zero Tolerance Law, drivers under 21 years of age may lose their license if they consumed any alcohol.

If you are caught drunk driving, your license may be taken away or punched (perforated) in some states. You will be able to drive for a period of only 10-14 days using a ticket issued to you at the time of your apprehension.

Solution: Apply for a formal hearing at the DMV (administrative suspension hearing) in a timely manner, or you will not be able to drive again. You will also face a criminal hearing in court. Noncitizens should hire an attorney to minimize the impact of a criminal case on their Green Card or naturalization.

Motorists also may lose their license for illegal purchase of alcoholic beverages using their state driver's license or even a non-driver ID as a proof of age. Their license or their privilege for applying for a license gets suspended.

Failure to Pay Parking Tickets

In some states (New Jersey, among others), a driver's license may be suspended by the municipal court or the DMV for failure to pay a parking ticket or appear at parking offense-related hearing. Low income divers receiving public assistance must be permitted to pay by installment, but they can still have their licenses suspended if they fail to make an installment payment. In most states, drivers with unpaid parking tickets cannot renew vehicle registration.

Some states will indefinitely suspend the driver's license of a person who paid for DMV services with a bad check.

Solution: Challenge the ticket or pay what you owe.

Failure to Pay a Traffic Ticket

Traffic tickets must be paid in traffic court of the county in which the citation was issued. Some traffic courts allow payment online via credit card. Check the traffic court website to determine how you can pay yours. Failure to pay will result in suspension.

Solution: Pay the ticket in the county court which issued it (listed on the ticket), and make sure the court clerk forwards the record of payment to the DMV. If your license is already suspended for nonpayment, get proof of payment from the court and bring it to your state DMV office. Call ahead or check the website to find out how to proceed.

Failure to Appear

When you get a ticket that says "Notice to Appear" and provides you with no option of paying a fine, you must come to the traffic court in the county where a traffic ticket was issued. If you don't, your license will be suspended indefinitely until you show up at court. Additionally, you may be punished by a fine or even jail if you knowingly fail to appear in court when required.

The court also may issue a warrant for the arrest of any person who fails to appear, as well as for those who failed to pay traffic tickets or court fines. If that happens to you, contact the court clerk in the county where your citation was issued and ask for instructions.

Out-of-state motorists must undergo the same procedure as locals. They must appear in court even if they live in another time zone; otherwise their home state will suspend their driver's license.

Solution: Contact the traffic court in the county where the traffic ticket was issued. Pay the fine and present proof of payment plus a reinstatement fee in a DMV office. Some traffic courts allow payments on-line via credit card. Check the traffic court website.

Driving Without Car Insurance

Most states require car owners to buy a minimum amount of bodily injury and property damage liability insurance before they can legally drive their cars. In those states you are supposed to show proof of insurance at registration and at the time of an accident, and you should carry the proof of insurance in your vehicle at all times.

> **Insurance Requirements and Punishments for Lack of Insurance**
>
> **California:** There is a minimum insurance of 15/30/5 (see explanation below); a fine for uninsured is $100-200
>
> **Connecticut:** 20/40/10, registration suspension
>
> **Florida**: 10/20/10, license/registration revocation
>
> **Illinois**: 20/40/15, $500-1,000 fine
>
> **New York**: 25/50/10, $150-1,500 fine, maximum 15 days in jail
>
> **New Jersey:** 15/30/5, $300-$1,000 fine, community service, 1-year license suspension
>
> Here's how to read minimum insurance. First number: bodily injury liability maximum for one person injured in an accident. Second number: bodily injury liability maximum for all injuries in one accident. Third number: property damage liability maximum for one accident.
>
> Thus in California, the minimum liability limits are $15,000 for injury liability for one person in an accident, $30,000 for all injuries in an accident, and $5,000 for property damage in an accident.

The DMV learns about the expiration or cancellation of your policy from your auto insurance company, which is required to notify the state immediately. The police will also inform the DMV if they catch you without car insurance.

If you drive an uninsured motor vehicle or you permit another person to drive your uninsured car, in most states your license will taken away. In addition, you may be fined and even put to jail. The penalty also applies when the Department of Motor Vehicles receives evidence that you were involved in an accident without being insured.

Solution: The only way to avoid problems is to purchase car insurance as mandated by your state law.

Note: Even if you don't drive your car for a while, you may not let the car insurance lapse. When you take the vehicle off the road, you must surrender the plates to the DMV, or otherwise you will face civil penalties, registration suspension and/or license suspension.

Only people who can show that they "inadvertently" drove without insurance and that the suspension causes an undue hardship on the person's family or dependents (because it interferes with work) are eligible for a hardship license.

Lack of Car Insurance at the Time of Accident

If you drove a vehicle without insurance and got into an accident in which you were at fault, the injured party may file a law suit against you for damages. The court may award a judgment against you for damages to the injured party. If you cannot pay the judgment, your driver's license may be suspended until the judgment is paid in full.

⚜ The Insurance Information Institute lists driving laws in all states. See www.iii.org.

Solution: If you can afford to regularly pay on the judgment, you can ask the court to order a repayment plan. Some drivers unable to pay big judgments are forced into bankruptcy.

Failure to Pay Child Support

A non-custodial parent may be subject to suspension of his or her license for failure to pay court-ordered child support. His license can be suspended in two ways:

- **Court-ordered suspension** happens when the court determines that a parent is intentionally withholding child support payments. The court orders the DMV to immediately suspend the parent's license indefinitely until he begins making payments satisfactorily to the court.
- **Administratively-ordered suspension** is ordered by the DMV. The local Child Support Enforcement Agency determines that a parent is behind in child support and the agency sends an order to the DMV requiring that the non-paying parent's license be suspended indefinitely until he pays up.

Under your state law, if your child support payments are two or more months behind, you may lose not only your driver's license but occupational, recreational, and sporting licenses as well.

Solution: Pay overdue child support promptly. Arrange to have payments automatically withheld from your paycheck. If you are not delinquent in child support payments, contest the fact by requesting a hearing. Your suspension notice will state the procedure.

Other Reasons for Losing Your License

Many states punish those who fail to pay child support, taxes, court judgments, or parking fines by revoking their driver's licenses. Juveniles can lose their driver's licenses, or their issuance may be delayed due to habitual absence from school. A license or state identification card can be taken away if it turns out that the document is false or altered.

Regulations vary from state to state. For example, in Wisconsin, residents can lose their driver's licenses for failure to pay library fines, shovel the snow from their sidewalk, or trim a tree overhanging a neighbor's property. In Florida, a license can be revoked for "an immoral act in which a motor vehicle was used." Montana residents are not allowed to drive if they default on college loans.

📖 Read *A U.S. Driver's License* to find out how to fight traffic tickets and license suspension or revocation (see the Appendix on page 262).

Summary: *You can lose your driver's license for more reasons than simply being a bad driver. The court or the state DMV can take your license away if you failed to pay a traffic ticket, didn't appear in court, haven't insured your car, or are delinquent in paying child support.*

14.4. Your Driving Record

How Your Driving History Is Created

Each state's Department of Motor Vehicles (reporting to the Secretary of State) keeps records of traffic violations and accidents of drivers residing in the state. In most states, traffic violations committed in another state are included on your record as though they happened in your home state. For example, if you are not a resident of Illinois and you are convicted of a traffic violation there, a record will be established for you in Illinois and the traffic violation also will be forwarded to your home state.

Definition: A driving record contains a history of violations and convictions, collisions, and departmental actions incurred by a driver over a period of time. A copy of the record is usually referred to as an abstract of a driving record.

Driving record information comes from DMV branch offices, police agencies, courts, other institutions, and other states. A driving record includes your personal information, driver's license information, convictions for traffic violations, civil infraction, failure to answer court judgments, car accidents, and license withdrawal actions or restrictions on driving privileges.

Information collected by Departments of Motor Vehicles is considered public information with exception of drivers' personal and confidential data. Law enforcement agencies have full access to driving records.

It may take several months before a piece of information appears on your record.

How Long Information Stays in Your Record

Information about traffic accidents, convictions for moving violations, and suspensions or revocations of your driver's license becomes part of your permanent driving record. Information is typically retained for these time periods:

- A moving violation conviction or an accident normally remains on a driver record during the year that the conviction or the accident occurred, and for the following three calendar years (up to 7 years in some states).
- A conviction that is alcohol-related or drug-related (DWI/DUI) remains on a driver record for 10 years, as well as some convictions and accidents of a serious type.
- A suspension or revocation of a driver's license that was not cleared or not terminated remains on a driver record indefinitely.
- A suspension or revocation that was cleared or terminated remains on a driver record for several years from the date of its termination. Note that the DMV uses the year when the suspension or revocation was cleared or terminated, not the year when it began.

The DMV normally deletes a driver record after the driver's license expires and is not renewed for five years. An incident that appears on the record can require the DMV to keep the record longer. Information on most serious violations is available to all 50 state DMVs for a period of 10 years after the conviction or license reinstatement.

Convictions remain on file indefinitely with the court which handled the case and in state and local criminal history files. Time limits and changes in your driving record do not affect court or criminal records in any way.

As laws vary from state to state, check your state regulations for exact information.

Summary: *State Departments of Motor Vehicles collect information on all people licensed to drive motor vehicles in the state: their personal information, driving history, convictions etc. The information stays in the record up to 10 years.*

14.5. How to Obtain and Clean up Your Driving Record

Check Your Own Driving History

If you have ever lost your wallet, became victim of identity theft, or shared your personal information with your countrymen, you should check your driving record often, even as frequently as once a year to make sure that no one uses a driver's license issued in your name.

It is important to have a clean driving record, because your car insurance rates and sometimes your job may depend on it.

You can obtain a copy of your own driving history by mail, e-mail or personally at the DMV office. Website www.dmv.org will help you locate your state Department of Motor Vehicles or, for a small fee, will get the driving record for you.

Who Can See Your DMV Record

Driver's license information, as well as vehicle and vessel records, is open to public inspection. Confidential information, however, such as Social Security numbers and residence addresses, may only be disclosed to law enforcement agencies, employers, attorneys, child support agencies, and insurance companies that have access for a "good cause" as specified under the Federal Driver's Privacy Protection Act and additional state laws. Your insurance company may only be concerned with offenses during the last several years when setting your premium.

For taxi drivers, truck drivers, domestic employees and many others, a clean driving record is a mandatory prerequisite for a job. Also, background checks for some professional licenses may include verification of DMV records.

For your protection, your confidential information (name and Social Security number) is not displayed on the driving record you obtain online. You are identified only by your driver's license number.

You will usually receive a notification when your information is released.

How to Clean up Your Driving Record

State Departments of Motor Vehicles compile driving history information and have the obligation to maintain the integrity of their databases. Corrections to your driving record, if any are needed, can only be processed by your state DMV. If your record contains erroneous information, request a correction.

Some states have forms available for removing errors from the records. For example, in California you would need to complete a Driver's License Record Correction Request (DL 207) or Traffic Accident Record Correction Request (DL 208), which can be downloaded from the Internet (www.dmv.ca.gov).

Unfortunately, most states do not explain their procedures online. You must contact your DMV directly for assistance.

✍ You can find addresses and phone numbers of all state Departments of Motor Vehicles in a telephone book or at www.dmv.org. When calling your state DMV, ask for a Request for Amendment of a Record or Record Correction Request.

Summary: It pays to check your driving history from time to time. Every state DMV allows drivers to order driving abstracts over the Internet, by mail, or in person. DMVs have procedures

to correct errors. You cannot access someone's personal information by looking at their driving record.

14.6. When Someone Steals Your Identity

Drivers' licenses are the most common identification documents in the United States. For this reason, driver's license numbers as well as Social Security numbers (SSNs) are critical pieces of information used by thieves to assume their victim's identity for fraudulent purposes. An imposter might apply for credit, buy a car, or rent an apartment, and then not pay the bills, leaving the victim with the bills and a bad credit rating. Moreover, when arrested or caught drunk driving, an imposter may give his victim's personal information to the police, instead of his own. The victim will have a criminal record and may even be arrested for a suspended license or failure to appear in court.

You may face similar consequences if you let your fellow immigrants use your documents.

Fraudulent Driver's License in Your Name

An identity thief can obtain a driver's license in your name. You could find out that this happened from strange activity on your driving or criminal records. If the imposter had an accident or got caught drunk driving, this event will be reflected on your driving history. If the imposter got arrested, this will appear on your criminal record. Maybe your driver's license has been suspended due to somebody else's irresponsibility and you even don't know about it!

If someone has been issued your driver's license for fraudulent reasons, file a report with your local law enforcement agency. Call your state DMV and ask how to contact your state driver special investigations unit. Your driver's license will be canceled and a replacement will be issued by the DMV.

The DMV may place a flag, alert, or comment on your record, or cancel or void your driver's license or ID card.

Traffic Tickets Issued in Your Name

It is possible for someone to put your name and information on his traffic ticket. If this happens, file a report with the local law enforcement agency that issued the ticket. Contact the appropriate court and request an identification hearing to contest the ticket.

To protect your driving privileges, you may also request that a comment about identity theft be placed on your record at the DMV. To request a comment, you must send to the appropriate unit of the DMV a written request, the police report, and the court document showing the reason for the dismissed ticket (wrong person cited, identity theft victim).

A New Driver's License for a Victim of Identity Theft

The DMV may issue another driver's license or identification card number to a customer whose name and number have been misused. You must provide evidence to the DMV that demonstrates how your name and license, or ID card number, have been used fraudulently. Submit at least one of the following types of documents to the DMV:

- a police report or a letter on police letterhead
- a report or letter from a credit card company, credit reporting bureau, or financial institution
- a report or letter from the state tax department or the U.S. Internal Revenue Service
- a document issued by a court or a letter from a District Attorney.

Include a completed driver's license application form and a signed statement explaining the fraudulent activity and why a new number should be issued.

Summary: A thief can use your personal information to obtain a driver's license in your name. Whatever trouble the imposter causes will be reflected on your driving and criminal record. The DMV may issue another driver's license to a victim.

15. CLEAN UP YOUR CRIMINAL HISTORY

An unfortunate incident, bad luck, or even a misunderstanding can result in your arrest and involvement with the criminal justice system. You must understand that a single arrest establishes your criminal record, regardless of the future outcome of the case. A criminal history has drastic immigration consequences for noncitizens, even Green Card holders. For that reason, it pays to keep your criminal history clean.

Noncitizens should be cautious even if they had a brush with the law a long time ago, and now they intend to apply for an immigration benefit (Green Card, reentry permit, etc.) or want to travel abroad.

15.1. What Is a Rap Sheet?

State Rap Sheet

Definition: "RAP" stands for Record of Arrests and Prosecutions. A "rap sheet" is a record of arrests and convictions of a person charged with crimes in his or her state.

> *If you have ever been arrested, even if the case was dismissed or you were found not guilty, you will still have a permanent criminal record, or rap sheet.*

A rap sheet contains detailed information about arrests, outstanding warrants, criminal charges filed, the disposition of those charges (final outcome, see page 249), the sentence you received, any supervised release time, and whether you were issued a certificate of rehabilitation. Information about juvenile delinquency and youthful offender adjudications will not appear.

State rap sheets are maintained by the state police department at the state criminal record repository. Each time an individual is arrested or fingerprinted, the police department sends a report of the arrest to its repository. Thus the state rap sheet contains only information about arrests and convictions in that state. The information is also forwarded to the Federal Bureau of Investigation (FBI).

FBI Rap Sheet

The Federal Bureau of Investigation is a federal police force that is the principal investigative arm of the U.S. Department of Justice. The FBI investigates alleged violations of federal criminal laws governing banking, gambling, white collar fraud, public corruption, civil rights, interstate transportation of stolen property, and elections.

FBI rap sheets are called Information Records or Criminal History Records. The Federal Bureau of Investigation compiles individuals' criminal histories from each state as well as from the federal government. The Criminal Justice Information Services (CJIS) – a division of the FBI – maintains FBI rap sheets.

Whenever you are fingerprinted due to arrest, federal employment, naturalization, or military service, the information taken from fingerprint submission is sent to the FBI and retained there. If the fingerprints are related to an arrest, the Identification Record includes the name of the agency that submitted the fingerprints to the FBI, the date of arrest, the arrest charge, and the disposition of the arrest, if known to the FBI. All arrest data included in an Identification Record is obtained from fingerprint submissions, disposition reports, and other reports submitted by agencies having criminal justice responsibilities.

Each criminal arrest for which the CJIS receive a fingerprint submission should have a disposition.

Definition: A disposition is a final action taken about the arrest. A disposition may state that the arrest charges have been modified, dropped, or may state the findings of the courts (conviction).

The following agencies submit fingerprints and dispositions to the FBI's Criminal Justice Information Services:

- State Criminal History Repositories
- arresting agencies such as police departments, sheriff offices, state police, prisons
- state, federal and local courts

- federal agencies such as the Drug Enforcement Agency, the Bureau of Alcohol, Tobacco and Firearms, U.S. Marshals, and the U.S. Citizenship and Immigration Service.

Law-enforcement agencies update disposition information to the Interstate Identification Index (III) through the National Crime Information Center (NCIC), in addition to reporting to the FBI. The Interstate Identification Index, known as "Triple I," is an "index-pointer" system for the interstate exchange of criminal history record information. Under the III, the FBI maintains an index of persons arrested for felonies or serious misdemeanors under state or federal law. (A serious misdemeanor is generally one that results in a jail sentence of one year or more.) The FBI handles non-criminal background checks outside of the Triple I system.

Summary: *A rap sheet is an informal term for a record kept by the police or the FBI listing all arrests and convictions of persons charged with crimes. If you have been arrested, you have a rap sheet. The FBI compiles criminal histories of individuals from all states as well as from the federal government. Each arrest record should have a disposition, or outcome.*

15.2. How to Check Your Rap Sheet

Why Check Your Criminal History?

Reasons for requesting a copy of your own FBI rap sheet (Identification Record) include:

- checking the record for mistakes
- providing correct information and explanations that are consistent with the background check done by a potential employer or the Immigration Service
- evaluating a chance of sealing or expunging of your criminal records
- for international adoption of a child – opening an account in a foreign bank, or satisfying a requirement to live or work in a foreign country (people with no criminal history may need a letter of good conduct or a police certificate).

SAMPLE CRIMINAL HISTORY REPORT

SP4-137B

PENNSYLVANIA STATE POLICE
CENTRAL REPOSITORY
1800 ELMERTON AVENUE
HARRISBURG, PENNSYLVANIA 17110
(717) 787-9092

COMPILED: 08/07/20XX

PAGE: 1

USE OF THE FOLLOWING CRIMINAL HISTORY RECORD FOR *SID/000-01-23-6*
REGULATED BY ACT 47, AS AMENDED.
III - SINGLE STATE OFFENDER

Single State Offender indicates Record only in PA. Multiple State Offender indicates fingerprints on file in another state

Name used when arrested

DOB: 08/25/44   SEX: M RAC: W SOC: 202-22-5555 FBI: 898989A

Date Arrested

NAME: TEST, RECORD   OTN: Q333333-0
ARRESTED: 08/25/87   PAPSP3600 HARRISBURG PSP   OCA: E19804
                           DISTRICT JUSTICE: 06306

OTN=Offense Tracking is assigned by the District Justice

Police Dept. Making arrest

07/24/87 CC5505   PUBLIC DRUNKENNESS - S   PLEAD GUILTY
07/24/87 CC5503A DISORDERLY CONDUCT - S   PLEAD GUILTY

Date of Offense

+++
NAME: TEST, RECORD   OTN: E123456-1
ARRESTED: 06/30/90   PA0350400 SCRANTON PD   OCA: B25000
DISPOSITION DATE: 10/25/90   COMMON PLEAS DOCKET: 90-1990

OCA=Number Assigned by the Police Department

Date Disposition made by Court

06/30/90 CC6106 FIREARM CARRIED W/O A LICENSE   GUILTY
                     - M1   CO. PROBATION
                                     05 YRS - 06 YRS

Common Pleas Court Docket Number assigned to the case.

Code charged with and the section number:
CC=Crimes Code
CS=The Controlled Substance, Drug, Device & Cosmetic Act

06/30/90 CC0908 PROHIBITED OFFENSIVE WEAPONS   GUILTY
                     - M1   CO. PROBATION
                                     05 YRS - 06 YRS

Disposition of the Charge

+++

Grade of Crime most serious to least serious:
F-1
F-2
F-3
M-1
M-2
M-3
S

NAME: RECORD, TEST   OTN: E949949-7
ARRESTED: 07/04/97   PAPSP54111 McCONNELLSBURG PSP   OCA: G12345
DISPOSITION DATE:

07/04/97 CS13A30   VIO CS/DRUG/DEV & COSMETIC ACT DISPOSITION
                                                        UNREPORTED

If the arrest is 3 years or less from the date of your request and we have not received a disposition from the clerk of courts, it is show as "disposition unreported" to let you know that charge(s) may be pending. If you desire a disposition on the charges, you must contact the clerk of courts in the county which the police department that make the arrest is located.

+++
F = FELONY, M= MISDEMEANOR, S = SUMMARY AND THE NUMERIC = THE
DEGREE

ARREST (S) SUPPORTED BY FINGERPRINT CARD (S) ON FILE.

RESPONSE BASED ON COMPARISON OF REQUESTER FURNISHED
INFORMATION AND/OR FINGERPRINTS AGAINST A NAME INDEX AND/OR
FINGERPRINTS CONTAINED IN THE FILES OF THE PENNSYLVANIA STATE
POLICE CENTRAL REPOSITORY ONLY, AND DOES NOT PRECLUDE THE
EXISTENCE OF OTHER CRIMINAL RECORDS WHICH MAY BE CONTAINED IN
THE REPOSITORIES OF OTHER LOCAL, STATE OR FEDERAL CRIMINAL

How to Get a Copy of Your FBI Rap Sheet

You may obtain a copy of your criminal record by writing to the Federal Bureau of Investigation. Include a letter stating why you are making the request, a set of fingerprints and a money order or certified check (no personal checks) at the amount of $18 payable to U.S. Treasury. Mail your letter to

📧 FBI Criminal Justice Information Services Div., 1000 Custer Hollow Road, Clarksburg, WV 26306. Telephone: 1-304-625-3878, web: www.fbi.gov/hq/cjisd/fprequest.htm.

A set of fingerprints taken on a standard form constitutes your proof of identity. You may have your fingerprints taken at a police station or any private fingerprinting service. Look under "Fingerprinting" in your telephone book or call your local police station. Ask for a fee and have a money order or certified check for that amount.

The FBI will respond to you in approximately 8-10 weeks. If you have no criminal record, you will receive the original fingerprint card stamped with the stamp "NO RECORD." Otherwise you will get your FBI Identification Record.

Letter of Request

Federal Bureau of Investigation
Ref: Criminal Record Request

Date: _____
Requestor's Name: _____
Requestor's Address: _____

I, _____, am requesting a criminal history background check for personal review pursuant to 28CFR§16.30-16.34. Please mail the results of the check to the following address: _____

I have a reason that requires expeditious handling (optional):

Date required: _____
Reason: _____

If you have any questions, please contact me at: telephone: ___ e-mail: ___

Sincerely,

Your signature

How to Get a Copy of Your State Rap Sheet

Your state criminal history can be obtained from the state police. Names and addresses of criminal record repositories (cri-minal information centers) for all states are listed at the end of this chapter.

On a request form, provide all pertinent data: your name, address, Social Security number, date of birth, race, sex, maiden name, and all prior married names. Enclose an original set of fingerprints and money order or certified check to cover the fee.

Make sure to specify that you need a certified criminal history record for the maximum number of years available.

Getting a Rap Sheet from a Private Company

Many private companies can do a criminal background check for a fee. You can conveniently order and receive your criminal record online. Here are some websites that provide background checks: www.docusearch.com, www.amerusa-criminal-records.com, or www.choicepoint.com.

You can find many other companies by searching the Internet for "criminal background check."

 Summary: Make sure that your criminal history is correct and complete. Get a copy of your FBI and state rap sheets and check for mistakes or omissions. You may do that by yourself or hire a private company.

15.3. How to Correct Your Rap Sheet

Since the FBI only compiles criminal information obtained from local, state, and federal agencies, the responsibility for correcting such data rests upon the contributing agencies. Therefore, to make corrections in your FBI Identification Record, you must contact the original agency that submitted the information – police department, county court, etc. The FBI is not authorized to modify the records without written notification from the appropriate criminal justice agency.

For instructions how to correct your record contact the state criminal record information center (central repository) in the state in which the arrest occurred.

Common Rap Sheet Mistakes

The following mistakes may occur:

- **Inaccurate information**. Sometimes records contain inadvertently made errors. For example, a date or the nature of a conviction may be wrong. A typing error could cause shoplifting (§155.25 – petit larceny) to appear as murder (§125.25).

- **Information on your rap sheet does not belong to you.** This "mistaken identity conviction" causes you to have a criminal record although you have never been arrested.
- **An incomplete record** is a rap sheet without disposition (see page 249). This may show arrest but does not explain what happened to your case.
- **Double entries.** If information about one arrest got split into two or more entries on your rap sheet, this can make your criminal record look worse than it is.
- **Cases that should be sealed but are not.** Arrests that did not lead to conviction, arrests for non-criminal violations, and arrests leading to convictions for possession of less than 7/8 of an ounce of marijuana can be sealed.

> **Letter Requesting Certificate of Disposition**
>
> Court, Court's address
> Ref: Certificate of Disposition
>
> Dear Sir/Madam:
>
> Please send me a Certificate of Disposition for the following case. I was the defendant in this matter.
>
> Arrest date _____
>
> Arrest charges
> _____
>
> Docket/indictment # _____
>
> Name/aliases _____
>
> Thank you.
>
> Your name

The truth is that while the police submit arrest information efficiently, local courts and prosecutors do not always follow up with submitting disposition information. Only in recent years have courts been automating their information systems (many small courts in rural areas still don't).

How to Proceed

If you believe that your rap sheet contains errors, you have to contact your state Criminal Justice Services Information Center (also called Division of Criminal Justice Services). Ask them how to challenge criminal history information and how to have errors corrected. You may find this information on the Internet.

Get a Certificate of Disposition for the case from the court where the case was heard. A Certificate of Disposition (disposition slip) is an official court record of the case and contains the following information: the docket number, date of arrest, disposition (the final outcome of the case) and the date of disposition. You may get your disposition slip from the court clerk in the court where your case was heard.

A Certificate of Disposition is official only if the seal of the court is pressed into the paper so that you can feel it when you run your finger over it. If certificate contains errors, discuss the issue with an attorney.

Write a letter requesting record challenge. In some states you will get an appropriate form in the mail with the requested rap sheet. Many states have forms available on the Internet. You don't need a specific form as long as you provide all information that is needed. For example, you may write a letter similar to the sample on this page.

Below your letter, list all information that may be necessary for your identification: your full name, your birth day, SSN, race, sex, address and phone number. Enclose a copy of your rap sheet and a copy of your fingerprints.

> **Letter Challenging Content of Your Criminal Record**
>
> State Criminal Record Repository
> Ref: Record Correction
>
> Dear Sir/Madam,
>
> I am hereby writing to request a record challenge. A criminal background check falsely indicates that I have a criminal record. I was never arrested or convicted and the convictions listed in the file do not belong to me. Because of these errors I just lost my job at the ABC Elementary School, where I was hired a month ago.
>
> Please correct my record as quickly as possible so I can try to get my job back. I enclose a copy of my background report and a copy of my fingerprints.
>
> Thank you for your prompt attention to this matter. My identifying information is as follows: _____
>
> Your name

On this and the following page are sample letters you could write if your criminal history contains mistakes.

Send your request to the state record repository (look up the address online or get it from your local police prescient). Call first or look them up on the Internet to confirm the address and fees. Include the original copy of your Certificate of Disposition (disposition slip), because copies are not accepted. Pay the appropriate fee by money order or certified check. Make copies of all documents you send and keep them for your records.

Where to Learn More

Many police departments and legal aid societies provide information how to obtain and correct your criminal history.

For example, the Legal Action Center with offices in New York and Washington DC provides an online booklet *How to Get and Clean up Your State Rap Sheet* for several states. This manual contains step by step instructions, sample letters, and an explanation of what types of offenses can be sealed or expunged. It also includes suggestions about completing an employment application. Free downloads are available for several states.

🕸 Legal Action Center, 225 Varick Street, New York, NY 10014, tel. 1-212-243-1313, toll free 1-800-223-4044, www. lac.org.

 Summary: *Fix errors or omissions in your criminal record. To do this, get a certificate of disposition from the court where your case was heard, write a letter requesting a change, and send it to the state record repository. The state repository will notify the FBI.*

Letter Challenging Content of Your Criminal Record

State Criminal Record Repository
Ref: Record Correction

To whom it may concern:

My rap sheet contains several errors which need to be corrected. Please make corrections listed below, according to information I provided on the enclosed Certificates of Disposition.

1. Information about my 12/12/20XX arrest is split into two separate entries and needs to be consolidated into one entry. Pertaining disposition with docket number 6543B is attached.

2. My arrest of 11/10/20XX is missing disposition information. The attached court transcript with docket number 9876A shows that all charges were dismissed following this arrest. Please include this information to your files.

I would appreciate your prompt attention in this matter.

Your name

15.4. How to Clean up Your Criminal Record

A conviction is never really "cleared" or "removed" from one's criminal record. It stays in your file permanently. Anyone who checks your background for criminal records will see that a conviction took place.

Also, any arrest will show up on your criminal record regardless of what later happened in court. You will have a criminal history even if your case was dismissed, you were acquitted, or the prosecutor dropped the case before or during trial (*"noll pros"*). You must file a petition and ask the court to expunge (or seal) your records in order to clear the arrest from your criminal history.

> *Unlike unpaid debts or a bankruptcy, arrest and conviction records are not automatically removed from your record after a period of years. It is up to you to clean up your past.*

What Is Expungement?

Definition: Expungement is a process by which a record of criminal conviction is removed by a court order. Depending on the jurisdiction, this process may be referred to as sealing, erasure, destruction, setting aside, expunction, or purging. The purpose of expungement is to conceal criminal records from the public if you did not break any law or if you served your sentence and were rehabilitated.

The laws pertaining to expungement of arrests and convictions vary from state to state, so you should conduct additional research about eligibility for expungement and the procedures. It is advisable to hire an experienced attorney.

Expungement is usually available only to those who have not been convicted of a crime. This means that you can erase from your record information about your arrest that did not lead to conviction. In some states however, expungement is available after conviction, but only depending on the severity of the crime and after the defendant is done serving the sentence and if he is facing no new charges.

The meaning of expungement varies as well. Some jurisdictions will deem the criminal arrest as never having happened; others will mean that the arrest will not be publicly disclosed but still available to law-enforcement officials.

Which Records Can Be Expunged

Eligibility for expungement is based on state law.

No conviction: If the case was resolved in your favor, you may be eligible for an expungement of arrest, investigation, or detention record if the following conditions are met:

- A minimum length of time has passed since the last arrest.
- You were acquitted (found not guilty). In some states, after acquittal, your criminal charge may be expunged from your records immediately, while in others you must wait up to 60 days.
- The proceedings were dismissed.
- You were discharged without conviction and no charges were re-filed.
- You were released without formal charges being filed.

Expungement of convictions: In states where state law allows expungement of convictions, your application may be considered if you meet the following main conditions:

- The required period of time passed since your prison sentence or probation has been completed.
- The severity of your crime does not preclude expungement. (Only some types of convictions are available for expungement. Many states exclude felony convictions: you are not eligible if you were convicted of murder, rape, vehicular homicide, crimes committed while you were armed, etc. Juvenile and misdemeanor convictions are most often subject to expungement).
- You completed your probation, community service, and paid all the court fees.
- Your case is closed and disposition information is available.
- No previous expungement exists.
- You have not committed sexual offense against a minor.
- You are not a registered sex offender.
- There are no arrests pending and no additional convictions.

Remember that each state sets its own standards. Have a competent attorney handle your criminal case, because your chance for expungement often depends on the process taken to complete the case without conviction. For example, it is quicker to obtain expungement when charges have been dismissed as opposed to when the case has been placed on a "stet docket" (a group of inactive cases which are generally not reopened if the defendant abides by certain conditions).

Expungement Procedure

In order to apply for expungement, you must file an application (motion) with the court in which you were convicted (or adjudicated as a juvenile). You may go back in front of the same judge who sentenced you, or maybe the case will be transferred to another judge. You may file on your own or use an attorney.

Every jurisdiction has its own procedures. The process is not difficult, but you must know which forms to file, which documents to include, and where to send the papers. Some states provide detailed instructions, some don't.

In most states you will need:

- an application (petition) for expungement (get copies with instructions from a court; attach proofs of your rehabilitation)
- one or two sets of your fingerprints
- a certified copy of your judgment of sentence or Certificate of Disposition (get this from the court where you were sentenced)
- a money order for the appropriate fee.

The procedure may require that you send sets of those documents to several institutions: the Attorney General Office, Prosecutor's Office, state police, and sometimes to a victim of the crime. In some states, the court sends the documents to those institutions seeking their opinions. Any of them may object to the expungement.

On a court date, you go to the court to answer any questions the judge may have. Most judges will want to see that you have demonstrated exemplary character since your conviction. Some judges are less strict and will grant expungement if you simply meet all the requirements. Be prepared to present proof of rehabilitation: a school diploma, a letter of appreciation for community service, or certificate of drug/alcohol treatment, etc.

If the judge grants your request for expungement, the court will keep the original order and will send a copy to the state police central records division. After a month or two, check your criminal record to make sure your conviction does not show on your rap sheet.

After Your Record Got Expunged

After your criminal record got expunged (or sealed), your finger-prints and "mug shots" are destroyed, and information is removed from your rap sheet. Then in the eyes of the law, the entire case never occurred. Therefore you can truthfully say to your prospective employer or a landlord that you have no criminal record.

Unfortunately, even expunged convictions must be reported for immigration purposes.

A record of your arrests will still remain in a confidential file on the state police computer. It will be released only in very limited circumstances – for example, if you apply for a license to carry a gun, or if you are arrested while on parole or probation. You will have to disclose your criminal past only when you apply for a public office or for some professional licenses.

 Summary: *Sometimes criminal records can be expunged or removed after the passage of a specified period of time and the fulfillment of some requirements. Also, some information about an arrest that did not lead to conviction can be erased from your criminal record. In order to apply for expungement, you must file an application with the court in which you were tried.*

15.5. What You Should Know About the Immigration Background Check

If you are still waiting for your Green Card, the U.S. Citizenship and Immigration Service (USCIS) will run a full background check on you before granting you permanent resident status. If you have a Green Card already, you will undergo the background check when you apply for citizenship. The Immigration Service will examine you carefully in many other circumstances: when you try to renew your Green Card, apply for travel document, or come back from a trip abroad.

In order to run a background check, the Immigration Service will fingerprint you and send your fingerprints to the FBI.

> **The FBI fingerprint check provides information related to your criminal background within the United States.**

The FBI results either indicate no record of a criminal history or provide your criminal history record (rap sheet). At that point, a USCIS officer reviews the information to determine what effect it may have on your eligibility for the benefit. About 10 percent checks uncover criminal history including immigration violations. In cases involving arrests or charges without disposition (see page 249), the USCIS requires the applicant to provide court certified evidence of the disposition (see page 254).

After September 11, 2001, the Department of Homeland Security started an efficient screening system at international airports to strengthen national security. As a result, many permanent residents are identified for past criminal convictions, even though they traveled before and their convictions go back 20 years or more.

 Suggestion: The Department of Homeland Security checks criminal records of people applying for immigration benefits as well as records of some non-citizens returning from abroad. If you were arrested before, you should complete information and certified records of disposition of your case.

APPENDIX: ABOUT THE NEW AMERICAN GUIDES

Helpful Guides for New Americans

The New American Guides is a series of books published for all immigrants who want to live and succeed in the United States. Written in simple language, the series explains what immigrants need to know in order to work their way into the middle class.

Whether you are starting your life in the U.S., starting it over, or you are already well established, the following guidebooks can help.

Surviving in the U.S. While Waiting for Your Green Card. This book explains how to live and work in the United States while waiting for legalization of your immigration status. It describes U.S. immigration laws, actions which may jeopardize obtaining your Green Card, how to detect immigration fraud, who is interested in your immigration status, when your status is relevant and when it is not, which institutions collaborate with the Immigration Service, how to avoid deportation, the rights of undocumented aliens, and much more. The book helps the reader to survive transitional period without legal immigration status while not violating any additional laws. $25.95 for printed book, $15.95 for e-book.

Starting Over in the U.S. After Getting Your Green Card: An Indispensible Handbook for Immigrants. This book tells you what needs to be done after obtaining permanent residency. It also helps you restart your life after a period of unauthorized stay or other problems such as unlawful employment, lack of credit history, debts, identity theft, loss of your driver's license, criminal record, and many other obstacles. $25.95 for printed book, $15.95 for e-book.

Citizenship: Overcoming Obstacles to Naturalization. This book provides a detailed description of naturalization requirements and how to become a citizen despite various complications such as a criminal record, long stays abroad, problems on the border, failure to register for military service, nonpayment of taxes, lack of English language, lack of cooperation of your American spouse, marriage fraud, and many others. $15.95 for e-book. Check www.NewAmerican Guides.com for availability of books in print.

Working as a Nanny in the U.S.: How to Earn Top Money in the Domestic Field, Make a Career, and Have the Adventure of Your Life. Topics include finding a top job, what needs to be done to work legally, taxes, insurance, employment contract, your rights, and much more. E-book only, $12.

A U.S. Driver's License: What Immigrants Need to Know About Licenses, Tickets, Driving Records, and Car History. The book covers: driver's license requirements for newcomers with and without legal status, fighting traffic and parking tickets, how to avoid losing your license and how to get it back, consequences of traffic violations, immigration implications of drunk driving, driving record and vehicle history at the Department of Motor Vehicles (DMV), and much more. E-book only, $12.

The books are available in printed as well as in electronic form at www.NewAmericanGuides.com. They are also carried by major booksellers throughout the country.

To Order

To order New American Guides, contact your local bookstore, or order directly from the publisher:

Polpress Services
255 Park Lane
Douglaston, NY 11363
Tel. 718-224-3492, newguides@gmail.com
www.NewAmericanGuides.com

Shipping and handling for printed books: $3.95 per copy anywhere in mainland USA. No shipping fees for 4 copies or more. International shipping: $10 for one book, $5 for each additional.

E-books can be downloaded from www.NewAmericanGuides.com.